Hamlet

ARDEN EARLY MODERN DRAMA GUIDES

Series Editors:

Andrew Hiscock
University of Wales, Bangor, UK and Lisa Hopkins,
Sheffield Hallam University, UK

Arden Early Modern Drama Guides offer practical and accessible introductions to the critical and performative contexts of key Elizabethan and Jacobean plays. Each guide introduces the text's critical and performance history, but also provides students with an invaluable insight into the landscape of current scholarly research, through a keynote essay on the state of the art and newly commissioned essays of fresh research from different critical perspectives.

Further titles in preparation

Hamlet

A Critical Reader

Ann Thompson and Neil Taylor

Bloomsbury Arden Shakespeare
An imprint of Bloomsbury Publishing Plc

B L O O M S B U R Y

LONDON • OXFORD • NEW YORK • NEW DELHI • SYDNEY

Bloomsbury Arden Shakespeare

An imprint of Bloomsbury Publishing Plc
Imprint previously known as The Arden Shakespeare

50 Bedford Square
London
WC1B 3DP
UK

1385 Broadway
New York
NY 10018
USA

www.bloomsbury.com

BLOOMSBURY, THE ARDEN SHAKESPEARE and the Diana logo are trademarks of Bloomsbury Publishing Plc

First published 2016

British Library Cataloguing in Publication Data
A catalogue record for this book is available from the British Library.

ISBN: HB: 978-1-4725-7138-0
         PB: 978-1-4725-7137-3
         ePDF: 978-1-4725-7140-3
         ePub: 978-1-4725-7139-7

Library of Congress Cataloging-in-Publication Data
A catalog record for this book is available from the Library of Congress.

Typeset by Fakenham Prepress Solutions, Fakenham, Norfolk NR21 8NN
Printed and bound in Great Britain

CONTENTS

SERIES
INTRODUCTION

The drama of Shakespeare and his contemporaries has remained at the very heart of English curricula internationally and the pedagogic needs surrounding this body of literature have grown increasingly complex as more sophisticated resources become available to scholars, tutors and students. This series aims to offer a clear picture of the critical and performative contexts of a range of chosen texts. In addition, each volume furnishes readers with invaluable insights into the landscape of current scholarly research as well as including new pieces of research by leading critics.

This series is designed to respond to the clearly identified needs of scholars, tutors and students for volumes which will bridge the gap between accounts of previous critical developments and performance history and an acquaintance with new research initiatives related to the chosen plays. Thus, our ambition is to offer innovative and challenging guides that will provide practical, accessible and thought-provoking analyses of early modern drama. Each volume is organized according to a progressive reading strategy involving introductory discussion, critical review and cutting-edge scholarly debate. It has been an enormous pleasure to work with so many dedicated scholars of early modern drama and we are sure that this series will encourage you to read 400-year-old play texts with fresh eyes.

Andrew Hiscock and Lisa Hopkins

NOTES ON CONTRIBUTORS

Catherine Belsey is Professor Emeritus in English at Swansea University and Visiting Professor at the University of Derby, UK. Her books include *The Subject of Tragedy* (1985), *Shakespeare and the Loss of Eden* (1999), *Why Shakespeare?* (2007), and *Shakespeare in Theory and Practice* (2008), as well as *Critical Practice* (1980, 2002), *Culture and the Real* (2005) and *A Future for Criticism* (2011). Her current project, a book on ghost stories, centres on *Hamlet*.

Mark Thornton Burnett is Professor of Renaissance Studies at Queen's University Belfast, UK. His books include *Masters and Servants in English Renaissance Drama and Culture: Authority and Obedience* (1997), *Constructing 'Monsters' in Shakespearean Drama and Early Modern Culture* (2002), *Filming Shakespeare in the Global Marketplace* (2002, 2012) and *Shakespeare and World Cinema* (2013).

John Lee is Senior Lecturer in English at the University of Bristol, UK. His publications on Shakespeare include *Shakespeare's 'Hamlet' and the Controversies of Self* (2000), 'Reanimating Criticism: Towards a Materialist Shakespeare' (2004), '"A Judge That Were No Man": Montaigne, Shakespeare and Imagination' (2006) and 'Shakespeare and the Great War' (2007). Currently he is editing *A Handbook of Renaissance Studies* for Wiley-Blackwell.

Frank McGuinness is Professor of Creative Writing at University College Dublin, Ireland. He has published widely on Irish, British, European and American Theatre. His plays include *The Factory Girls* (1982), *Baglady* and *Observe the Sons of Ulster Marching Towards the Somme* (1985), *Someone Who'll Watch Over Me* (1992), *There Came A Gypsy Riding* (2007), *The Match Box* (2012) and *The Hanging Gardens* (2013). His versions of Ibsen, Chekhov, Sophocles, Euripides, Racine and Lorca have been performed through the English-speaking world. He has published five volumes of poetry with the Gallery Press and a novel, *Arimathea* (2013), with Brandon/O'Brien Press.

Lois Potter is Ned B. Allen Professor Emerita at the University of Delaware, USA. Her publications include *Text and Performance: 'Twelfth Night'* (1985), *Secret Rites and Secret Writing: Royalist Literature 1641–1660* (1989), the Arden edition of *The Two Noble Kinsmen* (1997, 2015), *Shakespeare in Performance: 'Othello'* (2002) and *The Life of William Shakespeare* (2012). She has been a frequent reviewer of theatre productions for *The Times Literary Supplement*, *Shakespeare Quarterly* and *Shakespeare Bulletin*.

Neil Taylor is Professor Emeritus in English Literature at the University of Roehampton, UK. He has published widely on Shakespeare, Shakespeare on film and television, editing and other aspects of Renaissance and modern drama. He has edited an old-spelling *Henry IV Part 2* for Ginn (1972), *Henry VI Part 3* for the Norton Shakespeare (2015), all three texts of *Hamlet* (with Ann Thompson) for the Arden Shakespeare (2006, 2016) and *Thomas Middleton: Five Plays* (with Bryan Loughrey) for Penguin Classics (1988).

Ann Thompson is Professor Emeritus in English at King's College London, UK. She is a General Editor of the Arden Shakespeare and has (with Neil Taylor) edited all three texts of *Hamlet* for Arden (2006, 2016). Other publications include an edition of *The Taming of The Shrew* (1984, 2003) and an edition of *Cymbeline* for Norton (2015). Books include

Shakespeare's Chaucer (1978), *Shakespeare, Meaning and Metaphor* (with John O. Thompson, 1987), *Women Reading Shakespeare, 1660–1900* (edited, with Sasha Roberts, 1996), *In Arden: Editing Shakespeare* (edited with Gordon McMullan, 2003) and *Macbeth: The State of Play* (edited, 2014). Current projects include a book on Shakespeare and metonymy.

TIMELINE

1564: William Shakespeare born in Stratford-upon-Avon.

1570: Publication (in French) of François de Belleforest's *Histoires tragiques* containing a version of the Hamlet story first written down in Latin by Saxo Grammaticus.

1582: Shakespeare marries Anne Hathaway.

1583: Shakespeare's daughter, Susanna, born.

1585: Shakespeare's twins, Hamnet/Hamlet and Judith, born.

1589: Thomas Nashe refers to an earlier Hamlet play in his preface to Thomas Greene's *Menaphon*.

1594: Philip Henslowe records a performance of a play called *Hamlet* at Newington Butts.

1596: Thomas Lodge refers to an earlier Hamlet play in *Wit's Misery*.

1596: Death of Shakespeare's son Hamnet/Hamlet.

1599: Globe Theatre built in Southwark.

1599: *Julius Caesar* performed at the Globe (possibly Shakespeare's first Globe play).

1599–1601: Probable date of composition and first performances of *Hamlet*.

1601: Death of Shakespeare's father, John.

1601: John Marston's *Antonio's Revenge* (which contains some parallels with *Hamlet*) entered in the Stationers' Register.

1603: Publication of the First Quarto (Q1).

1604/5: Publication of the Second Quarto (Q2).

1605: The collaborative play *Eastward Ho!* by George Chapman, John Marston and Ben Jonson contains a number of references to Shakespeare's *Hamlet*.

1607: A performance of a Hamlet play recorded on board William Keeling's ship, the *Red Dragon*, anchored off the coast of West Africa.

1613: Globe Theatre destroyed by fire. It is rebuilt in 1614.

1616: Death of Shakespeare.

1619: Death of Richard Burbage. An elegy lists 'young Hamlet' as one of his great roles.

1619: *Hamlet* performed at Court.

1623: Publication of the First Folio (F).

1626: A company of English players performs a Hamlet play in Dresden.

1726: Lewis Theobald publishes *Shakespeare Restored*, an attack on Alexander Pope's edition of Shakespeare, using examples of alleged errors in his text of *Hamlet*.

1733: Voltaire dismisses *Hamlet* as one of Shakespeare's 'monstrous Farces'.

1742: David Garrick first performs the role of Hamlet at the Drury Lane Theatre in London.

1749: Henry Fielding's characters in his novel, *Tom Jones*, attend a production of *Hamlet*.

1776: Sarah Siddons performs the role of Hamlet in Birmingham and Manchester.

1783: John Philip Kemble first performs the role of Hamlet at the Drury Lane Theatre in London.

1795: Johann Wolfgang von Goethe's characters in his novel, *Wilhelm Meister's Apprenticeship*, get involved in a production of *Hamlet*.

1814: Edmund Kean first performs the role of Hamlet at the Drury Lane Theatre in London.

1823: The first (incomplete) copy of the First Quarto (Q1) is rediscovered.

1834–43: Eugène Delacroix produces a series of lithographs of scenes from *Hamlet*, using a female model for Hamlet.

1847: Charlotte Cushman first performs the role of Hamlet in Manchester and Dublin (later in Boston and New York).

1851: John Everett Millais paints 'Ophelia'.

1852: Herman Melville bases his novel, *Pierre, or The Ambiguities*, on *Hamlet*.

1853: Edwin Booth begins a long series of successful performances of *Hamlet* in New York, interrupted in 1865 when his brother, John Wilkes Booth, assassinates Abraham Lincoln.

1856: The second (incomplete) copy of the First Quarto is rediscovered.

1874: Henry Irving first performs the role of Hamlet at the Lyceum Theatre in London (Ellen Terry was his Ophelia from 1878).

1877: Horace Howard Furness publishes a two-volume *Hamlet* in the Variorum series, including a text of the First Quarto (Q1).

1880: The New Shakespere [*sic*] Society publishes facsimile reprints of the First and Second Quartos of *Hamlet* (Q1 and Q2).

1881: William Poel stages a production of the First Quarto (Q1) at St George's Hall in London.

1883: Teena Rochfort Smith publishes a sample of her *Four-Text Hamlet* (which was never completed).

1884: Wilson Barrett first performs the role of Hamlet at the Princess's Theatre in London, restoring many lines that had been cut for over 200 years.

1885: George MacDonald publishes an edition of *Hamlet* based on the First Folio (F).

1899: Sarah Bernhardt performs the role of Hamlet in Paris and releases a short silent film of the duel scene.

1909: Sigmund Freud begins his long development of a psychoanalytic reading of *Hamlet*.

1919: T. S. Eliot argues that the problem with *Hamlet* is the absence of an 'objective correlative' for Hamlet's sexual disgust.

1920: Asta Nielsen performs the role of Hamlet in a full-length silent film.

1922: In James Joyce's novel, *Ulysses*, his character, Stephen Dedalus, expounds his theory of *Hamlet*.

1925: Henry Ayliff directs Colin Keith-Johnston in the first modern-dress *Hamlet* at the Kingsway Theatre in London.

1937: Laurence Olivier first performs the role of *Hamlet* at the Old Vic Theatre in London.

1948: Release of Laurence Olivier's film.

1959: Jacques Lacan develops Freud's analysis in a series of seminars on *Hamlet*.

1960: Release of Akira Kurosawa's film, *The Bad Sleep Well*, an adaptation of *Hamlet*.

1964: Release of Grigori Kozintsev's film.

1967: Tom Stoppard's play, *Rosencrantz and Guildenstern are Dead*, first performed at the Old Vic Theatre in London.

1982: Harold Jenkins publishes an Arden edition of *Hamlet* based on the Second Quarto (Q2).

1985, 1986, 1987: Folio-based editions of *Hamlet* are published by Philip Edwards (New Cambridge), Stanley Wells et al. (Oxford *Complete Works*) and G. R. Hibbard (Oxford).

1990: Release of Franco Zeffirelli's film.

1991: Paul Bertram and Bernice W. Kliman publish *The Three-Text Hamlet*.

1992: Angela Carter's novel, *Wise Children*, includes a female Hamlet and a triumphant version of Ophelia.

1995: Peter Brook presents *Qui Est Là?*, a 'variation' on *Hamlet*, at the Bouffes du Nord in Paris.

1995: Robert Lepage first performs *Elsinore*, a one-man versions of *Hamlet*, at the Caserne in Quebec City.

1995: Robert Wilson first performs *Hamlet: A Monologue*, a one-man version of *Hamlet*, at the Alley Theatre in Houston, Texas.

1996: Release of Kenneth Branagh's film.

2000: Release of Michael Almereyda's film.

2000: John Updike's novel, *Gertrude and Claudius*, offers a prequel to *Hamlet*.

2006: All three early texts of *Hamlet* are published in the Arden Shakespeare series (edited by Ann Thompson and Neil Taylor).

2014–16: A company from Shakespeare's Globe Theatre in London takes a production of *Hamlet* on tour to every country in the world.

Introduction

Ann Thompson

Generally hailed until comparatively recently as Shakespeare's 'greatest play', *Hamlet* is still performed, read and studied more often than its only rival for this accolade, *King Lear*. It remains to be seen whether a mid-twentieth-century shift in taste towards *Lear* will be sustained or whether *Hamlet* will reassert its pre-eminence.[1] The sheer depth and breadth of tradition weigh heavily on those who tackle *Hamlet*, whether as actor, director, editor or critic. The part of Hamlet is the longest in the entire Shakespearean canon and has been treated as an initiation test or a mountain an actor has to climb to prove his skill and his commitment to his career. Or her skill and her commitment: as we shall see, many women have essayed the role. Numerous actors have 'made their mark' as Hamlet, establishing their 'star' status; by comparison, the role of Lear is of course usually undertaken by actors who are already well established and the performance is for that reason potentially less exciting for either actor or audience. *Hamlet* has attracted more productions, films, adaptations and off-shoots than any other play, as well as more commentary and criticism. Not just the story but many words and phrases from it are familiar, indeed over-familiar, to the modern reader or play-goer: it can seem like a tissue of quotations, and one of the challenges for performers is to make the lines sound fresh, as if they are being spoken for the first time. Hamlet's soliloquies are particularly well-known and actors often complain about audience members whispering the lines along with them.

There is, however, no single entity called *Hamlet*. As audience members, we are used to *Hamlet* as a play being different every time we see it. Of course every production is different, but even what is ostensibly the same production will be slightly different on different nights. Film might seem to give a greater degree of stability to individual performances, but even there we find variations such as the longer and shorter versions of Kenneth Branagh's *Hamlet*. Interpretations by readers and critics vary as widely as interpretations by actors and directors and will of course change according to chronology and geography. The *Hamlet* being performed from 2014 to 2016 by the touring company from Shakespeare's Globe Theatre in Rwanda or Tuvalu is inevitably quite a different phenomenon from the play presented at the original Globe in 1600, and it will be differently received by its audiences.

To take a snapshot view of some possible variations in what we refer to as *Hamlet*, let us look at what was available to audiences, scholars and readers in London from 1880 to 1885. In 1880 the New Shakspere [*sic*] Society sponsored facsimile reprints of the First and Second Quartos of *Hamlet* with Forewords by the Director of the Society, Frederick James Furnivall. Also in 1880, C. H. Herford and W. H. Widgery were jointly awarded the Harness prize for their essays on 'The First Quarto Edition of *Hamlet*, *1603*' (the two 'essays' were published together as a 200-page book). On 1 February 1881 William Poel wrote to Furnivall suggesting that the New Shakspere Society might like to sponsor an amateur production of the First Quarto; Furnivall agreed and the production took place on 16 April. Also in 1881, Richard Grant White published his essay on 'The Two *Hamlet*s' (meaning the First and Second Quartos) in *The Atlantic Monthly*. On 10 November 1882 at the 82nd meeting of the New Shakspere Society a paper by Teena Rochfort Smith on 'The Relation of the First Quarto of *Hamlet* to the Second, and on some of the Textual Difficulties of the Play' was read by Furnivall; Teena Rochfort Smith was described in the account of this meeting as 'the editress of the Society's four-text edition of *Hamlet*'. In 1883 she published a 36-page sample of her work. In 1884 Wilson Barrett first performed *Hamlet* at the Princess's Theatre in a version which challenged the dominant tradition of Henry Irving (who had been performing the play at the Lyceum since 1874) by restoring lines that had been cut for over 200 years. In 1885 George MacDonald published a Folio-based edition of the play.

Thus, there were a number of options available to someone proposing to produce *Hamlet* in the 1880s (as indeed there are today). And 'to produce *Hamlet*' includes 'to produce a book called *Hamlet*' as well as 'to produce a play called *Hamlet*' on the stage. Before 1823 everyone was aware that two versions of *Hamlet* had been published in the early seventeenth century and that a further version had been lost. A quarto text, which survives in copies variously dated 1604 and 1605, was called *The Tragicall Historie of Hamlet, Prince of Denmark*, and its title page claimed that it was 'Newly imprinted and enlarged to almost as much againe as it was, according to the true and perfect Coppie'. This implied that a shorter version had been published previously, but had not survived. (The 1604/5 quarto became the basis of most theatrical productions of *Hamlet* into the eighteenth century.) A somewhat different text was included in the First Folio of 1623 under the title of *The Tragedie of Hamlet, Prince of Denmarke*. This text lacked some 230 lines from the earlier version (including Hamlet's last soliloquy in 4.4 beginning 'How all occasions do inform against me') but added some seventy lines of its own (including Hamlet's assertion in 2.2 that 'Denmark's a prison'). It also had very numerous verbal variants, some of which seem to be corrections, but others of which are substitutions or new errors. In 1823 the lost shorter version finally turned up, a text called *The Tragicall Historie of Hamlet, Prince of Denmarke* and dated 1603.[2] Its title page claimed that this text was 'As it hath beene diverse times acted by his Highnesse servants in the Cittie of London: as also in the two Universities of Cambridge and Oxford, and elsewhere'. It was indeed about half the length of the 1604/5 version and its apparently garbled and carelessly printed text caused it to be categorized as a 'bad' quarto. This text became known as the First Quarto and the longer, 1604/5, text became known as the Second Quarto.[3] Much debate ensued as to the relationship between these two quarto texts with scholars at first assuming that the 1603 one was Shakespeare's first sketch of the play (a view initially taken by Furnivall, Rochfort Smith, Herford, Widgery and Poel) but later arguing that it in fact derived from a longer version (either the Second Quarto or the Folio), perhaps representing a script somewhat unevenly remembered by actors or audience members. This view still largely prevails today, although the First Quarto has had quite a respectable stage history in its own right,[4] and its placing of 'To be or not to be' at an earlier position in the play, in 2.2 rather than in 3.1, has been adopted by many productions of the longer texts in the twentieth and twenty-first centuries.[5]

Meanwhile, what of the text printed in the First Folio of 1623? Since Nicholas Rowe produced the first Complete Works of Shakespeare in 1709, it had been traditional for editors to combine (or 'conflate') readings from the quarto and folio traditions. Rowe himself conflated not Q2 and F1 but the Quarto of 1676 and the Fourth Folio of 1685 – presumably the texts that he happened to have to hand. His edition was primarily based on the folio, though he included some of the lines found only in the quarto, and where the texts differed in hundreds of minor variants he chose the readings he preferred. Subsequent eighteenth-century editors included more quarto lines and again made their own choices of readings, resulting in a maximally long but inherently unstable text. Gradually, a fully conflated text was established, and became dominant in the version published by William George Clark and William Aldis Wright in their Cambridge Shakespeare of 1866.[6] In 1885, however, George MacDonald was the first editor who refused to conflate quarto and folio texts. In his Preface he stated clearly his reasons for privileging the First Folio:

All the changes of importance from the text of the [second] Quarto I receive as Shakspere's [*sic*] own. ... A main argument for the acceptance of the Folio edition as the Poet's last presentment of his work lies in the fact that there are passages in it which are not in the Quarto and are very plainly from his hand. If we accept these, what right have we to regard the omission from the Folio of passages in the Quarto as not proceeding from the same hand? ... 'But when a man has published two forms of a thing, may we not judge between him and himself, and take the reading we like better?' Assuredly. Take either the Quarto or the Folio: both are Shakspere's. Take any reading from either, and defend it. But do not mix up the two, retaining what he omits along with what he inserts, and print them so. This is what the editors do – and the thing is not Shakspere's. With homage like this, no artist could be other than indignant.[7]

MacDonald, then, is firmly of the opinion that the text in the First Folio represents Shakespeare's own final revision of *Hamlet* and that the Second Quarto represents an earlier version. He does print the passages found only in Q2, but in smaller type at the foot of the page, indicating their position in the main text with an asterisk. *Hamlet* was the only play he edited and he complained in a letter to J. O. Halliwell-Phillipps, 'I have spent a labour over this work that might have served me to write three novels'.[8] He was (and is) better known as the author of adult and children's fiction such as *Phantastes* (1858), *At the Back of the North Wind* (1871) and *The Princess and the Goblin* (1872). His distinction between 'the editors' and the 'artist' in the quotation above indicates his partisanship on the side of the latter, and perhaps 'the editors' repaid him by ignoring his work almost completely. John Dover Wilson in 1934 attributed a suggestion to 'the novelist George MacDonald' without giving a precise source, and all his successors attributed this suggestion to Wilson himself. Even in the 1980s when several editors of *Hamlet*, including Stanley Wells and Gary Taylor, Philip Edwards, and

G. R. Hibbard, revived the view that the Folio is an authorial revision, they did so without reference to MacDonald.[9]

Current editing practice has turned against conflation, and Teena Rochfort Smith's attempt to produce a four-text *Hamlet* in the 1880s could be seen as an early example of a desire to keep the early texts separate rather than to mix them up: she proposed to print all three early texts, plus a conflated version, but was sadly prevented from completing the task because of her early death.[10] In more recent times, *The Three-Text 'Hamlet': Parallel Texts of the First and Second Quartos and the First Folio*, edited by Paul Bertram and Bernice W. Kliman (1991, 2003) and the Arden Shakespeare *Hamlet* and *Hamlet: The Texts of 1603 and 1623*, edited by Ann Thompson and Neil Taylor (2006, 2016), have fulfilled her ambition. On the modern stage, directors and actors are now more likely to be aware of the options available to them and theatre programmes are likely to carry an indication of which text has been chosen and why. The essays that follow provide a generous sample of the large number of *Hamlets* that have been available to actors, readers and scholars in the past as well as today.

John Lee's chapter performs the heroic feat of providing a survey of four hundred years of *Hamlet* criticism from the earliest responses to the play in its own time up to 2000. And those responses go beyond what we might think of as 'mere' literary criticism: some of the greatest writers and thinkers in the Western tradition have attempted to explicate this play. As Lee says, 'To read the history of *Hamlet* criticism is to read an abstract and brief chronicle of some of the main movements in the intellectual life of Europe and the English-speaking nations over the last four centuries' (17). Given that today we probably think of professional Shakespeare studies as being dominated by scholars from the USA, it is perhaps surprising how European the focus has continued to be: 'One could say that a French-influenced eighteenth century gave way to a German-influenced nineteenth century, which led on to a Franco-German twentieth' (15). In addition to the critics writing in English such as Johnson, Coleridge, Hazlitt, Eliot and Empson, the narrative would not be complete without reference to Voltaire, Goethe, Schlegel, Freud, Lacan and Derrida. The play itself encourages a European perspective, with characters moving between Denmark, Germany and France, and watching a play representing a murder committed in Vienna but based on an account written in 'very choice Italian'. They exist in a recognizably Elizabethan world, but one which has links to broader classical and early modern culture: their very names sound Roman, Spanish and French rather than English or Danish.

A further surprise, in the light of *Hamlet*'s current reputation as one of the greatest, if not *the* greatest of Shakespeare's tragedies (and therefore of all drama written in English), is the extent to which earlier generations of critics felt obliged to defend the play against charges asserting the 'indecorous' mixture of tones and especially the 'inappropriate' comedy of the gravedigger's scene. As Lee demonstrates, *Hamlet* presented a problem for eighteenth-century critics by offending against the neoclassical principles to which they were committed. Romanticism found a way around this with its new focus on character criticism, an approach which could be seen to culminate in the psychological analysis of Freud and his followers. Meanwhile political readings, influenced by Marx, led to movements within late twentieth-century academic criticism such as Cultural Materialism and New Historicism. And the 1980s saw the rise of both feminist criticism and new approaches to textual studies which argued for authorial revision and against the tradition of conflating different texts of the play.

The 'eccentricity' of *Hamlet* was also a marked feature of the early theatrical history of the play, as Lois Potter shows in her opening discussion of its imitations and parodies in contemporary drama: 'mad Hamlet' became an instant hit, with ghosts, skulls, madwomen and gravediggers proliferating on the seventeenth-century stage. Despite the disapproval of David Garrick, who actually removed the gravedigger's scene from the version he acted in from 1772 to 1779, the comic aspects of the play continued to be popular with audiences if not with critics. Again, the European dimension is important in the history of the transformation of *Hamlet* into a global phenomenon: by the 1620s it had probably been acted in Dresden, Prague, Gdansk, Warsaw, Konigsberg and Stockholm. Potter argues that it is no longer possible to polarize the French ('classical') and German ('Romantic') traditions of translating and performing the play as such specifically national responses have become invisible in the globalization process. *Hamlet* has proved to lend itself easily to appropriation by widely differing cultures in Asia and Africa as well as in the Anglophone world, and has spoken to the politics of countries as different as communist China, Soviet Romania and even Nazi Germany. Ironically, *Hamlet* 'has conquered the world by vanishing into it' (81).

Potter singles out some specific aspects of the staging of the play to illustrate the challenges it represents as well as the versatility of its interpreters. Hamlet's encounter with his father's Ghost and its later appearance in the 'closet' scene have proved to be some of the most memorable moments in productions, while his encounters with Gertrude and Ophelia have frequently been uncomfortable, especially for the performers of the female roles who have found the parts under-written. Many women have in fact succeeded in the role of Hamlet himself, from Sarah Siddons in the eighteenth century to Maxine Peake in 2015 – a phenomenon also discussed by Catherine Belsey in her chapter on '*Hamlet* and Gender'.

The play famously leaves many important questions unanswered, especially at its climax when the handling of the duel, the poisoning of the Queen and the appearance (or not) of Fortinbras have all allowed directors considerable scope for variation. In our own time, there is no longer such a thing as a standard performance text. It is perhaps impossible to generalize, beyond noting that 'directors' theatre' has led to 'interpretations that [do] not necessarily take the hero's viewpoint' (57); there are more unsympathetic Hamlets on today's stages than there were in the past.

Neil Taylor, in his chapter on twenty-first-century scholarship, confronts the suggestion that *Hamlet* studies may have reached a dead end – that after more than four hundred years there is nothing left to say about the play. He suggests however that, while it is difficult to claim that the last decade has seen a major new movement in Shakespeare studies, important work has been done by scholars prepared to revisit old sites of debate and rethink earlier habits of thought. He focuses his study on three significant books: Stephen Greenblatt's *Hamlet in Purgatory* (2001), Margreta de Grazia's *'Hamlet' without Hamlet* (2007) and Zachary Lesser's *'Hamlet' After Q1* (2015). Greenblatt reopens the question of *Hamlet*'s relation to medieval and early modern religious issues, including the Protestant rejection of Catholic doctrines regarding the afterlife. He and other scholars continue to be tempted to read the play in the light of Shakespeare's own biography, especially the death of his own son Hamnet/Hamlet in 1596 and that of his father John in 1601, despite the impossibility of pinning down with any certainty what Shakespeare personally did or did not believe and what his relationships were with members of his own family. De Grazia sets out to reject a post-Romantic reading of *Hamlet* as a play primarily concerned with an exploration of the inner life of its central character. She argues that this stress on the interiority (and supposed 'modernity') of Hamlet has blinded us to the fact that the play is as much a history as a tragedy and that its hero's behaviour is motivated by his uncle and mother's apparent conspiracy to dispossess him of his inheritance.

The extent to which the existence of three early texts of *Hamlet* seems to encourage readers to select a play of their own choosing has been emphasized by a number of studies discussed by Taylor which focus explicitly on the textual variations. Previously accepted positions – that the First Quarto is a memorially reconstructed text, for example, or that the First Folio represents Shakespeare's own revision of the play – have recently been challenged in what Ron Rosenbaum dubbed 'the Shakespeare wars' in 2006. The notion of an 'authoritative' text of the play is seen to have receded. Zachary Lesser's book demonstrates in sometimes surprising ways how the discovery in 1823 of the lost 1603 text not only made everyone rethink the status of the other two texts but influenced the entire phenomenon we call *Hamlet*. He succeeds in unsettling our previous interpretations through his detailed examination of the impact of the First Quarto's readings on familiar lines from the other texts and by his discussion of a famous Q1 stage direction in the closet scene: '*Enter the ghost in his night gowne*'.

'*Hamlet* and Gender' is an extremely complicated issue, as is illustrated by Catherine Belsey's chapter on this topic, which is also concerned, in a different way, with the ways in which every generation selects its own readings of *Hamlet* and reinterprets the play accordingly. A simplistic version of a feminist approach to *Hamlet* would look at the female characters and try to find positive things to say about them, even to 'redeem' them from the misogynistic attitudes of both the male characters and the male critics, but, as John Lee notes in his chapter, as far back as the 1980s feminist critics such as Lisa Jardine (and indeed Belsey herself), were pointing out that 'to be feminist Shakespeare's plays would need to be shown to actively seek changes in society's treatment of women, and this they did not do' (Lee: 47). Similarly, Belsey writes 'it has to be conceded that the women in this play do very little to challenge [Hamlet's] misogyny' (127). It is difficult to defend Gertrude from the charge of stupidity (at the very least) and Ophelia remains a 'curiously uncharacteristic Shakespearean heroine' in her failure to defy her father for love as Juliet, Hermia and Desdemona do. Perhaps the only way to 'redeem' these characters is to re-inscribe them in different fictions of their own as writers like Angela Carter and Margaret Atwood have done. But Belsey does not get around to discussing Gertrude and Ophelia until the final third of her chapter; she begins with a discussion of recent female performers of the title role and asserts that 'The story of *Hamlet* interpretation unfolds in line with the history of gender relations' (112).

How do we define masculinity and femininity? Does Hamlet's beard (mentioned by him and presumably worn by Richard Burbage, but inappropriate to most modern, clean-shaven actors in the role) signify that he is an adult male? How old is he anyway? Can he be legitimately played by a woman because he is too young, or too effeminate, or both? Did the eighteenth century's squeamishness about the excesses of revenge and the reasons for Hamlet's alleged delay solve one problem about the hero by transferring the focus to a different area, that of gender itself? As Belsey writes, 'In due course, Hamlet's hesitation would be ascribed to a particular weakness of will or a specific mental disorder; he was consti-tutionally indecisive, depressive, or just plain mad, conditions thought commoner among women than men' (119). This led not only to the triumphs of Sarah Siddons, Charlotte Cushman and others on stage but to the apotheosis of the female Hamlet in Asta Nielsen's representation of the prince in her 1920 film as a woman masquerading as a man.

Hamlet is of course one of the most frequently filmed narratives in world cinema, inspiring countless adaptations as well as straight versions. The films in the Anglo-American tradition, especially those by Laurence Olivier (1948), Franco Zeffirelli (1990) and Kenneth Branagh (1996), have been extensively analysed (see the 'Resources' section below, under 'Cinematic Resources', 'Adaptation and Appropriation' and 'Books'). By way of contrast, in his chapter on '*Hamlet*, Cinema, the World', Mark Thornton Burnett writes mainly about the 'global exposure' of the play, concentrating on lesser-known adaptations from China, Japan and Iran but comparing them with two films that are more familiar to Anglophone audiences, Michael Almereyda's *Hamlet* (2000) and Grigori Kozintsev's *Gamlet*[11] (1964). Like Lois Potter in her chapter on performance history, he emphasizes what he calls the play's 'manoeuvrability – its capacity for commenting on local situations and ideologies that run along divergent lines' (135). As he says, virtually every country in the world has crafted its own cinematic engagement with *Hamlet*, finding its own connections and relevancies.

In his first section Burnett explores the political critique of corporate corruption in post-war Tokyo represented in Akira Kurosawa's *The Bad Sleep Well* (1960) and draws parallels with Almereyda's dystopian vision of late-capitalist New York. Despite the earlier film being quite a distant adaptation of Shakespeare's play, the film-makers display 'a shared response to issues of moral accountability, corporate responsibility and government' (144). Next, two films made in China in 2006, Sherwood Hu's *Prince of the Himalayas* and Xiaogang Feng's *The Banquet,* can be seen as comparable adaptations of *Hamlet* in that each of them 'looks to an ancient world as part of a confrontation with the contemporary and each uses Shakespeare to reflect upon "Asia", broadly conceived and multiply understood, at a key stage of its recent global emergence' (144). Finally, not the tragic hero but Ophelia takes centre stage in a study of two apparently unrelated films, Kozintsev's relatively straightforward version of the play and the Iranian adaptation *Tardid*, directed by Varuzh Karim Masihi in 2009. While Kozintsev's Ophelia is seen as hopelessly incarcerated by the system in which she lives, Masihi's heroine is an independent agent who is able to question the similar constrictions of her situation in modern Tehran. It turns out that the parallels here are quite conscious ones as Masihi has mentioned his admiration of Kozintsev in an interview and even includes a shot of a poster advertising *Gamlet* in his own film, suggesting that it is 'an adaptation of an adaptation' (155). Burnett concludes that these and other cinematic encounters with *Hamlet* 'not only showcase the vitality of the play's afterlives but represent imaginative creations in their own right' (160).

Frank McGuinness, one of Ireland's leading contemporary playwrights, is well known not only for his original plays such as *Observe the Sons of Ulster Marching Towards the Somme, Someone Who'll Watch Over Me* and *The Match Box,* but also for his creative encounters with other dramatists, ranging from Euripides and Sophocles to Chekhov, Ibsen, Racine and Lorca. His versions of plays by these writers from other traditions have been widely performed on stages in Ireland, England, the United States and elsewhere. They could certainly be described as not just translations but 'imaginative creations in their own right'. In one of his own plays, *Mutabilitie*, he imagines a visit by an Elizabethan playwright called William (who bears some relation to William Shakespeare) to an English poet living in Ireland called Edmund (who bears some relation to Edmund Spenser). In his contribution to this volume, McGuinness sets *Hamlet* in the tradition of Greek tragedies as well as in relation to the poetry of T. S. Eliot and William Butler Yeats. The innate theatricality of the play carries a particular resonance for its audience: 'We enter the theatre to meet *Hamlet* as the living. We leave it as ghosts, drained, exhausted by the energy, the expense of spirit in a waste of shame happening in this text' (168). The focus here on the metatheatricality of *Hamlet* is particularly striking, coming as it does from a man of the theatre. Finally, Hamlet's provisional decision 'to be' brings us up against the realization that our own ultimate destiny is 'not to be'.

1

The Critical Backstory

John Lee

Given that this is an account of the critical history of *Hamlet* in English, it is remarkable how European an affair it remains in main outline, and from how early on. One could say that a French-influenced eighteenth century gave way to a German-influenced nineteenth century, which led on to a Franco-German twentieth. Sometimes that relationship was oppositional; many English and Scottish critics writing on *Hamlet* in the eighteenth century, though by no means all, aimed to repudiate Voltaire's judgement that the play was one of Shakespeare's 'monstrous Farces' (1733: 167). The nineteenth-century relationship was more companionate, with Goethe's and Schlegel's accounts of the play, and particularly its Prince, providing interpretations which English critics, now increasingly including critics from North America, naturalized, modified, and respectfully argued against. By the time the twentieth century arrived, and with it the profes-sionalization of the study of English literature in particular and the humanities and social sciences more generally, writing on *Hamlet* could be said to have become European in its spirit. The nineteenth-century philosophy of Hegel cast a long twentieth-century shadow first through A. C. Bradley's criticism, and then through a host of Marxist-influenced approaches (Taylor 1975). Freud became the single most influential figure, particularly in criticism from the second half of the century. Jacques Lacan and Jacques Derrida also emerged as important figures, and were themselves heavily indebted to continental theories of language. The play had become a settled part of a European intellectual and cultural landscape with which critics writing in English, wherever they were located, were intimately familiar.

Yet it is perhaps more remarkable how variously European a play *Hamlet* itself is, in its persons, scenes, and settings and times. That there is, perhaps, only one English name (or one name properly Englished), Gertrude, might not surprise – this is a play, after all, set in Denmark, in the mid-twelfth century. There are, though, not that many Danish names either; there is Hamlet, and presumably Rosencrantz and Guildenstern, and Osric. But the largest group of names are Roman: Claudius, Polonius, Marcellus, Cornelius and Horatio (which last might possibly be claimed as another Englished name). Then there are the Spanish-sounding Francisco, Bernardo and Reynaldo, and the French-sounding Fortinbras, along with the mentioned, though not seen, French-Norman Lamord (in the Second Quarto; in the Folio he is Lamound). Of the fictional persons Lucianus, the nephew of the King in the 'Mouse-trap' (as Hamlet calls it), seems Roman, as does the King's wife, Baptista, though the King himself, Gonzago, sounds more Italian, and the story itself is said to be written in the 'choicest Italian', although it is set in Vienna. Another of the play-within-a-play scenes draws on the *Aeneid*, the Roman epic poem, and takes us far back in time to the moment when Aeneas tells the Carthaginian Queen, Dido, of how Priam, King of Troy, was cut down by the sword of the Greek Pyrrhus. Polonius tells us that, while a student at 'university', he once acted Julius Caesar, a Roman emperor. That it was a university suggests that the play has moved forward in time much closer to Shakespeare's day; such a chronological move is of a piece with Hamlet having returned to Elsinore from the

German (Saxon) University of Wittenberg, which had been founded only in 1502. The Paris which Laertes visits sounds equally contemporary; the rapier with which he practises his duelling skills is a relatively recent, and fashionable, development in civilian arms. Elsinore itself seems to have more the architecture of a Renaissance great house or palace than that of a medieval castle (Everett 1990), and the players who visit it seem absolute contemporaries of Shakespeare: they have, according to Rosencrantz, been driven out of Wittenberg by the 'little eyases', or children's companies, amidst much 'throwing about of brains'. This controversy seems to reference the *Poetomachia*, or Poets' War, of the London theatres (Bednarz 2001), which broke out around 1600 between Ben Jonson, Shakespeare, John Marston and Thomas Dekker.

Hamlet is a play which locates its events, and in particular the central event of the killing of a king, in the long perspectives of a classicized and European literary culture. Jonson, the sharpest of Elizabethan and Jacobean critics, judged Shakespeare on a European level. In his dedicatory verse to the First Folio, the 1623 collected edition of Shakespeare's plays, he urged Britain to celebrate its possession of an author '*To whom all Scenes of* Europe *homage owe*' (Kökeritz 1955: n.p.). This chapter is the four-century story of that celebration and payment, in brief and as it has emerged in English-language criticism.[1] That brevity needs emphasis. *Hamlet* is probably the most written about play in English literature. Oscar Wilde, contemplating that vast body of work towards the end of the nineteenth-century, asked whether we should be wondering whether the Prince was mad, or his critics (Ellman 1987: 282). It is a fair point, nicely put, but its humour risks being a little mean-spirited. To read the history of *Hamlet* criticism is to read an abstract and brief chronicle of some of the main movements in the intellectual life of Europe and the English-speaking nations over the last four centuries. Time and again the great writers and thinkers of an age are drawn to explain *Hamlet*, and to explain their fascination for explaining *Hamlet*. That the resulting narrative might be, at times, baffling, or maddening, and perhaps even a little mad, is true; but it has a fascination in itself, and it offers to enrich our understanding of the play. The highly-selective history that follows favours the latter over the former; it chooses to follow the most critically productive and influential moments in the criticism of the play and leaves uncommented some of the less influential developments of the critical tradition. It also turns and returns its attention to the gravedigger's scene (5.1), both because that scene functions as a useful critical touchstone, and because it is representative of some of the most distinctive qualities of Shakespeare's literary and dramatic achievement.

The seventeenth century

While Europe, as will be seen, took some time to pay the homage Jonson declared it owed, *Hamlet* seems, from all that we know, to have been an immediate success in London. At the time of the play's first performance, 1600–1, there is little literary criticism *per se*, and less criticism of the new, and slightly suspect, professional theatre and its plays. The most immediate response, sometime before February 1601, was that of Gabriel Harvey, a Cambridge academic, who wrote in the margins of his copy of Speght's edition of Chaucer (1598) that 'the tragedie', along with *The Rape of Lucrece*, 'have it in them to please the wiser sort', while 'the younger sort', he thought, would prefer the more erotic *Venus and Adonis* (f.422v). More useful evidence of the play's popularity is provided by the number of allusions that were made to it, and particularly to the Prince, in other literary works (Munro 1932). These, particularly when compared with the number of allusions to other plays, suggest that Hamlet quickly became a recognizable and admired figure.

Written commentary very gradually increases as the century goes on, and is often hostile. Between 1661 and 1668,

Samuel Pepys in his *Diary* notes four visits to see *Hamlet* performed, as well as his and his wife's learning by heart of 'To be or not to bee' (Halliday 1949: 211). Earlier, in 1655, Abraham Wright had written in his commonplace book that the tragedy was 'but an indifferent play, the lines but meane'. Such a jotting may be of little consequence, but in 1661 John Evelyn, writing in his diary on 26 November, suggested a process of cultural change was under way. 'The old playe' had begun 'to disgust this refined age: since his Majestie being so long abroad' (Vickers 1974: I, 4). The abroad here was France, where Charles II had spent the interregnum after his father's defeat in the English civil war (1642–51). For Evelyn, France was characterized by the possession of different, more civilized, critical and cultural tastes, by which *Hamlet* was found wanting. Those values were seen to have travelled back to England with the restoration of the monarchy, and its court, in 1660. Central to those values was the notion of decorum, a single term which stood as shorthand for the complicated activity of the formulation of a set of criteria by which to judge what it was proper to represent on stage. As the title of Jeremy Collier's *A Short View of the Immorality and Profaneness of the English Stage, Together with the Sense of Antiquity upon this Argument* (1698) suggests, these values drew on classical precedent (and so are often referred to as 'neo-classical'), and they could be seen to rebuke contemporary theatrical practice. Where Euripides, a Greek tragedian, had ensured that Phaedra 'keeps her Modesty even after She has lost her Wits', Shakespeare's Ophelia both lost her wits and was seen to grow 'Lewd' on stage. This was both indecorous and unnecessary, Collier argued, relishing his hard-heartedness, since as Shakespeare 'was resolv'd to drown the Lady like a Kitten', he might 'have set her a swimming a little sooner', thus sparing the audience her sexually suggestive singing (10).

In the similarly critical *A Short View of Tragedy* (1693), Thomas Rymer argues that Shakespeare's talent lay in comedy; in tragedy, he 'appears quite out of his Element; his Brains are turn'd, he raves and rambles, without any coherence, any spark of reason, or any rule to controul him' (156). Shakespeare, here, looks a lot like his (to Rymer) mad Prince. This Hamletian Shakespeare cannot help but mix generic forms: 'But to him a Tragedy in *Burlesk*, a merry Tragedy was no Monster, no absurdity, nor at all preposterous' (157). This is, for Rymer, particularly terrible because of its moral consequences; such a mixture will 'delude our senses, disorder our thoughts, addle our brain, pervert our affections' (146). A mixed-mode tragedy will, in other words, lose its social purpose, and become an entertainment which tends to corrupt.

This was, in its description of Shakespeare's method, not news. Anthony Scoloker had written in 1604 that Shakespeare managed to please 'the vulgars *Element*' by making sure 'the *Commedian* rides' even then 'when the *Tragedian* stands on Tip-toe': 'Faith it should please all, like Prince *Hamlet*' (A2). That mixture of the comic with the tragic was not unique to *Hamlet*, or Shakespeare; but as the seventeenth century progressed, such a mixture of the comedian with the tragedian became ever more problematic for those wanting to praise Shakespeare. Evelyn had called the cultural shift correctly; the prestige of the classics within criticism was now overwhelming, and Greek and Roman literature and criticism, especially the Greek tragedy of Sophocles and Aristotle's commentary on it in the *Poetics*, were generally seen as authoritative. Greek tragic dramas contained very little comedy; why, then, should Shakespeare's, or other writers', tragedies be different? Aristotle, in the lecture notes that became the *Poetics*, had crucially provided a defence of the moral purpose of tragedy; if Shakespeare's tragedies did not fit Aristotle's model, were they immoral? And by the time Italian and French critics of the sixteenth and seventeenth centuries had elaborated that model with, most obviously, the notion of the 'three unities' of time, place and action, Shakespeare's tragedies began to look scandalously ungeneric.

The eighteenth century

Defending the presence of comedy even in some of the most tragic moments in *Hamlet* is central to the first 200 years of criticism. One scene in particular emerges as representative of this 'please all', mixed Shakespeare: that of the gravedigger. In the middle of tragic events, almost at the play's climax itself, the audience are whisked out of the world of the court, and put, graveside, amongst the banter and bad puns of the sexton and a second man, working up a thirst over the slow digging of a grave. For many critics, this was quite simply unbearable.

'It was the most imprudent thing that ever I did in my life; but I had sworn I would not leave the Stage until I had rescued that noble play from all the rubbish of the 5th act' (Garrick 1963: II, 845). David Garrick has strong claims to have been the greatest actor of the eighteenth century. He was also, famously, Shakespeare's great defender and champion. He had overseen the Stratford, or Shakespeare, Jubilee in 1769, which effectively crowned Shakespeare as the National Poet (Dobson 1992). Yet, three years later in 1772, towards the end of an illustrious career, he risked his reputation to produce a version of the play without the gravedigger scene. It was a particular risk because this was a particularly popular scene of a popular play; unusually amongst Shakespeare's performed plays, *Hamlet* had, up to this point, escaped wholesale radical revision.

Garrick's imprudence is a symptom of the critical pressure this scene had come under in the eighteenth century. The attacks on Shakespeare by Voltaire, a Frenchman, were often held responsible. This Voltaire features, in a relatively moderate portrait, in Elizabeth Montagu *An Essay* (1769), where he judges Shakespeare to be the writer of 'monstrous Farces, called by him Tragedies', and to believe that the English admiration of these show the nation's 'barbarism and ignorance' (2). This was not unfair: in his first widely published piece on Shakespeare, 'On Tragedy', translated into

English in 1733, Voltaire uses almost exactly those words as
he examines *Hamlet*, and takes the gravedigger's scene as its
defining absurdity. What this portrait downplays, however,
is Voltaire's praising of the natural dramatic effectiveness of
Shakespeare's plays: 'The shining monsters of Shakespear,
give infinite more Delight than the judicious Images of the
Moderns' (179–80).

This two-dimensional Voltaire, typically seen as a zealous
nationalist and a dogmatic theorist, offered to divert attention
from the dominance within English criticism of neo-classical
critical dissatisfaction with the mixed modes of *Hamlet*.
Some Remarks on the Tragedy of Hamlet Prince of Denmark
(1736) praises Shakespeare for his 'Nobleness and Sublimity
of Thought' (2), and is typical of its period in singling out
the Ghost scene as especially representative of those qualities.
No other scene is 'more capable of stirring up our noblest
Passions', as the audience's natural 'Terror' fights with its
sense of 'Filial Piety' (22). Yet that praise, and that scene, is
counterbalanced by what emerges almost as its evil twin: the
gravedigger's scene. Though 'much applauded' by audiences,
it is 'very unbecoming such a Piece as this' (37).

Some Remarks are thought to have been written by Sir
Thomas Hanmer. If so, they are also representative of their
time in being the work of an amateur critic. At the other
end of the century, William Richardson is, largely, a professional critic. By the time he wrote his *Essays on some of
Shakespeare's Dramatic Characters*, he was the Professor of
Humanity at Glasgow, a position which saw him writing and
lecturing mainly on the language, literature and history of
classical Rome and Greece. *Hamlet*, uniquely, he treated in
two essays (1774 and 1784). His account of the play is fuller,
more detailed, and more theoretically and methodologically
coherent than that of *Some Remarks*. In its increasing focus on
the Prince and the Prince's character it is also representative of
one of the main developments in the century's criticism.

Hanmer had been interested in character; drawing on
Alexander Pope's preface to *The Works of Shakespeare* (1725),

Hanmer had declared Shakespeare's 'particular Excellency' to consist of 'the Variety and Singularity of his Characters, and in the constant Conformity of each Character to it self from its very first setting out in the Play, quite to the End' (2). The difficulty with this, as it concerns *Hamlet*, is that it is not clear how the Prince demonstrates this excellence. That was a part of the problem with the 'very unbecoming' scene in the graveyard. Hanmer saw such deviations from the Prince's proper 'Heroical Disposition' (18) as examples either of Shakespeare pandering to the low tastes of his age or, following John Dennis (1712), of Shakespeare's lack of classical learning. Richardson, by contrast, has a far more complex model of the mind than Hanmer. Richardson is fascinated by Shakespeare's understanding of how the human mind works, and especially by the ways in which the mind may control the passions. Richardson anticipates Coleridge and what has been called the Romantic Hamlet, by arguing for a Prince whose inconsistencies of character are incidental; Hamlet is a 'young person of good sense, of strong moral feelings, possessing an exquisite sense of character, great sensibility, together with much ardour and constancy of affection' who is put in a very 'peculiar' situation which, given his fine qualities, admits of no simple response or resolution (1797: 124).

Yet Richardson continues to share Hanmer's worries about the indecorous mixture of tones within the play. He, too, loves the scene with the Ghost. Benefitting from Edmund Burke's explication of the sublime (1757) as something different in kind from the beautiful, he is able to offer a richer account of its 'awful horror': he notes that the Ghost does not describe what he calls the 'secrets' of his 'prison-house' (1.5.14) itself, but rather the *effects* these would have on Hamlet as a viewer (1797: 97–8). Just as with Hanmer, though, Richardson finds the gravedigger's scene deeply problematic. In his essay 'On the Faults of Shakespeare', he uses it as a key example of how Shakespeare has been misled by the standard maxim given to poets: to '"follow nature"' (1797: 377). Gravediggers may speak grossly, he argues, but fine writing needs above all a consistency in passion, emotion and sentiment, and Richardson appeals to other arts for his proof: 'We find nothing in music or painting so inconsistent as the dissonant mixture of sentiments and emotions so frequent in English tragedy' (1797: 382).

Eighteenth-century criticism of *Hamlet* found itself in a bind. The play came increasingly to be seen as representative of Shakespeare's achievement, and did so at a time when Shakespeare was being increasingly seen as the National Poet on account of the outstanding nature of that achievement. Yet giving positive accounts of the play remained deeply problematic for critics given the neo-classical principles to which they were largely committed. What was needed was for criticism to step outside its neo-classical perspective; but stepping outside a critical paradigm takes an enormous amount of intellectual effort. The neo-classic critic who came closest to achieving such a move was Samuel Johnson (1765). Johnson states, as a *positive* observation, that '*Shakespeare*'s plays are not in the rigorous or critical sense either tragedies or comedies, but compositions of a distinct kind' (xiii), which kind he later calls 'the mingled drama' (xiv). It is not that he dismisses neo-classical criteria; it is rather that Johnson simply has the confidence to back his own judgement, and declare that another literary genre is to be seen here at work, which has its own aims. That leads him on to one of the greatest paragraphs of descriptive Shakespearean criticism, as he notes that Shakespeare's plays are concerned with 'exhibiting the real state of sublunary nature, which partakes of good and evil, joy and sorrow, mingled with endless proportions and innumerable modes of combination' (xiii). 'When *Shakespeare*'s plan is understood,' Johnson continues, by which he refers to Shakespeare's compositional method of varying between seriousness and merriment, 'most of the criticisms of *Rhymer* and *Voltaire* vanish away. The play of *Hamlet* is opened, without impropriety, by two sentinels [...] and the Grave-diggers themselves may be heard with applause' (xvi).

The earlier nineteenth century:
The romantic *Hamlet*

When the American H. N. Hudson writes, in 1848, of the gravedigger's scene as one of the 'manifold excellencies' of *Hamlet*, it is clear that many eighteenth-century critical preoccupations have been left far behind. 'The heterogeneous elements which are brought together in the graveyard scene, with its strange mixture of songs and witticism and dead men's bones, and its still stranger transitions of the grave, the sprightly, the meditative, the solemn, the playful and the grotesque, make it one of the most wonderful yet most natural scenes the poet has given us' (2.133). What is new here is Hudson's utter lack of anxiety about the admixture of the scene, and of the play in general. Hudson's enjoyment of the 'complexity and versatility' (2.90) of the Prince is of a piece with this, but has a longer heritage; Aaron Hill, in an essay in *The Prompter* in 1735, talked of the Prince as having being adorned by Shakespeare 'with a Succession of the most *opposite* Beauties, which are *varied*, like *Colours* on the *Chameleon*, according to the *different Lights* in which we behold him' (Vickers 1974: 3.35). Henry Mackenzie, a contemporary of Richardson, perhaps most nearly anticipates Hudson. In a pair of essays in *The Mirror* in 1780, Mackenzie advances an account of Hamlet as a 'melancholy man' (*The Mirror* 1793: 332). This 'leading idea' (320), as Mackenzie terms it, explains the variable and uncertain nature of the Prince: such a man 'feels in himself [...] a sort of double person' (332). For Mackenzie, it is the gravedigger's scene which is particularly illustrative of this doubleness. Shakespeare has departed from the rules of drama, to delineate 'the passions and affections of the human mind, as they exist in reality, with all the various colourings which they receive in the mixed scenes of life' (333). The scene and the play illustrate the 'irregularities' of genius which may depart from the 'common rules' of criticism (319).

In making this argument for genius and its irregularity, Mackenzie is indebted to Edward Young's *Conjectures on Original Composition* (1759). To Young, classical tradition was not a simple good. It held obvious risks; there were now fewer original works of literature because 'illustrious examples *engross, prejudice*, and *intimidate*' the present (17). Shakespeare is the great example of the modern original, and 'Who knows whether *Shakespeare* might not have thought less, if he had read more?' (81). Mackenzie still feels, however, as Hudson does not, the need to respond to neo-classical criteria. In between Mackenzie and Hudson, and perhaps responsible for that change, lies the literary criticism of Samuel Taylor Coleridge.

Coleridge supplied a series of intellectually satisfying formulations with which to declare, and mark, the break with neo-classical traditions that in large part defined the Romantic movement; in particular he offered an account of literary genius that stressed not its irregularity, but rather its regularity, or organic unity: 'the power of acting creatively under laws of its own origination', as he phrased it in his 1812–13 lectures (Foakes 1989: 52). Modern tragedies were now to be judged by what they set out to do, not by what Greek tragedians had set out to do. They were also to be read, as much as, if not more than, to be watched. This stance is most famously associated with an essay of Charles Lamb (1811). Lamb was a great theatregoer, and he makes clear that he is 'not arguing that Hamlet should not be acted, but how much *Hamlet* is made another thing by being acted' (302). It is an important distinction. The play becomes one of his main examples of the paradoxical conclusion his theatre-going has led him to, that 'the plays of Shakespeare are less calculated for performance on a stage, than those of almost any other dramatist whatever' (300). The soliloquies' lack of relationship to the plot had long been noted; Lamb now suggests that they are in tension with the dramatic medium itself. The text becomes a more complicated space under Lamb's gaze; performance, in his eyes, reduced and flattened this complexity, tending to draw the audience's attention to the actor's skill. For Lamb,

Hamlet's anger at Ophelia is a sign of residual love; for actors it is an opportunity to stand centre-stage.

Hamlet's treatment of Ophelia had been written of before; but Ophelia now becomes an object of critical interest in herself. Anna Jameson (1832) looks to substantiate Ophelia's importance, arguing against the tradition that had seen her a trivial character unworthy of Hamlet's attention. To Jameson she is a kind of second-Hamlet of the play, Hamlet's nearest equal in the complexity of her character. Her madness comes about as her feelings gain their full force before her nature learns to bear them; it is as if 'burning fluid [was] poured into a crystal vase' (137). Jameson is here offering a parallel to what was becoming one of the most famous Romantic descriptions of the Prince, given by the protagonist in the German J. W. von Goethe's *Wilhelm Meister's Apprenticeship* (1795, translated 1824). The play showed 'a great action laid upon a soul unfit for the performance of it [...] There is an oak-tree planted in a costly jar, which should have borne only pleasant flowers in its bosom; the roots expand, the jar is shivered' (II.74–5). Ophelia, however, is a relatively briefly drawn character; with the exception of one, important, monologue (3.1.149–60), we hear little from her about her own experience. Mary Cowden Clarke (1850–2) looked to rectify this by describing Ophelia's childhood. It is, in its details, deeply disturbing, being repeatedly punctuated by threats and examples of male sexual violence. It is no surprise that, later, she finds her brother's and father's advice to her about Hamlet's intentions persuasive.

The earlier nineteenth century: Hazlitt

Clarke's *The Girlhood of Shakespeare's Heroines* is a good example of the way in which, under Coleridge's influence, character criticism looked to treat Shakespeare's dramatic persons as, in effect, real people. (The reverse was also true;

the nineteenth century saw a succession of distinguished psychiatrists, in England and North America, publishing works which discovered Shakespearean characters amongst their patients.[2]) Coleridge had sought to explain the 'germ' of the Prince's character which, once grasped, explained away all the seeming inconsistencies of Hamlet's behaviour. For Coleridge this was the fact that the Prince was 'a man living in meditation, called upon to act by every motive human and divine, but the great purpose of life is defeated by continually resolving to do, yet doing nothing but resolve' (Foakes 1989: 72). For the Shelley of 'Byron and Shelley on the Character of Hamlet', the Prince 'represents the profound philosopher; or, rather, the errors to which a contemplative and ideal mind is liable' (331). Such a notion of solution put Byron 'fast asleep' (336); others were more impressed. Jonathan Bate, in his introduction to *The Romantics on Shakespeare* (1992), refers to Coleridge's Prince as the 'single most influential act', which laid 'the foundation for more than a century's thinking about Shakespeare's most celebrated play' (2). Yet it was not the only romantic Hamlet. H. N. Hudson had noted with approval Coleridge's remark 'that Shakespeare's characters are classes of men individualized' (87), while adding that a distinction needs to be made for Hamlet, 'undoubtedly the most complex character in dramatic literature' (90): 'Hamlet, in short, is the very abridgement and eclecticism of humanity: in the words of another, it is *we* who are Hamlet' (87). The 'another' was William Hazlitt (1817). Hazlitt's Prince is often discussed as a variation on Coleridge's, and is often used particularly as an example of the way in which critics, trying to understand the inner working of a character, tend to find themselves in the characters they study. Hazlitt's Prince, in fact, is distinct from Coleridge's, and Hazlitt intends something rather more interesting than is usually allowed when he says 'it is *we* who are Hamlet' (1817: 104). Lamb had noted how the reader or spectator 'oftentimes mistake the powers which he [Shakespeare] positively creates in us, for nothing more than indigenous faculties of our own minds'

(1811: 304). Hazlitt's suggestion is more radical. Coleridge's interest in psychology was genuinely innovative (Vickers 2007), and yet, following a notion of identity deriving from Descartes, he saw identity as something which was basically fixed and essential to the person. Hazlitt, by contrast, has a more Montaignesque notion of identity, which sees it as something largely processional which is constituted by the person's own actions and experiences (Lee 2000). Within this self-constituting, as opposed to self-mastering, notion of identity, our constant experience of the Prince makes him in some ways a part of us. Oscar Wilde, in 'The Decay of Lying' (1905 [1891]), would put it more directly: 'Schopenhauer has analyzed the pessimism that characterises modern thought, but Hamlet invented it. The world has become sad because a puppet was once melancholy' (34). This is quite different from any Coleridgean projecting of ourselves onto a character; Hazlitt and Wilde imagine the character opening up kinds of experience and selfhood for our selves. Bound together with the work of Sigmund Freud, it underlies the claims of its most expansive modern proponent, Harold Bloom, that we owe to *Shakespeare*, in the words of one of his work's subtitles, *The Invention of the Human* (1998).

The later nineteenth century

'Verily, given a printing-press upon German soil', says Dr. Furness, 'and lo! an essay on Hamlet' (1904: 3). So begins Albert H. Tolman's 1898 essay: the Dr Furness quoted is H. H. Furness, the editor of the *New Variorum Shakespeare*. Furness, in this multi-volume edition of the plays, began with the remarkable aim of drawing together all the critical commentary of significance on each play up to the date of publication. *Hamlet* was the third play to be published, in 1877, and it was the only play to require two volumes. The *New Variorum Shakespeare* was a landmark event, a sign that Shakespeare studies were essentially professionalized. The nature of Tolman's essay represents a smaller statement of the same professional fact. Tolman, thanks in large part to Furness, is aware not only of the amount of criticism of *Hamlet*, but its availability. His opening goes on: 'England and the United States, as might be expected, vie with Germany in contributing to the literature of this play. All the sister nations of Europe, too, have their own essays on Hamlet'. Europe, as Ben Jonson suggested it must, had begun paying homage.

Tolman, cautious of adding to that already huge body of work, instead attempts to classify it. Starting from what he sees as the Ghost's three-fold command, that Hamlet should revenge his father, not taint his mind in doing so, and not act against his mother, Tolman identifies eighteen kinds of critical explanation. Of the particular critics he names, sixteen are German, seven North American, seven English and three French. Such a crude counting understates the German influence; for Tolman it is by and large clear that the *important* critics are German, and above all Karl Werder. Werder, in *The Heart of Hamlet's Mystery* (1907 [1875]), argued that Hamlet's delay was a result of the nature of the task he is required to do, which is no simple act of revenge, but rather the exposure of Claudius's misdeeds to public justice and public retribution (49). Given the nature of the crime, the evidence Hamlet possesses, and the nature of the political governance of Denmark, this is no easy matter. Werder sees himself as flatly dissenting from the previous, Goethe-inspired criticism of the prince; where Goethe offered a subjective reading, that is a reading which looks to the Prince's character to explain the Prince's actions, Werder sees himself offering an objective reading, that is one which looks to the Prince's circumstances. As Tolman points out, under such an objective view what had been seen as a tragedy of character becomes a tragedy of fate.

In *Shakespearian Tragedy* (1904), A. C. Bradley pushed back against such a view, in two chapters which are often seen as the culmination of the nineteenth-century line of subjective, or character, criticism of *Hamlet*. If the task is such as Werder describes it, Bradley asks, why does the Prince not once mention it, or its implications? Bradley, by contrast, is remarkably attentive to the whole of the text. He points out the characteristic 'strange lightning of the mind' (151) produced by Hamlet's quibbles, and notices Hamlet's verbal tic of repeating words and phrases. He reconstructs, from textual evidence, the Prince's character before his father's death. Modifying the 'Schlegel-Coleridge' (105) picture, Bradley insists that Hamlet's irresolution is a symptom of the 'state of profound melancholy' into which he has been thrown by recent events (108). Bradley is one of the first to insist on the centrality to the play of the Prince's horror at his mother's actions subsequent to the death of his father (118). He constructs a picture of a once healthy and vigorous Prince of action, who is seen becoming a brooding and irresolute, passive onlooker.

Like Coleridge, Bradley is willing, as Hudson had put it, 'to go round behind the text' (1848: 91), treating the dramatic persons as if they were living people. Yet Bradley is not only, or finally, a psychological critic. Edward Dowden had been the great British critical figure before Bradley. His *Shakspeare: A Critical Study of His Mind and Art* (1875) was built upon the work of the New Shakespere Society. The NSS was, alongside Furness's *Variorum* edition, the other great marker of the professionalization of Shakespeare studies. Members of the society applied the new 'science' (as they claimed it to be) of bibliography to Shakespeare's works. One consequence was the development of a more accurate chronology of Shakespeare's plays. Dowden used this chronology to argue that a developmental (not biographical) arc could be seen within Shakespeare's works. *Hamlet*, for Dowden, marked a key moment in Shakespeare's artistic development: it is the play which shows, in large part by its rejection of any single controlling idea (and here Dowden can be seen pushing back against Coleridge's influence), that Shakespeare had reached 'the full maturity of his manhood' (142). The play's mystery and obscurity was 'vital' (112) – both, that is, central, and that which gives life to the play. The Prince, like life, is in some ways inexplicable, because he is of life-like complexity; as life cannot be finally explained, neither may works of great art which deal with life; both are finally, to some extent, mysterious.

Bradley disagreed. He acknowledges that life, in its complexities, may finally be inexplicable to us, if we seek answers to questions of causation. However, while 'the mysteriousness of life is one thing, the psychological unintelligibility of a dramatic character', Bradley argues, 'is quite another; and the second does not show the first, it shows only the incapacity or folly of the dramatist' (1905 [1904]: 93). Dowden had misplaced the source of the play's mystery; the mystery does not reside in the character, but in the nature of Hamlet's relationship with his world. (See also Bradley 1909 [1901], 1929.) Views such as Dowden's, according to Bradley, made the mistake of not distinguishing between the psychological point of view and the tragic point of view, which was itself also distinct from the objective point of view. Our sense of the play's mystery is not the result of the unintelligibility of the Prince, but rather our constant sense that there is 'some vaster power' (171) at work, pushing the dramatic persons 'through devious paths, the very paths they take in order to escape' (172), towards the play's dreadfully inescapable conclusion.

The early twentieth century and the *Ur-Hamlet*

The ongoing academic professionalization of the discipline of literary criticism did not, of course, lead to any diminution in the number of competing accounts of the play. Indeed, the play itself, the object of critical attention, became seen to be more various and complicated. The fact that Shakespeare's

Hamlet was not the first play of that name was not news; Richard Farmer (1821 [1767]) had drawn attention to the mention, by Thomas Nashe, of a *Hamlet* in 1589. Farmer had assumed this play was an earlier version by Shakespeare; Edmond Malone suggested, in 1778, what would become the more widely accepted position, that this earlier play was written by another dramatist, Thomas Kyd (1790: 183). The nature of this play, which Boas (1901: xlv) named the *Ur-Hamlet* (the German 'Ur' meaning 'Original'), and in particular its relationship with Shakespeare's *Hamlet*, and *Hamlet*'s relationship with the genre of revenge tragedy, now once again became prominent questions. Elmer Edgar Stoll (1919) argued that Hamlet's delay was to be explained strictly in terms of generic convention; without the revenger's delay, there would be no time for the play. J. M. Robertson (1919) took an opposite view: Shakespeare had tried to differentiate his play from the barbaric *Ur-Hamlet*; had, by and large, succeeded; but areas remained where 'the construction is incoherent' (67), especially where Shakespeare's complex new Prince failed to fit the old revenge plot. As Graham Bradshaw (1987) snappily summed up the envisaged situation, the *Ur-Hamlet* was *Hamlet* without our Prince (112).

William Empson (1953a, 1953b) turned both Stoll's and Robertson's arguments around. For the first audience, Empson argues, there was no incoherence, but this was not because of their willingness to accept revenge convention. Rather, they shared the Prince's sense that what the revenge plot asked him to do was absurdly old-fashioned; the Prince embodied the audience's frustrations with 'old' revenge conventions and the *Ur-Hamlet*. In doing so, the play initiated a self-consciously theatrical exploration of identity as a kind of willed and unwilled performance of a role one could not fully escape, and which one felt, at different times, to define one more or less badly. The Prince and the play grew interpretatively problematic, however, when knowledge of the *Ur-Hamlet* was lost. Bradshaw (1987) saw the clash between the different kinds of play within *Hamlet* creating a situation in which one dramatic person, the Prince, is asked to embody the 'opposed views of Nature and Value' (12) which in others of Shakespeare's plays are given to two or more dramatic persons. The result is a Prince who shares the intellectual incoherences and sceptical tendencies of his age.

After so much praise, such willingness by various critics to allow (again) that *Hamlet* might be, in some ways, imperfect, could seem healthy, almost liberatingly iconoclastic. T. S. Eliot (1950 [1919]) offers the most famous example; he declares the play to be, not Shakespeare's masterpiece, but 'most certainly an artistic failure [...] the "Mona Lisa" of literature' (98–9). This failure owed much to Shakespeare's failure to integrate the new play with the old, especially where Hamlet's sense of his mother's guilt was concerned. Shakespeare's Hamlet's emotional response was far 'in *excess* of the facts as they appear' (101). *Hamlet*, Eliot argued, 'like the sonnets, is full of some stuff that the writer could not drag to light' (100), as Shakespeare had failed to find the necessary '"objective correlative"' to express Hamlet's emotion (100). For Eliot, the real puzzle was why Shakespeare had attempted such a revision.

The early twentieth century: Freud, and Freudian readings

'Fleetingly the thought passed through my head that the same thing might be at the bottom of *Hamlet* as well.' This line, in an 1897 letter of Sigmund Freud's to Wilhelm Fliess charting the progress of Freud's self-analysis, announces what would become the twentieth century's most influential reading of the play. That reading, and the psychoanalytic method it is a part of, develops over many years (Freud 1979 [1909] to 1997 [1927]). But here, at the start, some of its most recognizable features are present. Hamlet is seen as a hysteric, a neurotic type who suffers from an Oedipus complex: Hamlet, like all (male) children, including Freud, desires the love of his

mother, and so, being jealous of his father, wishes to kill him.
For most boys such love and hatred is only a stage in their
psychosexual development, and they successfully repress such
Oedipal desires as part of their maturation. Hamlet has failed
to do this, and so, unconsciously, he identifies himself with
Claudius, recognizing in Claudius's actions the fulfilment of
his own deepest wishes. How can he judge or take revenge on
Claudius without judging and taking revenge on himself? That
conscience makes cowards of us all becomes, for Freud, an
unconscious statement of Hamlet's recognition of the 'obscure
memory' of his desire for his mother and his resentment of
the father who was the focus of her sexual attention (Freud
1985: 273).

Freud published expanded versions of this reading in section
5.D.b of *On the Interpretation of Dreams* (1985 [1900]), and
in 'Psychopathic Characters on the Stage' (1997 [1905–6).
Where Sophocles' *Oedipus Rex* was archaic and religious in
the dream-like way in which it staged this universal childhood
fantasy as a struggle against a divine fate, Shakespeare's
Hamlet, Freud argued, was representative of the modern
epoch in that its dramatic struggle was centred wholly within
an individual and unfolded the plot as, in part, a psycho-
pathology whose motivating drive 'remains repressed' (1985
[1900]: 366). Freud's explanation of Hamlet's delay was
expanded on and developed within psychoanalysis. Norman
Holland's *Psychoanalysis and Shakespeare* (1976) is the best
guide to this, tracing ninety or so readings through to 1964.
The most famous Freudian reading within literary studies
remains that of Freud's follower and biographer, Ernest Jones,
whose *Hamlet and Oedipus* (1949 [1910/29]) elaborated the
methods and degrees of the play's repressions, seeing the play's
anti-hero being split or 'decomposed' into three father figures
– Claudius, the Ghost and Polonius – as well as the play's
hero being split into four (or more) brother figures – Horatio,
Laertes, Fortinbras and 'Rosencrantz-and-Guildenstern'. Yet
neither these expansions, nor Freud's reading of *Hamlet*,
turned out to be the most critically influential aspect of Freud's

engagement with the play. That was rather Freud's method, his increasingly sophisticated grammar of subjectivity. Where Freud had been released into his work by *Hamlet*, critics in the second half of the twentieth century would return with Freud's, and later psychoanalysts', insights into *Hamlet*.

Janet Adelman's *Suffocating Mothers: Fantasies of Maternal Origin in Shakespeare's Plays, 'Hamlet' to 'The Tempest'* (1992) is one of the most productive. Like Eliot, Adelman notes the disjunction between how little the audience knows of Gertrude, and how significant she seems to Hamlet. But for Adelman the disproportionate response of Hamlet to his mother is explainable; it is seen to 'reiterate infantile fears and desires rather than [to demonstrate] an adult apprehension of the mother as a separate person' (16). In seeing the process by which boys differentiate themselves from their mothers as a site of particular male anxiety (as opposed to the more traditionally Freudian emphasis on the father), Adelman is borrowing from object-relations psychoanalysis. (Coppélia Kahn [1981] had given a particularly clear exposition of this approach, and why Hamlet's anxieties were a particularly sixteenth- and seventeenth-century concern.) Adelman argues that Gertrude's sexuality is so disturbing to Hamlet because, in loving both Old Hamlet and Claudius, she collapses the two father figures upon whose distinctiveness Hamlet has fashioned his own identity; this, in addition to the physical loss of his father, threatens to re-absorb Hamlet within the maternal conception of identity that Gertrude represents; and thus she threatens to suffocate the Prince.

Where the eighteenth century had seen a son exemplary in his consciousness of his filial duty, Adelman sees a son exemplary in his unconscious fear of his mother. The closet scene (3.4) now becomes central to the play; Gertrude's acknowledgement of her sins allows Hamlet to re-imagine her as a good mother, which allows him to begin 'to rebuild his masculine identity' (34). The play is, more than anything, about familial relationships, and in this, it is not unusual. For Adelman, *Hamlet* marks the moment when Shakespeare realizes that the premise of his tragedy will be a male confrontation with a sexualized maternal presence.

Adelman's reading of the closet scene fits in with a tradition of seeing the Hamlet of 5.1 as in some way a different Prince or the Prince starting afresh. For Stanley Cavell (1987), by contrast, the Hamlet that stares at the skull in the graveyard is representative of the Hamlet of the play. This is how the Prince sees everything; Hamlet sees life in its inhuman truth, and is disgusted by it. Cavell, a philosopher and a literary critic, sees this disgust with life as an anticipation of what philosophy would later conceptualize, most famously in the work of Descartes (1596–1650), as the problem of doubt. Cavell argues that these different modes of response, the dramatic and the philosophic, are complementary and of equal intellectual validity. *Hamlet*'s treatment of doubt is the more radical; where Descartes would bring in God as the guarantor of an external world, in Shakespeare's tragedies, Cavell believes, there is no such divine guarantee.

Cavell had used the principles of organization by which Freud understood the actions of the unconscious to work in order to detect meaningful patterns in *Hamlet*, and had done so as part of an argument about the importance of scepticism to modern subjectivity. Jacques Lacan had earlier detected patterns in those Freudian principles of organization themselves. Influenced by structuralist theories of linguistic meaning, Lacan saw Freud's notions of substitution and transference as forms of metonymy and metaphor. He proposed that the unconscious was structured by language, and that this structuration was a key moment in the psychosexual development of the child, and one which explained, in particular, the nature of desire. *Hamlet*, Lacan argued in a series of 1959 seminars published as 'Desire and the Interpretation of Desire in *Hamlet*' (1977), provided an exemplary series of dramatizations of the workings of this process. (See also Lacan 2002 [1960].)

For Lacan, *Hamlet* was 'the drama of Hamlet as the man who has lost the way of his desire'. That use of 'way' is important, in its suggestion of a preformed route (or organized set pattern of relationships between desired objects) which the person follows. There is, for Lacan, 'a level at which [Hamlet] is merely the reverse-side of a message which is not even his own' (12). For it would be truer to say that the person is constituted as a subject by desire, rather than that he or she constitutes him- or herself as a subject by desiring something or someone; and that the play shows us more about desire, its 'topology' as Lacan puts it, than it does about the subject, Hamlet. Gilbert Murray, exploring the similarities between Orestes and Hamlet (first noted by Rowe in 1709), suggested they were the results not of imitation, but of the universal presence in human cultures of 'a strange unanalysed vibration below the surface, an undercurrent of desires and fears and passions, long slumbering yet eternally familiar' (1919: 26). For Murray, this undercurrent manifested itself in vegetation myths, in which the battle between summer and winter, life and death, were given personified forms. Frye (1967), a later mythic critic, is less directly concerned with vegetation myths, but agrees, in *Hamlet*'s case, that the centre of the play's dramatic interest is on the killing of the Agamemnon or father-figure (that is, Old Hamlet), and sees *Hamlet* as therefore being a social tragedy of order. Lacan's notion of a universal structuring desire which was external and yet constitutive of the hero emphasized a new factor: the qualified withdrawal of agency from the subject. It was an innovation that would become highly influential.

The mid-twentieth century: Historicism and making sense

G. Wilson Knight, however, had had enough of the Prince at 'Harley Street' by 1930. *Hamlet* on Knight's street becomes the play of a Claudius who is 'a good and gentle king' (38), very human for all his many faults, standing against an inhuman Hamlet who, in the 'sickness of his soul' (21), is both 'enduring and spreading Hell on earth' (42). The paradox, clear to Hamlet as to us, is that the Prince is set off on this Macbeth-like course by Claudius's crime; and yet Claudius can recover his spiritual health while the Prince cannot. That he cannot is part of his greatness; in a later note (49) Knight suggests his Hamlet is an expansion of the Prince sketched out by Nietzsche in *The Birth of Tragedy* (1872 [trans. 1909]). Nietzsche's Hamlet was not the Romantic Prince who thought too much, but rather an example of Dionysian man, the person who has, in experiencing 'the rapture of the Dionysian state with its annihilation of the ordinary bounds and limits of existence [...] looked truly into the essence of things'. That understanding, when combined with the return of everyday reality, produces a nausea when the 'horrible truth' is realized that nothing he or she can do can change the eternal nature of things.

The criticism of Knight's time was, in fact, more historicist than it was psychoanalytic. Lily Bess Campbell (1930) explains that *Hamlet* accurately illustrates contemporary Elizabethan thinking on the dangers of excessive grief, and notes that different religions have different views on ghosts: for a Catholic the Ghost might be the spirit of Old Hamlet returned; while for a Protestant it would have to be an agent of the Devil. This was essentially the position adopted by J. Dover Wilson, in *What Happens in 'Hamlet'* (1935). The omission of a question mark in that title is important. Wilson sought, in his book, to respond to W. W. Greg's 1917 article 'Hamlet's Hallucination'. Greg had argued that Claudius's lack of textual response to the dumb scene suggests both that he had not poisoned Old Hamlet, and that the Ghost's account of his death was inaccurate. Dover Wilson offers a knowledge of the Elizabethan staging of the play as a way of answering questions raised by such seeming inconsistencies. With its mixture of listings of the play's interpretative puzzles and its provision of historicist dramatic solutions, *What Happens in 'Hamlet'* became one of the classic mid-century introductions to *Hamlet*. Eleanor Prosser (1967) would later disagree about

the nature of the Ghost; and would herself be corrected by
Roland Mushat Frye (1984). Frye's *The Renaissance Hamlet*
(1984) is a remarkable gathering together of the past century's
progress in recovering the Elizabethan context. He notes
that while Prosser is correct in her sense of the official views
on ghosts, that they were damnable to both Protestant and
Catholic Elizabethans, individual responses from within the
Elizabethan church were far less clear cut. Frye's monumental
work marks the high tide of historicism; and yet it seems to
have no ocean behind it.

In part this was a result of critiques of this kind of literary
criticism. C. S. Lewis (1942) cautions against the habit of calling
the 'thing' (1.1.20) that may be Old Hamlet a 'ghost'. Invoking
such a single concept and category misses the dramatic point;
Shakespeare introduces an indeterminate object as a means to
announce the 'breaking down of the walls of the world and
the germination of thoughts that cannot really be thought:
chaos is come again' (148). Pneumatology and the history of
the dramatic uses of ghosts may be of use; but then again, they
may not. More important than such critiques, however, was
what Norman Rabkin would celebrate, in his introduction to
Reinterpretations of Elizabethan Drama (1969), as a Kuhnian
(Kuhn 1962) paradigm shift in the practice of criticism. The
new critics included within this collection of essays refused,
Rabkin said, to reduce works to meanings, seeking instead to
understand the work of art as 'a complex and highly determined shaping of an audience's responses' (viii).

Thus Stephen Booth's essay 'On the value of *Hamlet*'
(1969) is interested in what the play does, rather than in what
it might say. For Booth, it is not just that the play questions
the concept of 'ghost'; rather it questions, or drops, all 'the
humanly necessary intellectual crutches of compartmentali-
zation, point of view, definition, and the idea of relevance'
(151). It does this by offering an often mutually contradictory
series of frameworks within which to view and make sense
of its actions. Yet, through the nonsignificant coherences of
dramatic prosody such as parallel scenes and the rhetorical

patterning of language, Shakespeare gives structural coherence to 'undeniably incompatible and undeniably coexistent' truths (171). (See also Hartwig 1983 and Stockholder 1987.) Booth's *Hamlet* is a play that preoccupies Western man, not because it is incoherent, but rather because he or she cannot explain its coherence. '*Hamlet* is the tragedy of an audience', for Booth, 'that cannot make up its mind' (1969: 152).

This was a position close to Rabkin's own. What makes *Hamlet* problematic, as Rabkin (1967) sees it, is exactly what makes it Shakespearean. The play, not its persons, employs a 'dialectical dramaturgy', offering up competing views on its own events on a 'both/and' not 'either/or' basis (11). Yet this Shakespearean dialectic has no synthesis; rather the play simply offers complementary, yet conflicting, ways of seeing the same events, which ways become 'a mode of vision' (12). This differs from Booth, but shares with him a sense of the anti-utopian, non-rational nature of the plays, and the focus on the dramatic experience as driver of this recognition. What the play is not, under these approaches, is a reflection or mirror of its society (though it may *also* be that). Rather the play exists in what Maynard Mack (1959) had characterized as an interrogative mood. Mack's short essay perhaps puts most concisely and convincingly the argument against the possibility of 'solutions' to the play. Harry Levin's *The Question of 'Hamlet'* (1959) works well as a longer companion piece; and it places its critical emphasis more fully on the verbal structure of the play: 'Now *Hamlet* without Hamlet would, of course, be altogether unthinkable; but Hamlet without *Hamlet* has been thought about all too much' (5). Questions, doubt and irony constitute the play; the graveyard scene providing a particularly fine example with seventy question marks in 322 lines (19). Where figures like Caroline Spurgeon (1935) and Wolfgang Clemen (1951) had followed Wilson Knight by exploring the play's image clusters, Levin moved the focus onto rhetoric more generally. The play offers the Prince a 'grammar of doubt' with which he 'parses every affirmation' (43). Spurgeon's and Clemen's studies were themselves largely superseded by Maurice Charney, *Style in 'Hamlet'* (1969). Rightly pointing out the relative absence of studies of style *per se*, A. C. Swinburne (1880, 1909 [1905]) having promised more than he delivered, Charney makes a case for seeing the play as Shakespeare's 'most stylistically inventive' (xviii), and the Prince as having the most styles of expression. Gordon Braden (1985) would later show how the 'declamatory exorbitance' (170) of rage in the style of the Senecan tradition became, in *Hamlet*, an expressive resource to articulate a felt sense of disjunction between the self and its world, marking out, rather paradoxically, an area of inner 'emotional privacy' (223).

Charney wished to better understand drama as its own mode of thought or expression. James L. Calderwood gives perhaps the best exposition of how the play's 'mode of being is the ground for its meaning' (xiv). Anne Righter (1962) had noted how *Hamlet* was full of the vocabulary of the theatre. In *To Be and Not To Be: Negation and Metadrama in 'Hamlet'* (1983), Calderwood sets off in pursuit of small questions, taking Sigurd Burkhardt (1968) as his model. Asking why Shakespeare is so parsimonious with names, Calderwood formulates a Shakespearean 'law of the included middle', that is 'a thing may be both A and non-A' (xiv): 'Fortinbras' may also be (old) 'Fortinbras', and 'Hamlet' may also be (old) 'Hamlet'. This law, which gives his book its playful title, sets Calderwood off on the pursuit of the play's *'via negativa'* (189), its seeming love of dissolutions and erasures. Yet, amongst all this taking apart is a putting back together, on a variety of levels. Hamlet achieves his identity by defining what he is not; Shakespeare defines his *Hamlet* by defining how it is not like the *Ur-Hamlet*; and in the exploration of its own form, the play explores the consciousness of its own hero.

The later twentieth century: Marxism and Cultural Materialism

Rabkin's claim for a paradigm shift in the late 1960s overstates the case, but there does seem to have been a shift away from attempts to determine the play's meaning. Much historicist criticism now appeared out-of-date; similarly left behind was the normative and earnest moralism of British New Criticism represented by figures such as D. A. Traversi (1938) and L. C. Knights (1960). For Traversi, Shakespeare shared Hamlet's inability to master his emotional world, too often preferring the abstract and artificial over the real and alive. For Knights, Hamlet lacked the correct, 'mature self-knowledge' (61), especially in his attitude towards sex and death, a personal failing of character which held him back from developing the proper adult attitude to life. For both critics, the political world of the play was a dangerous snare, and their literary-critical politics tended towards a humanist curation of the self.

Yet, elsewhere, criticism was becoming increasingly interested in politics and more generally anti-establishment. To begin with, this more openly political criticism largely shared the values of the more established critical tradition. *Shakespeare in a Changing World* (1964), a collection of essays edited by Arnold Kettle, self-consciously announces the arrival of a Marxist Shakespearean criticism. Taking aim at Jan Kott's *Shakespeare Our Contemporary*, published in the same year (1964), Kettle insists that the pastness of Shakespeare's plays matters. For Kott, *Hamlet* was like a 'sponge' (54), being particularly brilliant in the way in which it was able to absorb and present contemporary problems. For Kettle such a presentist approach loses what is key to the play's real power. A Marxist critic is expected to look to both *Hamlet's* place in its Elizabethan world, which world was changing, and its place in our world, which is also changing – and to do so in order to see how Shakespeare may enable that continuing historical process of social progress. Hamlet is a prince, for Kettle, who gains class consciousness; he is to be celebrated for embodying 'something of the actual aspirations of humanity in its struggles to advance its condition' (158). Those aspirations may end in 'almost total defeat' (157), but Hamlet has testified to the possibilities of a better future. Hamlet is overcome 'not by his enemies or by his weaknesses but by history' (171).

Kettle's argument against a wilfully anachronistic use of *Hamlet* is largely an argument against Modernism, as Richard Halpern (1997) has shown. Halpern himself employs a more eclectic Marxism. Drawing on Marxist analysis of capitalism, but also on Modernist, Freudian and Lacanian positions, he constructs a history of a late-nineteenth and twentieth-century Prince whose traditionally anguished repetitions begin to look more like the stuttering movements of a broken machine denied full subjectivity. This is the Prince first imagined in W. S. Gilbert's and Alfred Cellier's *The Mountebanks* (1892), who has the inhuman and traditional madness of 'Antic-tic, tic-tic, tiquity' (235).

Kettle had a clear awareness of a tradition of the popular use of Shakespeare and *Hamlet* for progressive political ends (Rose 2001; Bartolovitch 2012). He believed the key contemporary struggle for academics to be the removal of the barriers separating the working class from coming into a full possession of Shakespeare. Such optimism had, by the 1980s, largely disappeared. In its place came a criticism, Cultural Materialism, which, while still Marxist in spirit, was both less convinced that literature had any intrinsic power, and more certain that radical, self-consciously anti-institutional political activism would be needed if any genuine political progress was to be seen. *Hamlet* remained central, but did so in a way that made much previous criticism of the play a part of the political problem. The Prince of Francis Barker (1995 [1984]) and Catherine Belsey (1985) lacked agency; or as Barker would memorably formulate it: 'At the centre of Hamlet, in the interior of his mystery, there is, in short, nothing' (33). There were good arguments in support of this position; as

Anne Ferry (1983) had pointed out, the vocabulary of modern interiority was almost non-existent in 1600. 'The project of humanist criticism', as Belsey saw it, had been 'to fill this gap' (49). Filling that gap had produced the founding myth in the creation of the bourgeois, normative, modern state; that we were all, like Hamlet, subjects with agency. Where Kettle had seen the state as obstructive to political progress in the pitiful support it gave to Shakespeare, then, Cultural Materialists saw Shakespeare and *Hamlet* deployed as a key part of an overweening state's mechanisms of ideological production (Althusser 1971 [1970]). The critic's role was now to reverse such institutional *Hamlets*, in order to undo the repressive state; what was wanted, as Terence Hawkes put it memorably, was 'Telmah' (1985).

The later twentieth century: Post-structuralism

Another significant influence in the 1980s was the post-structuralism of Jacques Derrida (1967). Linguistic meaning, in post-structuralist accounts, was a more diffuse and slippery affair than it had been under structuralist accounts. In some ways this made little difference. Where structuralists tended to think that language determined thought, post-structuralists might argue that thought could have no individual determination or origin; both approaches, however, saw little scope for individual agency. However, in its critical attention, post-structuralism turned out to be more focused on the text. Margaret Ferguson (1985) is above all interested in the Prince's concern with 'matter' and its relationships to art, spirit and those things which are of 'no matter'. Those relationships are seen to be, for the Prince, in every case questionable; and the Prince is seen to share Derrida's deconstructive interest in the impossibility of stable discrimination or differentiation between supposedly antithetical terms. Hamlet's wordplay is seen to have metaphysical and political implications. Such an interest in wordplay *per se* was not new: Molly Mahood (1957) had pointed out that Hamlet had more puns (she counts ninety quibbles) to his name than any other character (166); George T. Wright (1981) had observed how *Hamlet* featured more uses of hendiadys than any other of Shakespeare's plays. (Hendiadys is a scheme of rhetoric in which two words, usually nouns, are joined by 'and' into a single more complex notion, as in 'the very age and body of the time' (3.2.23–4).) Wright argued that the figure called into question 'all relationships, familial, political, cosmic, and even artistic' (179). For Ferguson, the Prince's destabilizing wordplay is seen as a hesitation to signify, which is in turn read as a moral quality. (See also Derrida 1994 [1993].) When Hamlet chooses one meaning, as he does increasingly towards the end of the play, he commits himself to an act of destructive reduction which tends to have deadly consequences. A simple or unitary meaning is seen to be, within *Hamlet*, a kind of impoverishing act of violence; meaning is seen to be murderous.

The later twentieth century: Feminism and textual criticism

The lack of agency central to the founding assumptions of much literary critical writing in the 1980s, and most obvious in the dominance of Cultural Materialism's North American sibling, New Historicism, was particularly troubling to Feminist critics. On first publication, Lisa Jardine's *Still Harping on Daughters: Women and Drama in the Age of Shakespeare* (1983) had been seen as a New Historicist text, and not unreasonably; Jardine brought a combination of recent social history and non-canonical texts to bear on Elizabethan and Jacobean drama. Yet, by the time of the publication of the second edition of the text (1989), Jardine was clear herself why she was not a New Historicist: 'in my case, the move *forwards* towards a new fusion of methodologies and material from cultural history and text studies was made in order to retrieve *agency* for the female subject in history' (viii).

Without the notion of agency, the particularity and distinctiveness of female experience tended to be erased; quite how to recover that history was a question central to Elaine Showalter's influential article on Ophelia (1985). Showalter observed that Ophelia, while a minor character in literary criticism, was second only to Hamlet in European cultural mythology. Showalter provided a history of the representation of Ophelia, both for its own interest and for the light it sheds on the cultural associations between female insanity and female sexuality. Critics had been attending to the experience of female characters from the nineteenth century, and there were earlier twentieth-century examples (MacKenzie 1924); modern feminist criticism, though, is generally thought to have begun with Carolyn Heilbrun's essay on 'The Character of Hamlet's Mother' (1957), developed in Smith (1980), which challenged the stereotypically shallow and feminine Gertrude of the critical tradition, and with Juliet Dusinberre's book-length study, *Shakespeare and the Nature of Women* (1996 [1971]). Dusinberre casts Elizabethan and Jacobean drama as a whole as feminist in sympathy, and sees in Hamlet's delayed revenge a serious recognition of the Puritan ideals of companionate marriage; thinking of Claudius and Gertrude as 'one flesh', an attack on Claudius must harm Gertrude. For Jardine, this was too accommodating a use of 'feminist'; to be feminist, Shakespeare's plays would need to be shown to actively seek changes in society's treatment of women, and this they did not do. The Prince, for Jardine, finds Gertrude's sexuality disturbing, and his reading of that as an unreasoning act of sub-bestial lust is typical of the society of the time, and expressive, in particular, of a male fear of 'female interference in patrilinear inheritance' (92). Far from criticizing such a fear, the play is seen to support it.

The lack of agency disconcerted other voices on the left. Howard Felperin (1990) detected in the Hamlet of the

Cultural Materialists a politically regressive valorization of the
past, which abandoned Marxist dialectic for a 'nostalgia for
the future' (162). Robert Weimann (1985) argued that critical
theories which based their approaches on models of authority
derived from the study of language largely missed the point;
language was only one form of mimesis, and *Hamlet* was the
play, above all others, which put various incommensurate
mimetic strategies into play against one another to make up
its drama.

Textual criticism was meanwhile being rethought about the
argument that the various texts of *Hamlet* might represent
different, and not simply corrupt, versions of the play. Major
single-volume editions (Edwards 1985; Hibbard 1987) and
complete works (Wells and Taylor 1986) chose to print largely
Folio-based texts of *Hamlet*, passing over Q2. Underlying
these new editions were arguments for authorial revision and
against the conflation of the different texts of the play. These
arguments were not new (Werstine 1988), but were made
with a newly available detail (Wells and Taylor 1987) and
persuasiveness. The multitudes of Princes to be seen in critical
studies were now joined by Folio and Quarto Princes who
were textually distinct, saying both more and less than one
another, and being part of rather different plays. Quite what
difference this made was a matter for debate (Werstine 1988;
Ioppolo 1991; Clayton 1992; Marcus 1996). John Jones
(1995) argued that the different texts should be seen less as
revisions than revelation, a kind of 'creative confirmation'
(113) that occurred when Shakespeare had the opportunity
of seeing his play staged. Jones manages the difficult task of
marshalling plausible arguments from single-word variants,
suggesting how the presence of Yorick's skull on stage impels
the script from Q2's 'Alas, poor Yorick', via Q1's inaccurately
remembered version of a stage performance, to the Folio's
'Let me see. Alas, poor Yorick' (71). The added phrase gives
'spatial pointing' (72) to the transfer of the skull, shining a
verbal spotlight on 'one of the most famous inanimate things
in world drama' (71).

The late twentieth century

Given the self-consciously radical attacks on institutional authority and the theoretical challenges to the notion of authorial agency, and given the general suspicion of tradition and the status quo, it was surprising, as Marjorie Garber (1987) observed, that critical attention remained so focused on the uber-canonical works of Shakespeare. Garber's answer to this paradox was to draw together much of the critical writing of the previous two centuries within a Freudian paradigm. Marx, Nietzsche, Freud, Lacan, Derrida – Shakespeare was seen to have written them all; Shakespeare was their Ghost, the father-figure whose command they repress, which act of repression then manifests itself in their acts of writing. Western culture, in fact, may be read as a sublimated response to *Hamlet*. In 1623, the homage Ben Jonson had judged Europe to owe Shakespeare was theatrical; here, almost 400 years later, was a North American critic suggesting that debt was more properly ontological; *Hamlet* and Europe have become parts of one another.

Joel Fineman saw this rather differently. In a dense and difficult book on *Shakespeare's Sonnets*, there are what are perhaps the most illuminating two pages (184–5) on Hamlet's strange words to Ophelia about her honesty admitting no discourse to her beauty (3.1.102–14). Fineman sees these as part of a larger epistemic shift, from a notion of language as offering a true representation to a notion of language as offering an opaque performance of the object represented in a different medium. Our modern sense of subjectivity arises out of this shift, the implications of which the theoretical discussions of our own time are still trying to unpack. The claim, like Garber's, is so large as to be questionable; but the point about the Prince's modernity being a function of the play's lyric and linguistic sophistication is vital. Hamlet's sense of self is not finally about the vocabularies he uses, but rather about the ways in which he uses those vocabularies. Here

Helen Vendler's arguments (2007) for the achievement of the complexity of the lyric 'I' in the *Sonnets* might well be applied to *Hamlet*.

William Kerrigan's *Hamlet's Perfection* (1994) saw itself in a more polemic mode, being both more dispirited by political criticism, and more celebratory of the general critical tradition. Kerrigan places himself in the Romantic tradition of character criticism, a tradition which he summarizes as the attempt 'to discover the new forms that unity, structure, character, action, and style assume in Shakespeare's post-classical drama' (8). Kerrigan draws attention to the importance of night to the play and the prince, showing how a simple phrase like 'Good night' can be 'formal, intimate, poignant, comic, mad, unflappable, ordinary, sweet, and prayerful, a thing of childhood and a thing to be said at the end of a life' (62). No one has better demonstrated the madness and sanity in Hamlet's 'Goodnight, mother' (3.4.215). His Hamlet regains balance as he gains a sense of God's providence. In the graveyard the Prince comes to recognize that death is the best revenger; this is the larger point of the imaginative detail with which death's digestion of its many victims is followed. Through this elaboration 'Christianity is made to *seem* [my emphasis] fully compatible with Hamlet's vengeful spirit' (138). God becomes Hamlet's fellow counter-plotter, and so the Prince commits himself into His hands.

Robert N. Watson reaches almost the reverse position in *The Rest is Silence: Death as Annihilation in the English Renaissance* (1994). Watson's starting point is historicist. Revenge tragedy is seen as a substitute for the rituals of the Catholic afterlife that Protestant England had banished, as it shows how our desires may operate beyond our deaths. The ghost becomes a symbol of all our hopes for an afterlife, tempting us to deny the absoluteness of death. The play thus shows us 'the crimes to which religion leads', as Watson quotes Lucretius (98). In its black humour, the gravedigger's scene is seen to offer up to us 'a parody of the Last Judgment: skulls rise from their graves to endure Hamlet's sentences, and the gravedigger, Hamlet, and Laertes all climb from graves under their own power' (89). The scene becomes the equivalent of a Black Mass, and, in reading it so, Watson perhaps captures best its scandalousness for the eighteenth century. It was not just the mixture of tragedy and comedy that caused the critical discomfort, but rather the subject matter of the jests – the parodic presentation of the great pieties of Western culture.

*

Michael Neill's chapters on *Hamlet* in *Issues of Death: Mortality and Identity in English Renaissance Tragedy* (1997) make a fitting end point to this chapter. They are to an extent historicist; like Watson, Neill looks to recover the changing attitudes to death brought in by the Reformation, a set of attitudes which he takes to mark a secularizing moment, and movement, in European culture, and also to see the role literary depictions of death play amongst those changing attitudes. The chapters are also indebted to post-structuralism in their willingness to commit themselves to the minutiae of verbal play, especially of figuration, and see in that verbal play the social import of linguistic forms. Yet Neill also maintains a sense of the agency of individuals, resisting the tendency to see the individual, in this case largely the Prince, as primarily a product of the social and linguistic networks in which he finds himself. Criticism is a complex business, and, as Neill's work shows, the best is often quite distinct, though not detached, from the movements of its times.

Neill's description of the gravedigger's scene is one of the finest. He catches well its abrupt departure from and constant integration into the main modes and interests of the play; quoting Claudius to remind us how the final act of the play is of a part with its opening, Neill talks of the 'indecorum' with which the scene plays 'eldritch variations on the theme of "mirth in funeral and dirge in marriage"' (234). As has been seen, Neill's description of this scene is by no means the first, but it is astounding how long it is before any critic writes well on this scene, a scene which is so brilliant, and so central to the play's ways of working, with its doublings of figures, its staging of the interior world of Hamlet's imagination, its movements from the particular to the universal, its ability to suggest that it deals with the whole of human history – that one man's life story, so vital to that person, might at the same time be able to be caught up, and seen to be so small a fragment, in a larger story of the lives and deaths of humankind, acted upon by social and historical forces of which they have little comprehension. Life and death may be, to answer a question Gertrude puts to Hamlet in one of the play's opening scenes, both common and particular. Presenting the one perspective as a part of the other provides the vertiginous experience that is so important a part of our experience of *Hamlet*.

2

Performance History

Lois Potter

Hamlet loves the theatre, and the theatre has returned his love. The play itself refers obliquely to other plays: perhaps to a lost *Hamlet* by (perhaps) Thomas Kyd, certainly to Kyd's *Spanish Tragedy*, and probably to other plays featuring the characters that Hamlet names – Aeneas, Pyrrhus, Hercules. It also refers to other acting companies, to acting styles, and perhaps to the actors associated with these styles. Imitations and parodies of *Hamlet* in contemporary drama (it is often hard to tell one from the other) suggest what was most memorable. In *Antonio's Revenge* (1600–1), by John Marston, *three* ghosts urge the hero to take revenge; the collaborative *Eastward Ho!* (1605) includes, among other obvious echoes (perhaps also by Marston), a coachman named Hamlet who enters only to be asked, 'What, Hamlet, are you mad?' Madwomen sing and gather flowers in numerous other plays of the period. Skulls are significant props in Middleton's *The Revenger's Tragedy* (1607) and Cyril Tourneur's *The Atheist's Tragedy* (1611), and the entire scene between Hamlet and the Gravediggers was published in 1662 in a collection called *The Wits, or, Sport upon Sport*, extracts of 'Humours' intended (according to the publisher) for private reading or amateur performance.

The scene may have been acted separately during the period when the public theatres were closed. At the Restoration, *Hamlet* was one of the first plays to be revived. By the end of the seventeenth century, it was the best known of Shakespeare's works, and, in other countries, was often the first to be translated and performed. This chapter will look first at how a work once regarded as eccentric became a worldwide icon. I will then focus on some of the transformations of more specific characters and situations resulting from its movement through time and/or space.

From the Globe to the global

Nothing certain is known about most of the original cast. In the Induction that Webster wrote when the King's Men played Marston's *The Malcontent* in 1604, a minor actor called Sinklo (Sinclair) has some comic business with a feathered hat, which may allude to his having played Osric earlier. That Polonius claims to have acted Julius Caesar may be a theatrical joke, meaning that Burbage, as Brutus, had already killed the Polonius actor as Caesar. Lowin, who often played villains and soldier heroes, may not have been the first Claudius, as he seems to have joined the company only in 1602, but he may have taken on the role later. Shakespeare, according to a not very reliable tradition, may have played the Ghost.

What is known is that Richard Burbage was famous in the title role. An anonymous elegy of 1619 lists 'young Hamlet' (contrasted with 'old Hieronimo' in *The Spanish Tragedy*) among his great roles. It also seems to refer to a specific moment in his performance:

> Oft have I seen him leap into the grave,
> Suiting the person, which he seem'd to have,
> Of a sad lover, with so true an eye
> That there I would have sworn he meant to die.[1]

There is some debate as to whether Hamlet did indeed leap into the grave (as Q1 indicates, though only Laertes is directed to do so in Q2 and F), and the 'sad lover' is not how most people remember Hamlet; this could instead be a confused recollection of Romeo breaking into the Capulets' monument. Yet it is possible that its earliest spectators enjoyed the play primarily as a tragic love story. When Marvin Rosenberg was writing his mammoth study of *Hamlet* in the theatre, he found that 'naïve' spectators (those who had never read or seen the play) 'were caught up in a love story' and devastated when they heard of Ophelia's death: 'Until this moment they had hoped, first for a reconciliation, later, at least a joint dying.'[2] Many productions and adaptations (starting perhaps with Q1?) have catered to this audience desire by emphasizing the romantic rather than the political or philosophical.

One reason for the play's lasting success is that most major actors have wanted to play Hamlet. In the past a successful actor could keep the part in his possession for the whole of his career, as Burbage and his successor, Joseph Taylor, evidently did. The Restoration Hamlet, Thomas Betterton, was still playing it when he was over seventy. Many of Burbage's most successful roles (Richard III, Othello) involved an element of impersonation but Hamlet, as Michael Pennington wrote, is 'the greatest straight role ever written',[3] one in which the audience is likely to identify the actor with the character and in which the actor therefore feels particularly exposed. In a period still lacking in inexpensive, well-annotated and accurate Shakespeare texts, many spectators felt that they understood the plays best when they were acted. Colley Cibber saw Betterton as almost equal to Shakespeare, and many eighteenth-century spectators felt the same about David Garrick (who was a collector of early plays and had the benefit of expert opinions on his acting texts). As more scholarly editions appeared (beginning with Edmond Malone's in 1790), the gap between scholarship and the theatre widened: some readings of the play became so philosophical that it is hard to imagine any production that could do them justice and some productions were so heavily cut that there was no room for philosophy anyway.

The early history of the Anglo-American Hamlets is tied to that of the major London theatres, two of which, before the repeal of the Licensing Act in 1843, had a virtual monopoly on Shakespeare productions. It was often the leading tragedian who chose and prepared the acting text. That text had, however, been largely the same since the Restoration, as far as can be deduced from the early acting editions. Someone (possibly Betterton, or the theatre manager and playwright William Davenant) cut many minor characters, topical references (and metatheatrical ones like the advice to the Players), and nearly everything to do with Fortinbras, though he was still allowed to end the play. Fortinbras disappeared entirely after 1732, and eighteenth- and nineteenth-century productions were focused on Hamlet's major scenes, with other characters seen largely in relation to him. At its worst, this star-centred approach could lead to the sort of behaviour attributed to one Hamlet during Claudius's first speech: 'While the wretched monarch was speaking of "our sometime sister, now our queen, the imperial jointress to this warlike state", etc., the supposedly silent Hamlet was muttering "Get on with it ... they aren't listening ... no one's interested ... quicker, quicker ... cut it short."'[4] One reason why the history of Shakespearean acting is so often restricted to the performances of the leading actor is that it was actors, not productions, that travelled. Outside the major metropolitan centres, most audiences saw Shakespeare's plays performed by a visiting star who had only limited rehearsal time with the local company. It was in everyone's interest to stick to traditional 'business' and interpretations. On the other hand, the short rehearsal period and the absence of direction in the modern sense meant that actors who specialized in comedy could make the most of the parts traditionally given to them: Polonius, the gravediggers and Osric. Vanessa Cunningham points to a playbill of 1754 on which Osric (or Ostrick, as he was usually called), played by a popular comedian, gets the best billing next to David Garrick's Hamlet.[5] The fact that this tragedy has so much room for comedy (even in the form of Hamlet's comments on 'those that play your clowns' [3.2.36–7]) is another reason for its popularity.

There was one brief attempt to create a more classical – more purely tragic – Hamlet, near the end of Garrick's period as manager of Drury Lane (1747–76). Though he had played the traditional Hamlet text for much of his career, the actor had many friends among scholars and writers, and was well aware of how Hamlet looked to non-English eyes and even to some English intellectuals.[6] In 1772 he created a version that eliminated the gravediggers and Osric and avoided the pile-up of onstage deaths in the last act. Gertrude was not poisoned, but collapsed, and perhaps went mad or died, offstage. Hamlet killed Claudius quickly, then let himself fall on Laertes's sword and, dying, urged Laertes and Horatio to join forces to calm the troubled state. Horatio spoke his two-line elegy on Hamlet, plus Fortinbras's last two lines. This Hamlet was clearly not popular: it was acted only from 1772 to 1779. Not only were the comic characters restored soon after Garrick's death, they became even more irrepressible. By the early nineteenth century the First Gravedigger had somehow acquired a totally irrelevant piece of business – apparently continued for several decades – that involved the elaborate removal of one waistcoat after another, to the delight of (some of) the audience.[7] The arrival of 'directors' theatre' in the twentieth century would eventually produce the kind of harmonious production that Garrick seems to have wanted, though it would also lead to interpretations that did not necessarily take the hero's viewpoint.

The play's theatrical history was gradually affected by developments in scholarship, criticism and editing. The greatest American Hamlet of the nineteenth century, Edwin Booth, corresponded with H. Howard Furness, the editor of the 1877 New Variorum. A copy of the first Quarto of Hamlet was discovered in 1823, but it was some time before its significance was recognized. The great German Hamlet,

Emil Devrient, apparently used it in the theatre,[8] but its first
English production was William Poel's in 1881. Poel tried to
place Shakespeare in his theatrical context, performing the
play on a bare stage and in Elizabethan dress rather than the
early medieval tunics that had become customary. He also
drew on some of the stage directions of Q1, such as the one
for Ophelia to accompany her songs on a lute. The production
was considered a curiosity, but it was the beginning of a
recovery of Shakespeare's text. Bernard Shaw, who had
constantly complained of the reshaping of Shakespeare to
fit Irving's elaborate stagings at the Lyceum, wrote a famous
review of Johnston Forbes-Robertson's *Hamlet* (1897) in
which he describes his amazement at realizing that Cornelius,
Voltemand, Reynaldo and Fortinbras were all included in
the cast.[9] The text had been cut by 1,329 lines, but it was
still considerably longer than usual. It was soon followed by
Frank Benson's uncut *Hamlet* (a conflation of Q2 and F) in
Stratford-upon-Avon (1899–1900). The movement towards
greater 'authenticity' (fuller texts, simpler staging, more or less
inspired by the Elizabethan theatre, costumes from the period
of the play rather than of its supposed setting) continued
through much of the twentieth century. Towards the end of
that century, however, it was countered by several factors,
particularly the growing awareness of, and interest in, other
cultural traditions.

Like other English plays, *Hamlet* was played on the
European continent at an early stage, though probably in a
shortened version. Fynes Morison, who saw English actors at
the Frankfurt Fair in September 1592, reported that they lacked
the costumes, props and numbers for a full-scale production
but performed 'peeces and patches of English playes'.[10] Later,
whole companies travelled to German-speaking countries,
where professional actors were unknown but where many
princes had well-equipped private stages. After 1621, continental Europe was a battleground, but touring actors found
various safe havens. Some version of *Hamlet* was probably
seen by audiences in locations as widely scattered as Prague,

Gdansk, Warsaw, Königsberg and Stockholm, though it is mentioned by name only once, as part of the repertory performed at Dresden in 1626.

The Dresden *Hamlet* may have been a shorter version of Q1 with additions from the recently published Folio text. If this is the source of the German play that was printed in 1710 under the title of *Der Bestrafte Brudermord* (or, Fratricide Punished), it had changed drastically over the years, probably passing through the hands of several authors.[11] Ironically, in view of Hamlet's joke about becoming an interpreter to puppets (3.2.239–40), it may have been performed as a puppet show.[12] Its story is recognizably *Hamlet*'s, but it is much shorter than even Q1, perhaps allowing for improvisation, and it includes a great deal of interpolated material, such as a classical prologue; its clown absorbs several other roles, including that of Osric, but is among Hamlet's victims at the end when he admits that he knew about the poisoned foil and cup. As Zdeněk Stříbrný has pointed out, 'the clown, who was expected to learn foreign languages quickly, formed the chief link between the actors and the spectators, introducing other characters and commenting on the action.'[13] This character remained an important part of traditional theatre in central and eastern Europe – for example, in Alexandru Tocilescu's Romanian production of 1985, two white-faced clowns accompanied the action; the dying Hamlet wiped the make-up from the face of one of them and spread it on his own.

The point at which it became worthwhile to learn English well enough to read and translate a very difficult author like Shakespeare was also the point at which English-speaking countries began to be taken seriously on the world stage. There is a tendency to polarize French (classical) and German (Romantic) responses to Shakespeare, but this contrast existed only for a brief period. Since Shakespeare's name had not been associated with the versions of his plays in popular German theatre, German-speakers in the early eighteenth century first heard about *Hamlet* from French translations of English

literary periodicals in which Shakespeare was discussed, and
from Voltaire's qualified praise in his widely published *Lettres
sur les Anglais* (1733) – as well as from his later attacks when he
became alarmed at the growing enthusiasm for Shakespeare.[14]
The *Lettres* included Voltaire's version of 'To be or not to be'
in alexandrines, and, as Michèle Willems notes, it was one
of three French translations of this soliloquy in that year.[15]
Between 1746 and 1749, Pierre-Antoine de la Place published
an anthology of English drama including paraphrases of the
highlights of ten Shakespeare plays, linked by summaries of
the untranslated scenes. It was on the basis of this version
that Jean-François Ducis, who knew no English, created his
versions of Shakespeare adapted to classical tastes (the cast
was greatly reduced in size; the Queen was unequivocally
guilty; the Ghost did not appear). When the great actor Joseph
Talma took over the role of Hamlet in 1803, he drew on his
knowledge of Shakespeare in the original to persuade Ducis to
include more of Shakespeare's text, including the hero's most
famous soliloquy. But when English actors brought the play to
Paris in 1827 it was the first time that French audiences had
seen the duel scene. Ducis's versions were the only ones staged
at the Comédie Française before 1851 and they were the
means by which most non-Anglophone readers and audiences
for the next fifty years became acquainted with Shakespeare:
as Michèle Willems points out, they 'were translated, or freely
adapted, into Italian, Spanish, Dutch and into the languages
of Latin America.'[16] When a Brazilian actor in 1835 attempted
to stage a *Hamlet* directly translated from the English, its
failure forced him to return to the Ducis version.[17] In 1848
Alexandre Dumas and Paul Meurice produced a livelier and
closer adaptation that gave Ophelia and Hamlet an early love
scene and ended with Hamlet becoming king, though he was
prevented from suicide only when the Ghost reappeared and
insisted that it was his duty to reign. The first Arab version was
based on this play, as was the opera by Ambroise Thomas.[18]
Sarah Bernhardt's *Hamlet* in 1899 was in fact the first French
production to use a text translated directly from the English.

The first German Hamlets also played heavily cut and adapted texts. Even the version by Friedrich Schroeder (first performed in 1776 in Hamburg), which was to be the basis of the first translations into Polish and Hungarian, made a number of changes to the action. Germany's long identification with Shakespeare began with August Wilhelm Schlegel's translation of sixteen plays between 1797 and 1801 (with a seventeenth in 1810), which was completed in 1825–33 by Ludwig Tieck, his daughter Dorothea, and Wolf Heinrich. This version (still considered a classic of German literature) survived, sometimes revised or updated, into the twentieth century – it was, for instance, used for subtitling and dubbing the BBC Shakespeare series from 1978 to 1985 – and is still occasionally played. Because Hamlet's studies at Wittenberg are often mentioned in the play, and because Goethe made it an important part of the plot in his *Wilhelm Meister's Apprenticeship*, it was a particular favourite with German actors, who often played fuller texts than in England. When a German company visited London in 1852, the critic Henry Morley disliked the fact that the Ophelia spoke rather than sang her songs; however, he recognized that the production not only had a superb Hamlet in Emil Devrient, but also gave equal care to all the lines and to the performances even of minor characters.[19] In the same decade, the visiting German writer Theodor Fontane (who, by contrast, disapproved of the singing of Ophelia's songs) discovered that in London theatres Polonius was invariably a comic role and that his advice to his son, taken seriously in Germany, was either cut or made ridiculous.[20] In 1877 Furness dedicated his *New Variorum Hamlet* to the German Shakespeare Society and devoted a separate section to German criticism of the play, apologizing for not being able to cover it all.[21] As late as 2005 Rodney Symington contended that 'The reason for Shakespeare's hold on the German theatre is simple: his plays are performed in a "modern" translation that captures their poetry and the magnificence of their language, while clarifying all the archaic words and expressions [...] The German theatregoer experiences the plays as richly as does his or her English-speaking counterpart.'[22] It was for this reason that in 1934 the Nazi government, when it tried to enforce a policy of performing mainly German works in the theatres, made an exception for Shakespeare.[23] The French and German responses to Shakespeare can no longer be polarized. In France as in Germany, as Nicole Fayard wrote in 2006, 'Decades of appropriation have transformed Shakespeare into France's "other" national playwright.'[24] France has seen uncut *Hamlets* (Antoine Vitez, 1983–4, gave it in both a cut and an uncut version – *Hamlet, avec les episodes ignorés* – and Patrice Chéreau performed a complete text in 1988). Both countries have numerous accurate and effective translations from which to choose. Elsewhere, too, Shakespeare translation has become a major literary interest. The opening up of Spain to foreign influences after the death of Franco led to Shakespeare's becoming more popular than the Golden Age writers to whom he has often been compared. This is partly because he sounds more 'modern' in translation and partly because actors found it easier to speak his blank verse than the complex and varied rhyme schemes of their own dramatic tradition.[25]

Curiously, many Europeans seem to have identified more deeply with Hamlet than did English-speaking spectators. The condition known as 'Hamletism', first encountered in the 1844 statement by Ferdinand Freiligrath that 'Germany is Hamlet', was identified in the nineteenth century as a national malaise in France, Spain and Russia, among others.[26] But, if North American and antipodean actors initially thought of themselves as in a continuous line of descent from the great British Hamlets, the way in which the English language developed in these countries over a few generations soon created a divide between them. Could Hamlet with a non-British accent sound credible? Was an acting tradition designed for the highly verbal classical drama of Britain right for Americans and Australians, especially as their populations came less and less from British ancestry?

The famous performance of *Hamlet* by crewmembers of a merchant ship off the coast of Sierra Leone in 1607 and

1608 has come to seem highly symbolic in the history of
Shakespeare's globalization – although, as has been pointed
out, African countries have largely ignored the play since that
time. The authors of a recent survey of 'Shakespeare and Africa'
suggest that one reason is 'impatience' with its 'introspective
nature'.[27] (*Macbeth*, by contrast, has received a number of
imaginative productions.) In many cases, it is a country's
relation to British culture that has determined its response
to its most famous play. This response has been particularly
complex in countries that were also subject to British imperialism. India had an English-language theatre in Calcutta in
the time of Garrick, who indeed donated some playbooks to
it.[28] By the nineteenth century, as Poonam Trivedi has shown,
however, there were really two Shakespeares in India: an
elitist one for British-educated Indians, who read the plays
in the original, and a more popular one that used the stories
(much as in seventeenth-century Germany), assimilating them
into local theatrical traditions and incorporating music and
dance.[29] It was the story rather than the text of *Hamlet* that
entered other non-European cultures, often through the *Tales*
of Charles and Mary Lamb.[30] As Alexa C. Y. Huang writes,
the dramatist's early reputation in China 'was not the result
of translation, teaching, performance, or any other form that
would have entailed a substantial engagement with his texts,
but took the form of informants' references and an abstract
panegyric.'[31] Increasingly, instead of studying English in order
to read Shakespeare, people studied Shakespeare in order
to gain entrance into a dominant culture. Huang quotes
an illuminating passage from the principal of the National
Drama School, Yu Shangyuan, at the time of a *Hamlet*
performed during World War Two in a Confucian temple: in
the first place, the production was meant to depict 'Hamlet's
progressive and revolutionary [*geming jinqu*] spirit, which
is what the Chinese people need during the Anti-Japanese
War'. But it had a larger function: 'Those countries that
produce the most high-quality Shakespearean productions are
the countries with the highest cultural prestige'.[32] Similarly,

Japanese Kabuki actors chose to perform Shakespeare in the early twentieth century 'because Shakespeare was a part of the "modern", that is western, world they wished to enter.'[33] For Koreans, it has been argued, playing Shakespeare was a way of distancing themselves from Japanese dominance.[34] Political emancipation did not necessarily mean cultural rejection. The writer Amrit Rai translated *Hamlet* into Hindi in 1963, arguing that 'the ability to translate the ideas and emotions of Shakespeare is a touchstone of a language's maturity and capability'.[35]

Politically, as well as culturally, *Hamlet* has been a crucial play in many countries. The authors of *Painting Shakespeare Red*, which looks at the dramatist's career in eastern Europe, effectively summarize the reasons why Shakespeare lends himself so well to appropriation: his plots 'belong to a common pool of narrative heritage'; his varied settings 'can be endlessly diversified in theatrical productions'; and his dialogical form is so open, even at the end where one usually expects some transcendent statement, as to allow multiple interpretations.[36] *Hamlet* can be used to diagnose and criticize apathy – political or generational – and advocate a cult of violence, or (particularly through its treatment of Fortinbras) it can attack the assumption that military action and the imposition of a new dictatorship can rescue an evil society. A Japanese translator in 1995 pointed out that *Hamlet*, a play about going abroad, speaks to 'a peculiarly modern sense of powerlessness', both individual and national.[37] In the Arab world, where Shakespeare was a cosmopolitan rather than a specifically British influence, Margaret Litvin has found that 'Liberals, nationalists, and Islamists have enlisted Hamlet for their causes.'[38] Rather than blame Hamlet for his inaction, other productions have played Claudius as someone the audience would recognize as a contemporary tyrant – Kaiser Wilhelm II in Leopold Jessner's 1926 Berlin production or Ceaucescu in Tocilescu's Romanian one of 1985, or, more recently, an American president. Sometimes they have equated the sinister efficiency of the Claudius–Polonius–Osric bureaucracy with government in general.[39] For Marxist theorists, in the Soviet Union, Maoist China and much of the Arab world, Hamlet was a hero crushed, not by his psychological state, but by a corrupt society; his death was a heroic sacrifice for the sake of the future.

Yet it is often difficult to untangle ideological intentions. The 'correct' view of Hamlet, for Hitler's ministers of culture, was of a Nordic hero who, contrary to Goethe's view, was an energetic political activist, but there is no consensus on whether this is how Gustav Gründgens actually played him in the famous *Hamlet* directed by Lothar Müthel (Prussian State Theatre, 1936), which ran for nearly 200 performances. One writer thought him decadent and neurotic; others saw him as a determined avenger from the start.[40] But many productions were regarded, then and with hindsight, as 'subversive' if they engaged in 'debunking the previous romantic conception of the heroes in defiance of the official requirement to fashion them after the True Man of socialism.'[41] Adolf Dresen's 1964 production of *Hamlet* in Greifswald, East Germany, which did precisely this, was taken off after only five performances; the director was fired 'and sent to work in a nearby oil refinery.'[42] Ironically, many Western productions of the play were also engaged in debunking the hero. This was sometimes because they saw Shakespeare as an Establishment figure, sometimes because they wanted to attack Hamlet's refusal of political commitment. Kate Flaherty suggests that 'By being an intellectual and a philosopher, Australian Hamlets transgress locally dominant tropes of masculinity in ways that a British, German, or American Hamlet never could.'[43] In fact, the last part of her statement may not be true for Americans either. As Dennis Kennedy has said, the 'greater political stability' of much of the Anglo-American-Antipodean world 'has robbed Shakespeare of some of the danger and force that other countries have (re)discovered in his texts.'[44] This is one reason why productions in English have often focused on the psychological and domestic side of the play.

Aspects of performance

The Ghost

The confrontation between the hero and a figure who may bring 'airs from heaven or blasts from hell' was so memorable that Colley Cibber, trying to give an idea of the intelligence and power of Thomas Betterton's performance, chose to describe this moment, which became a touchstone for later Hamlets. Yet Cibber says nothing about the performance of the actor playing the Ghost. The history of the play's production includes many exasperated accounts of the difficulty of making his appearances effective: he emerged from a creaking trap door that often got stuck; his armour clanked when he moved, and, more important, he rarely spoke the lines well, which is why Bernard Shaw decided that Shakespeare played the part himself (as tradition has it) because he 'would not trust anyone else with it'.[45] Yet Voltaire was so impressed by the theatrical effect that, contrary to neoclassical practice, he introduced a ghost into two of his own plays.[46] (Ducis, on the other hand, kept it offstage.) The illustration to the play in Nicholas Rowe's 1707 edition depicts Hamlet and the Queen with the Ghost (in 3.4), but, as Barbara Hodgdon has said, the image has the effect of a composite reminder of what seem to have been the play's two most memorable moments: Hamlet's first sight of the Ghost and its appearance in the 'closet' scene.[47]

Productions on some version of an early modern stage, of which 'Shakespeare's Globe' in London is the best known, play the ghost scene in a manner that Gielgud found hard to imagine in 1937: 'a noisy, fidgeting, mostly standing audience, no darkness, afternoon sunshine streaming on to a tidy little platform.'[48] But technology, from the most rudimentary to the elaborate, has usually attempted to make the Ghost as ghostly as possible. An early device in the opening scene was the use of a second Ghost, or even more, to appear in different places in rapid succession as the soldiers attempt to strike at it. (This continues to be used, most recently in Yukio Ninagawa's *Hamlet*, seen in London in 2015.) Patrice Chéreau's production of *Hamlet*, designed for the outdoor theatre in Avignon (1988), brought the Ghost on horseback from under the stage, as if from under the earth. As the animal reared up in front of the terrified soldiers, Horatio's action in 'crossing' it became genuinely daring. The Faction touring production of 2013 used a video of Simon Russell Beale as the Ghost to create a genuinely disembodied spectre. Robert Lepage, in his one-man show, used a pre-recorded version and played the scene opposite himself. Sometimes – starting, apparently, in 1868 – the Ghost has been invisible to the audience as well as to the other characters.[49] In productions that treat Hamlet as a study in abnormal psychology, the effect, of course, is to suggest that he is hallucinating. In Richard Eyre's Royal Court production of 1980, Jonathan Pryce's Hamlet seemed to produce the voice of the Ghost from his own stomach. On the other hand, despite the Queen's assurance to Hamlet that she sees 'Nothing at all', in John Barton's RSC production of 1980 Gertrude (Barbara Leigh-Hunt) clearly *did* see it, and then lied because she could not face the implications of the sight. Samuel West writes that in Stephen Pimlott's RSC production of 2001 'we chose to make a ghost who could be touched' but that this made no difference to the power of the scene.[50]

'Filial Piety' was the title given to *Hamlet* to conceal its identity when it was staged in anti-theatrical Philadelphia shortly after the War of Independence,[51] and many Hamlets (for instance, Garrick and Sarah Bernhardt) were remembered most for the reverence they showed towards the Ghost.[52] It was one reason why the play was so quickly popular in Asian countries, where reverence for one's parents was highly valued and where (as in Noh drama) the protagonist of classical drama is often a ghost. Recent Korean productions have drawn on shamanism in the Ghost's scenes, often with Ophelia becoming a medium through whom it speaks.[53] In productions with a political emphasis, the Ghost is more likely to represent the weight of the past, as in the title of Margaret Litvin's 2011 study, *Hamlet's Arab Journey: Shakespeare's Prince and Nasser's Ghost*. Yet a production that makes Hamlet the child of a modern nuclear family rather than of a royal household is likely to import an element of inter-generational conflict, suggesting that the student Hamlet has little in common with his military father. The Ghost in the 1989 RSC *Hamlet* towered over his son (Mark Rylance) and said 'I find thee apt', as if surprised that the boy might after all be competent to carry out revenge.

Women and Hamlet

The playing of Ophelia and Gertrude has inevitably reflected archetypes of femaleness (mistress and mother) at the time of performance. The first actors of these roles were boy apprentices, accustomed to the often-brutal ways in which children were punished. Some of this brutality may have carried over into Hamlet's treatment of them. Ophelia finds Hamlet's offstage behaviour frightening, but neither she nor the eavesdroppers on the 'nunnery' scene say anything about his resorting to physical violence. Eighteenth-century actors seem to have shouted and slammed doors. Nineteenth-century Hamlets sometimes tried to soften even the character's verbal harshness, as when Edmund Kean returned to kiss her hand at the end, while Herbert Beerbohm Tree stole back and, as she lay sobbing on a couch, silently kissed her hair.[54] Some modern productions, however, make Hamlet come close to raping her, something that makes sense only when the couple are played as having been lovers. In an Australian production of 2001, she and Hamlet were having sex in 2.1; Hamlet hid when Polonius came to her room, and her story about being 'affrighted' was a cover-up. Later, they played the nunnery scene as her revelation ('you know right well you did') that she was pregnant.[55] As this extreme interpretation indicates, her relationship with Hamlet also affects her relationship to her father. Tony Church, who played Polonius in two very different productions, found it difficult to carry out a sympathetic interpretation: 'why, when Hamlet rushes from the stage having brutally abused Ophelia, does Polonius wait for a soliloquy by Ophelia before going to comfort his daughter? [...] I compensated by comforting her physically, while speaking to the King; but the problem remains, particularly as Hamlet not only berated Ophelia in this production but slapped her face very hard as well.'[56]

It was Ophelia's very gentleness and the lyric beauty with which she interpreted her madness that made visiting productions from England so thrilling to nineteenth-century French audiences, accustomed as they were to the powerful and often terrifying heroines of Corneille and Racine. They fell in love with Harriet Smithson in 1827 and with Helena Faucit, who played opposite William Macready, in 1844. Faucit, who always presented herself as frail and helpless, later wrote an account of Ophelia that fully embraces the idea of a fragile creature unable to cope with court life and misunderstood by everyone. Chinese and Japanese theatre found Ophelia more sympathetic than Hamlet, perhaps because she resembled one female type that had often been played by traditional male impersonators. A modern Ophelia, Frances Barber, who played the role opposite Roger Rees in 1984–5, was convinced that she was 'acutely intelligent' and 'the female counterpart and counterpoint' to Hamlet.[57] She emphasized the parallel between the characters by wearing black after Polonius's death. (When Ellen Terry, Irving's Ophelia, had wanted to do so, she was told, 'My God! Madam, there must be only one black figure in this play, and that's Hamlet!'[58]) Some Ophelias have researched the behaviour of mental patients to give a performance as far removed as possible from the favour and prettiness that Laertes describes.

Hamlet, in the 'closet scene', may have been even more violent with his mother. As Ann Thompson and Neil Taylor point out in their note on 3.4.13, the Q1 Gertrude tells

Claudius that Hamlet had thrown and tossed her about.[59]
If this does reflect the way in which the scene was originally
performed, it is likely to have been only verbally violent after
the Restoration, when a woman played Gertrude. Hamlet
sometimes forced his mother to sit down, and they may
have touched when he assured her that his pulse was beating
normally, but their physical closeness depended on what
happened when Hamlet told her to 'Look here upon this
picture, and on this' – that is, the images of Old Hamlet
and Claudius (3.4.51). The actor, as Sprague concisely puts
it, 'has traditionally chosen one of three possibilities: he
has pointed at large portraits visible on the wall; he has
examined two miniatures; or he has conjured up, by means
of impassioned description, imaginary pictures.'[60] If the actor
is wearing a miniature of his father, and the Queen one of
Claudius, his action in seizing it will bring him close to her.
When the 'closet' (a small private place in which to read and
pray) becomes a bedroom, there is a further opportunity
to emphasize an Oedipal interpretation of the mother–son
relationship. In 1989, Mark Rylance stabbed Polonius on his
mother's bed, and she later crawled back into it, despite its
bloodstained sheets.

Imogen Stubbs – who vividly describes her attempts to
make Gertrude interesting, despite the character's silence at
crucial moments, and the difficulty of her speech reporting
Ophelia's death – says, in words that could apply to many
performances of both Ophelia and Gertrude, that 'actresses
spend about 50 per cent of their lives crying and much of
the rest of the time taking their clothes off.'[61] In a profession
overcrowded with women, many actresses have longed to
escape from this narrow range into the great roles that
Shakespeare wrote for men. And some have done so. The
great Sarah Siddons was one of several who played Hamlet in
the eighteenth century. Unfortunately, Siddons played the role
only in the provinces; after her retirement, she read the play
aloud before select audiences. In 1846 Charlotte Cushman
had unsuccessfully urged a contemporary dramatist to write

a part for her: 'I long to play a woman of strong ambition, who is at the same time very wily and diplomatic, and who has an opportunity for a great outburst when her plans are successful – in short, a female Richelieu.'[62] (Bulwer Lytton's *Richelieu* had provided a great part for Macready, particularly interesting for its emphasis on intellect and its absence of 'love interest'.) Unable to find such a play, Cushman, who had already played Romeo, began in 1847 to play Hamlet herself, with great success. In the closet scene she found a new reading of the lines:

> You are the Queen, your husband's brother's wife,
> And, would it were not so, you are my mother (3.4.14–15)

These words, as punctuated in Q2, seem cruel throughout, though F's replacement of 'And' by 'But' might justify a change of tone in the second line. Cushman's performance, recorded in her promptbook with commentary, put a pause after 'would it were not so', making the anger apply only to her previous words; then, as if recalling himself, Hamlet spoke 'you are my mother' 'with much feeling and respect.' As Tony Howard comments, 'few previous Hamlets, after all, had played Gertrude first'.[63]

Sarah Bernhardt was already famous when she played Hamlet in 1899, which is why her performance received more attention than any other female Hamlet; there is even a short film of the duel scene. Macready said of Hamlet, 'I believe no man ever played it with any approach to completeness until he was too old to look it.'[64] One of Bernhardt's justifications for playing the role was that a woman in male costume could look much younger than a man of the same age. This has been true of a number of female Hamlets (Maxine Peake's, the most recent at the time of writing, looked like an adolescent even though she was forty). When Bernhardt took her production on tour, she inspired many other female Hamlets worldwide, including two in Egypt.[65] During World War One, with many male actors fighting overseas, the Old Vic cast women in men's roles, so that, as Tony Howard notes, women playing men could be seen as patriotic and acceptable even after the war. The first radio Hamlet was probably Eve Donne, who performed the famous soliloquy for a Shakespeare's Birthday celebration in 1923.[66] Trying to explain why female Hamlets largely disappeared in England between then and the 1970s, Howard suggests two reasons: after World War One the recognized phenomenon of shell-shock in men made it possible for men to play qualities in Hamlet that had been considered 'female', while the growing uneasiness over homosexuality (and lesbianism, which Parliament attempted to criminalize in 1920) meant that reactions to female Hamlets were sometimes both homophobic and misogynistic.[67] One reason sometimes given for the fact that *Hamlet* is not Shakespeare's most popular play in Spain is its lack of good female roles in a country where there are many important female performers. Nuria Espert, who played Hamlet in Franco's Spain, was greeted with both cheers and angry shouts from the audience. She had made no attempt to look male, as she wanted to bring out the sexual and homosexual dimensions of her portrayal.[68] Similarly, an East German Hamlet of 1989 (Cornelia Schmaus) 'seemed to have slept with Horatio, Rosencrantz, Guildenstern, Ophelia, Gertrude, and maybe the Ghost'.[69] Schmaus's Hamlet had a female Polonius (Marianne Wünschler) who 'smoked cigars, and cooked meals in a pan' – something that Tony Howard relates to the complex expectations for women in a country supposedly dedicated to gender equality.[70] The all-male *Hamlet* of Glasgow's Citizens' Theatre (1970) was a deliberate 'queering' of the play, designed to question every aspect of its assumptions about manliness and womanliness.

The ending

Almost everything about the play's ending is ambiguous. Does Gertrude know that she is drinking poison? Does Hamlet know that he has an 'unbated' sword when he wounds Laertes? Does Fortinbras just happen to be passing through Denmark at exactly the right moment to gain the crown (and incidentally revenge his father)? Shakespeare may have been saying something about the divinity that shapes our ends, or he may simply have been trying to avoid the difficult moral issues involved in all these situations. Theatrically speaking, the ending is exciting (Steven Berkoff comments wryly that 'this is the "bit" the audience has suffered a lot of dialogue to get to … THE FIGHT … the eventual *coup de theatre* when the roof falls in'[71]). Critics, however, have disliked the pile-up of deaths, and the final entry of Fortinbras and the ambassadors can be anticlimactic. Many actors have complained of having to fight a duel at the end of a long and difficult role. (This was at least partly why David Garrick, aged fifty-five and in poor health, altered Act 5 to reduce the amount of fencing he had to do.) The business by which Hamlet and Laertes change rapiers is particularly difficult to make clear to an audience. Emphasizing the corruption of the old that destroys the young, a Czech production showed Laertes wanting to get rid of the poisoned rapier (at 'This is too heavy'), but being prevented by Claudius and Osric.[72] More usually, Hamlet forces the exchange on Laertes, once he realizes that the latter has an 'unbated' sword, but what happens next depends on the production's conception of his character. The nineteenth-century French 'translation' inserted lines to make clear that Hamlet, in offering his own foil to Laertes, was only being courteous.[73]

When John Caird deleted Fortinbras from his National Theatre production in 2000, he argued that this part of the plot might have been a later addition to the story.[74] This seems unlikely, since Fortinbras is present in all three texts. Even in the heavily cut *Bestrafte Brudermord* Horatio declares his intention to take the crown to Norway after the royal funerals. The treatment of Fortinbras – initially a hothead looking for someone to fight, in 4.4 a 'delicate and tender prince' whom Hamlet apparently admires, and in 5.2 someone that Hamlet wants as a successor -- sends mixed messages. Perhaps the play takes account of English uneasiness about the prospect of a foreign ruler succeeding Elizabeth I by providing the elaborate backstory that gives Fortinbras, like James VI of Scotland, a genuine claim to the kingdom. Since the Stuart succession, like the Tudor one, was an embarrassing political problem, it is not surprising that this part of the play was already being cut in the Restoration. It is in keeping with the 'emphasis on the domestic' that Anthony Dawson, in his performance history of *Hamlet*, distinguishes as 'a dominant aspect of English revivals at least since Irving.'[75] For most non-Anglophone countries, on the other hand, the contrast between Hamlet's failure and Fortinbras's success was interpreted as a political lesson.

When Fortinbras was re-introduced, he was generally seen through Hamlet's approving eyes and his final speech was played as a fitting tribute to the hero. Gaston Baty's production of Q1 (Paris, 1928) contrasted the black-dressed Hamlet with a Fortinbras all in white, a figure of hope for a sick country. By contrast, in a Romanian production of 1989, he wore a red uniform.[76] This is typical of his increasingly frightening treatment in many productions after World War Two, either because of widespread anti-militarism or because so many countries had suffered under foreign occupation: he is now likely to break down the doors and to silence or kill Horatio, thus destroying one of the few consoling aspects of the ending.

As Zdeněk Stříbrný points out, the fact that 'In Czech, as in Russian, the safety curtain is traditionally called "iron curtain"' has made possible a number of visual puns with political meanings. A Moscow *Hamlet* of 1954 became known as the Iron Curtain production because 'its central metaphor was a massive pair of metal gates', while in 1982 a Prague production, whose actors had already been warned by a government official not to make political interpretations of 'this rotten intellectual Hamlet', expressed its sense of imprisonment through a set designed by Josef Svoboda: most of the play took place in a cramped space in front of the safety curtain; only at the end was it lifted so that the Prince's body could be carried up a long flight of stairs and into freedom.[77] Yuri Lyubimov's *Hamlet* (in Moscow in 1971–80, revived in an English production in Leicester in 1989) began with the gravediggers shovelling real earth for the burial of Hamlet senior, and the grave remained visible throughout, as if beckoning Hamlet, who was always aware of its presence. A knitted curtain served various functions: among other things, it represented the Ghost and, at the end, swept Claudius onto Hamlet's sword.

The theatre

The curtain also evokes a sense of theatre. The presence of a company of actors in *Hamlet* opens it up to both metatheatricality and topicality. Productions aiming for realism generally avoid both: hence, Hamlet's dialogue with Rosencrantz about the child actors and his 'advice to the players' were usually cut in pre-twentieth-century productions. So was the archaic dumbshow, thus evading one of the questions frequently asked: why does Claudius not react as soon as he sees it instead of sitting through so much dialogue? Now, on the other hand, these discussions of contemporary theatrical fashion offer the opportunity for a production to be topical in its own way.

Shakespeare initially represented a totally different kind of theatre from those indigenous to most non-European countries. To perform his plays 'authentically' might require an all-male theatre to allow women performers, as in Japan; it might require compromises in the playing of love scenes, as in India. The earliest Japanese productions omitted all the soliloquies,[78] and sometimes imitated English ones to the point of giving the actors red wigs and even having them speak in an English-accented Japanese.[79] Some directors have treated Hamlet's advice as transhistorical: it was 'reproduced regularly (particularly in the first decade or so of the twentieth century) as advice to Catalan actors'.[80] At the same time, theatre practitioners are aware of the danger of losing their own rich theatrical tradition and now productions outside the English-speaking world often use *The Murder of Gonzago* to draw on – for instance – African dance, *commedia dell'arte*, Noh drama, or children dancing. (These often make the dumb show, as Hamlet says, 'inexplicable', at least to Claudius.) Productions sometimes historicize the play by having the Player Queen played by a boy. Some directors have also been tempted to create characters for the actors and even suggest the existence of their own 'story' alongside the main play.[81]

International theatre festivals, and festivals devoted (at least in name) to Shakespeare, have proliferated since the 1980s. For example, the opening of the 'Globe' theatre in Tokyo (1988) was accompanied by a festival to which Ingmar Bergman brought his controversial *Hamlet*. An event which started as a tribute to the 'historical' Shakespeare thus led to a surge of experimental, 'postmodern' productions by Japanese directors.[82] The short-lived period of optimism following the fall of the Berlin Wall in 1989 was the catalyst for 'East–West' theatrical exchanges. In 2012, coinciding with the Olympics in London, the RSC offered an international festival in Stratford, and Shakespeare's Globe, in its 'Globe to Globe' season, was able to advertise '37 plays in 37 languages in 6 weeks'. Two years later, in a return gesture, the Globe sent its production of *Hamlet* to visit every country in the world.

Because *Hamlet* is long, and what survives of it is the purely verbal dimension, there is always likely to be a conflict over the extent to which the words should dominate a production. There is no longer such a thing as a standard performance text. Each director (or dramaturg) usually creates a new *Hamlet*, and the director of a non-English production will often commission a new translation to fit the intended inter-pretation. Major theatres are now capable of rapid scene changes, so playing a full text does not have to mean forgoing beautiful scenic effects. When the play is cut, as it usually is, it can express a directorial view; thus, John Caird has said that to play the full text is 'to shirk the responsibility to make the evening coherent.'[83] Kenneth Branagh, who has played both cut and uncut versions (and agrees that 'arguments will always rage about what constitutes a full text'), found that playing the longer version enriches the roles of Polonius and Claudius and allows the Hamlet actor to pace himself better.[84] Some directors compare the quarto and folio texts and decide either to follow a specific one or to rely on an edited (often conflated) text to make choices for them. Every textual choice is also a performance choice. For instance, to take a very minor example, the line 'What, has this thing appeared again tonight?' (1.1.20) is given to Horatio in Q2 but to Marcellus in F. As Marvin Rosenberg notes, the choice of speaker will affect the delivery of the line: if it's Horatio who asks the question, the word 'thing' is trivial, as Horatio at this point doesn't believe in the reality of the Ghost; if the line belongs to Marcellus, '*Thing* is then loaded with intimations of the unspeakable.'[85]

In some ways, the twenty-first-century *Hamlet* text is simply a reversal of the eighteenth-and nineteenth-century one: where productions once deleted everything 'low' and sexually suggestive, now they are more likely to delete anything that seems too 'high' or moralistic. But there are now so many *Hamlets* that generalization seems impossible. At present I see two contrasting trends. On the one hand, there is the desire for the *frisson* of reality, usually achieved by reconnecting with the play's historical context: the reconstructed indoor and outdoor playhouses, many of them experimental, as far away as Gdansk, Prague, Western Australia and Tokyo; the experiments with historical lighting, casting and costuming; even the more dubious kinds of knowledge to be derived from guided tours of Kronborg Castle in the company of Horatio. Real human skulls have been used in the graveyard scene, and even bequeathed for that purpose.[86] Richard Eyre's 1989 *Hamlet* at the National Theatre may be best remembered because one Hamlet-actor (Daniel Day-Lewis) gave up the part because he had become obsessed with his father's ghost and another (Ian Charleson) died of AIDS seven weeks after his last performance. Similarly, for audiences of Yuri Lyubimov's famous *Hamlet* for the Taganka Theatre in Moscow, the identification between actor Vysotsky and the character he played was virtually total.[87] Less grimly, Samuel West was pleased to realize, as he started rehearsing the role in 2001, that references to an 'election' might seem relevant to the controversial context of George W. Bush's inauguration.[88]

The visibility of the standing audience at an outdoor theatre has a particular effect in *Hamlet*, given the play's metatheatricality and its hero's fondness for self-questioning. Already, in the populist nineteenth-century theatre, audiences in the upper gallery were likely, as in Dickens's account of Mr Wopsle's Hamlet in *Great Expectations*, to respond to the hero's famous soliloquy ('some roared yes, and some no, and some inclining to both opinions said "Toss up for it"'). The groundlings at the Globe in 2000 loved Mark Rylance's delivery of the line about splitting the ears of the groundlings, especially when, after announcing that they were 'capable of nothing but inexplicable dumb show', he waited for the predictable laugh and, with a withering look, added, 'and noise'.[89] When he asks, 'Am I a coward?', there is now the possibility that someone will say, 'Yes', thus setting up his 'Swounds, I should take it', which, as Tim Carroll observed, gave the moment 'an electric charge'. Samuel West once actually had this experience, though he was in the darkened RSC auditorium.[90] Audiences seem to be reclaiming their right to be part of the play. The candlelit Wanamaker Theatre will some day show how *Hamlet* looks when both characters and audience are straining to see the action clearly, while the Blackfriars Theater in Staunton, Virginia, uniformly lit by electricity, renounces theatrical illusion in favour of a frank playing to the audience that, at its best, brings out the humour of the plays while still capturing its attention in moments of high tension.

Opposed to this hyperrealism, however, there is a competing tradition of productions that are unlocalized, decontextualized, or, paradoxically, so full of contexts that they cancel each other out. The sheer amount of writing about *Hamlet*, exhilarating for some actors and directors, is depressing for others. Robert Stephens felt that 'You cannot play Hamlet, but you can give an edited opinion of him, which is what the best actors do.'[91] For Simon Russell Beale, on the other hand, the abundance of choice means that 'The part just adapts itself to you, it's one of the most hospitable an actor can play. It says, Come and get me, I've got everything here, just pick what you want. But it does demand that you strip everything away.'[92]

Beale was in fact playing in a heavily cut production that had already done a good deal of picking and stripping to produce the 'edited opinion' that Stephens meant. Explaining why he cuts even seemingly crucial scenes, the Japanese director Tadashi Suzuki has said that he assumes 'that people already know the story' and Margaret Litvin recognizes the same assumption in recent Arab adaptations of *Hamlet*.[93] Words no longer belong to specific characters but to a kind of collective imaginary, and thus can be transferred to someone else – as in Charles Marowitz's 'Collage *Hamlet*' (1972), where Hamlet, an unheroic and unromantic young man, was constantly being bombarded with advice and commands from everyone else in the play. The 'post-modern' *Hamlet* of the late twentieth century deliberately incorporates the play's own history in theatre and criticism. The heterogeneity that used to baffle neoclassical critics has been embraced and extended to a variety of performance styles. What has been called 'a recognizably Australian approach to Shakespeare, an approach which is iconoclastic, energetic, physical, carnivalesque and excessive',[94] might equally well be a description of many English-language productions, which seem to resent the word-based theatre.

Productions in other languages are aware of, and exploit, their distance from the 'real' play. A Cantonese Hamlet in 2001 played the part against the background of Olivier's film, which continued running even after all the characters except Hamlet had been machine-gunned in the final battle.[95]

In 2006 an *Ur-Hamlet* at Kronborg Castle had 'a cast of Nō, Balinese, Indian, Afro-Brazilian, and European performers'.[96] The English theatre, which learned from the ensemble acting of the German company from Saxe-Meiningen in 1881 and from the visit of the Berliner Ensemble to London in 1956, has continued to benefit from contact with other theatrical traditions. Peter Brook's production of *Qui Est Là?* (1996), based on a French translation, was made up of lines from *Hamlet* (80 per cent), with the other 20 per cent consisting of critiques of the play and passages from theorists of the theatre like Brecht and Artaud, spoken in a number of languages. His more conventional though stripped-down production in English (2000) nevertheless retained some of the redistributions of the French version: the play began and ended with Horatio, alone onstage, calling out, 'Who's there?'. The question was allowed to reverberate in the mind. Brook's decision to move 'To be or not to be', so that Hamlet spoke it later in the play (in fact replacing 'How all occasions do inform against me' in 4.4), was followed in the production starring Maxine Peake, who spoke it after the murder of Polonius, with blood on her hands. The 2015 *Hamlet* at London's Barbican, directed by Lyndsey Turner, began the play with this speech at early previews, but by opening night, perhaps because of critical reactions, had moved it back to its conventional place. These experiments with the most famous lines in Shakespeare seem to have been attempts to encourage a focus on the theatrical event in the present, rather than on memories of the text.

What Andy Lavender says of Robert Wilson's *Hamlet: A Monologue* (a one-man show, treated as a flashback from the moment immediately before the hero's death) might apply to many modern productions of *Hamlet*: 'Theatrical effects are not there to produce meaning. They are there to produce an *experience* of the theatrical.'[97] Whereas one used to go to a major performance of *Hamlet* hoping to learn something about the play, one is now more likely to go in order to watch actors and directors pushing the boundaries of what theatre can do – something that is most easily seen in the context of a well-known work. Of course, there is still a need for productions to cater for the sophisticated theatregoer, the student reading *Hamlet* as part of an English course, and the 'naïve' spectator (in so far as such a person exists). There also remains a thirst for the living presence of the actor: tickets for all performances of the 2015 RSC *Hamlet* were sold on the day booking opened, a year in advance of the production, even though many of the buyers must have known that the performance was sure to be available as a live transmission in cinemas. The desire to see Hamlet interpreted by Benedict Cumberbatch, an actor famous for playing Sherlock Holmes as a 'high-functioning sociopath', may also reflect the basically psychological, apolitical stance that still characterizes most Anglophone productions.

This *Hamlet* has also profited from a belief that his home is still the English language. Yet it will be seen worldwide by spectators who will rely on sur- and subtitles to understand it. Spectators at Ninagawa's *Hamlet*, on tour in London in 2015, were also given surtitles. Though the actors were speaking in modern Japanese, their words were 'translated' back into Shakespeare's seventeenth-century language. By contrast, the surtitles for the foreign-language productions in the 'Globe to Globe' season gave only brief summaries of the action, recognizing that Shakespearean English was not really equivalent to what was being said. Perhaps some day an English-language *Hamlet* will be accompanied by surtitles in modern English. This would be a logical conclusion of the process by which Shakespeare's play has conquered the world by vanishing into it.

3

The State of the Art

Neil Taylor

'Today, *Hamlet* studies have, one suspects, reached something of a dead end.' That was the view of Adrian A. Husain, writing in 2004. 'The noted Shakespeare scholars', he continued, listing some illustrious names from the twentieth century, 'seem to have said it all.' We are, as he put it, 'in limbo'.

If one accepts Husain's metaphor of the dead end, then one way forward is to go back – to turn round, retrace one's steps, and find a different route. Today, more than a decade further into the new millennium, one can see that, while no major new movement in Shakespeare studies may have yet emerged, there has been some most illuminating work involving revisiting old sites and rethinking earlier habits of thought. This chapter concentrates primarily on three important and absorbing books by three noted scholars who have decided to look back in order to look forward. But it also takes note of recent and interesting work by others working in the same or related areas of Shakespeare studies.

Stephen Greenblatt and the old religion

In the case of Stephen Greenblatt, going back has meant rediscovering a feature of medieval religious thought and feeling. It has meant finding a route, not from Limbo, but from Purgatory.

His *Hamlet in Purgatory*, which was published in 2001, spends much of its time researching medieval documentation of the institution of Purgatory, that afterlife state where those who die with sins unshriven must have them burnt away before they can get to Heaven. In 1563, the year before Shakespeare was born, the Protestant Church of England officially relegated belief in Purgatory to the Roman Catholic past, along with the practice of praying for the souls of the dead. Nevertheless, Greenblatt finds in the language and feeling of Shakespeare's play (to which he devotes his two closing chapters) sufficient echoes of the old Catholic doctrine to persuade him that an important element in the power of the play to enthral and move us is its capacity to make us participate in the fearful idea, shared by Hamlet and the Ghost alike, that the dead might be forgotten and their suffering doubted.

Greenblatt's title, *Hamlet in Purgatory*, is nicely ambiguous: the 'Hamlet' in question could be Prince Hamlet or it could be the late King Hamlet. Both of them seem to be in purgatory – the son metaphorically, the father literally. The grieving son's emotional confusion and suffering is there at the outset of the play, but then his encounter with the Ghost provokes a new, profounder level of suffering, both psychological and intellectual. As for his father's spirit, while it fails to state explicitly that it is suffering in Purgatory, its language, and other parts of the play's verbal texture, together persuade Greenblatt to draw that conclusion. Or, at least, he thinks Shakespeare's audience would have drawn that conclusion, and we would do well to entertain it.

The Ghost presents Hamlet with a set of interlinked problems. Firstly, it informs him that his father's death was not from natural causes but at the hands of his father's brother. The play invites a degree of scepticism about the authenticity of ghosts and therefore of the truth of what they have to communicate. Hamlet is in doubt from the moment he sees the apparition, his first thought being, is it 'a spirit of health' or is it a 'goblin damned' (1.4.40)? He is in doubt again at 2.2.533–5, and then again at 3.2.78. Horatio, who has seen the Ghost in the opening scene, warns Hamlet that it might be the devil in disguise (1.4.69–74), while Gertrude, who cannot see it at all, thinks it is the product of Hamlet's deranged imagination (3.4.135). Determining the true identity of the Ghost taxes Hamlet's intellect. But there is another conundrum, which is not just intellectual but moral and theological as well. The Ghost demands that the son avenge the father's death, by killing and sending to Hell the man who is, at one and the same time, his uncle, his mother's husband, and the King. If this Ghost's habitat really is the Christian Purgatory, whose inhabitants are assured of a safe, if temporarily painful, passage to Heaven, then young Hamlet's initial confusion can only now be compounded, for revenge, murder and regicide are surely outlawed by the Church. And this moral and theological problem is, of course, a problem for the audience and the reader, too. How can we be expected to share Horatio's vision of the man who does indeed kill his uncle, father-in-law and King (along with a few others) being finally released like souls released from Purgatory in medieval paintings, and finding his way to Heaven accompanied by flights of angels (5.2.344)?

At least one scholar has suggested that we do not allow the concept of the Christian ethic to deny the force of other deeply felt human imperatives at work in the play. Marguerite A. Tassi's *Women and Revenge in Shakespeare: Gender, Genre, and Ethics* (2011) argues that, while revenge in Early Modern drama appears to be condemned on the grounds that it is unchristian, the fundamental passion motivating revenge can be read as a positive moral imperative, namely a love of justice. Gertrude and Ophelia share a deep, inward sense of injustice, and their words are the revenge drivers: Gertrude's 'I am poisoned', more than the Ghost's command, is really what prompts Hamlet to kill Claudius, while Laertes kills Hamlet in response to Ophelia's call that he remember their father's death.

Greenblatt would probably not deny this. Indeed, he reckons that ghosts provided Shakespeare with rich and complex 'theatrical capital' (157), coming as they might from any of three locations – Hades (the source of Seneca's ghosts with their powerful call for justice and revenge), Hell (home of the Devil who can drive you into insanity and sin) or, finally, Purgatory (whose lodgers call on your imagination, your sympathy, your empathy and your humanity, pleading as they do that your prayers might bring an end to their suffering). This particular ghost Greenblatt finds particularly compelling: 'amazingly disturbing and vivid', it is like no other ghost, he says, 'not only in Shakespeare but in any literary or historical text that I have ever read' (4). While it certainly cries out for vengeance, its 'solemn command upon which young Hamlet dwells obsessively, is that he *remember*' (206).

This emphasis on an internal response, this 'inwardness' as Greenblatt terms it, is corrosive and becomes 'the hallmark of the entire play' (208). Yet the memory of the dead father recedes. The Ghost has to return in 3.4 to remind Hamlet of his mission. But that is it, it never again returns. When Hamlet finally kills Claudius he fails to mention his father, merely bidding his uncle to 'Follow my mother' (5.2.311). The play's emphasis on the psychological dimension seems to be at the expense of the Ghost 'as ghost', but Greenblatt argues that the psychological dimension is constructed almost entirely out of the theological – 'and specifically out of the issue of remembrance that … lay at the heart of the crucial early sixteenth-century debate about Purgatory' (229).

Why should this relic of the Old Faith so inform *Hamlet*? The play is much to do with death, and it is also much to do with fathers and sons. In August 1596, while Shakespeare was away from Stratford earning his living as an actor and playwright in London, he had lost his only son Hamnet. This death must surely have affected him deeply and contributed something to the creation of *Hamlet*. Then, five years later, he lost his father too. In 1757 a workman mending the roof of Shakespeare's birthplace in Stratford-upon-Avon found an old document bearing the supposed signature of John Shakespeare, the playwright's father. It was a so-called 'Borromeo will', stating that before his death he intended to have the sacraments of confession, Mass and extreme unction in order not to have a lengthy stay in Purgatory. Shakespeare would therefore seem to have been brought up in a Roman Catholic household, and even if he ended up a loyal member of the Church of England, Greenblatt surmises that 'the Protestant playwright was haunted by the spirit of his Catholic father pleading for suffrages to relieve his soul from the pains of Purgatory' (249).

But John's death surely comes too late for it to have inspired a central theme in *Hamlet*, for the play seems to have been written in 1600 or 1601, and he did not die until September 1601. It is hard to overcome this obstacle in the path of Greenblatt's argument. Nevertheless, as Greenblatt puts it, the Protestant attack on 'the middle state of souls' did not necessarily destroy 'the longings and fears that Catholic doctrine had focused and exploited' (256–7). The removal of John Shakespeare from the argument doesn't entirely demolish the idea that Shakespeare's play draws on the power of the old Catholic belief that the dead wish to communicate with the living and need our prayers. As Graham Holderness argues in a 2007 essay entitled '"I covet your skull": death and desire in *Hamlet*', this impulse goes far beyond Hamlet's relationship with his father, for we can find it both in Hamlet's need to converse with Yorick's skull and, almost three hundred years later, in Victorian scholars' interest in disinterring Shakespeare himself. Both of these, Holderness argues, are expressions of a vision of the dead as 'alive, speaking, still accessible to inquiry, prayer and love' – a vision which he describes as 'early modern Catholic' (236) but which Greenblatt, in a deeply personal introduction, claims to find active in his own Jewish twenty-first-century self.

(One of the more interesting responses to the problem of the biographical element in Shakespeare's play is actually a deflection from it. Writing in the journal *ELR* in 2014, James J. Marino sees no merit at all in the idea that *Hamlet* is autobiographical in respect of the influence of the deaths of either Hamnet or John Shakespeare. Rather, he sees quite another father and son reflected in the play – James Burbage, who died in 1597 and was builder in 1576 of the first purpose-built playhouse, The Theatre, where many of Shakespeare's plays were performed in the 1590s; and his son Richard Burbage, who was the leading actor in Shakespeare's company and played Hamlet, possibly at his father's playhouse in 1594, but definitely, after his father's death, at the Globe. However, Marino believes that, even though the contemporary audience would have expected the actor's performance to invoke thoughts of his relationship with his late father, Shakespeare's play 'proposes its hero's interiority as a defence against its star's celebrity' (76), thereby artfully deflecting attention away from Richard's autobiography.)

Other scholars have also published material on Shakespeare's supposed Catholic background and beliefs. Richard Wilson's book on the topic, *Secret Shakespeare: Studies in Theatre, Religion and Resistance* (2004), contains a useful chapter entitled 'Ghostly fathers: Shakeshafte and the Jesuits', in which he goes back and rehearses in some detail the theory, first proposed by Oliver Baker in 1937 and taken up again by E. A. J. Honigmann in *Shakespeare: The Lost Years* (1985), that the young Shakespeare spent a period in the 1580s in Lancashire as a tutor or actor in a Catholic household. After 1576 John Shakespeare had stopped attending Stratford corporation meetings and started refusing to go to Church, pleading 'fear of process of debt'. Wilson doubts that this was the reason, preferring to believe that it was his Catholicism, and that his son too was initially caught up in Counter-Reformation zeal. The Jesuit martyr, Edmund Campion, entered the country and travelled from Warwickshire to Lancashire in 1580 seeking support. The following year, the year of Campion's arrest and execution for treason, a 'William Shakeshafte' is mentioned in the will of Alexander Hoghton, whose home of Hoghton Tower was used throughout Elizabeth's reign as an academy for boys preparing to train abroad as Catholic priests.

It is in the nature of drama that it is impossible to know which if any of the characters' opinions or attitudes are shared by the author, but that hasn't deterred scholars and others from trying to deduce from his plays whether Shakespeare, despite living in an officially Protestant country, might actually have been, as some have argued, a Catholic. Since the turn of the century, a surprising number of established scholars have taken up the challenge of writing Shakespeare's biography, and almost all have shared René Weis's conclusion in 2007 that the issue was impossible to determine (Weis 2007: 49); the following year Jonathan Bate described the debate as fierce but inconclusive (Bate 2007: 73), and in 2010 Katherine Duncan-Jones repeated her belief, first published in 2001, that most of the evidence, including most of the literary evidence, could be read in contradictory ways (Duncan-Jones 2010: 282). John Shakespeare's Borromeo will has divided opinion, with Weis believing it was probably genuine (269–70) and Bate thinking it was probably not (73). As for Shakespeare's supposed sojourn in Lancashire, Duncan-Jones, in her 2011 *An Ungentle Life*, was sure that Douglas Hamer had produced enough evidence in a 2002 *Review of English Studies* article that the William Shakeshafte in Hoghton's will was not a seventeen-year-old from Stratford but a middle-aged man born and bred in Lancashire, to persuade her that the theory that Shakespeare had spent a year at Hoghton Hall had been 'refuted' (Duncan-Jones 2011: 160). Lois Potter argued in 2012 that 'If (which is unlikely) he was to be involved in undercover Catholic activities, it would have made more sense to send him abroad than to Lancashire, especially since Shakeshaft is not much of an alias' (Potter 2012: 49); she also thought it unlikely that Shakespeare was a committed Catholic by the time he married, since Anne Hathaway's brother was to become a churchwarden a few years later (58).

The identification of Shakespeare with Shakeshaft is, of course, speculation, but important to the argument of Wilson's book, which is that Shakespeare was a Catholic but learned to keep his Catholicism secret. David Scott Kastan observes in his book, *A Will to Believe: Shakespeare and Religion* (2014), that a play like *Hamlet* may be 'intensely saturated with religious language, religious practices, and religious ideas, but their presence neither exhausts nor explains the play's mysteries, and they function neither as an index of Shakespeare's faith nor as a prompt or challenge to our own' (143). Wilson would agree that Shakespeare is effectively silent on the matter of his own religious position. 'This is a book', he writes, 'about what Shakespeare did not write', and 'The silence in question is his total effacement of the religious politics of his age' (ix). But Wilson's argument goes further. He believes Shakespeare's silence is eloquent of his moral position: he deliberately rejected overt and violent opposition to the official Protestant religion, and this 'resistance of the resistance' provides a model of responsible behaviour, as much for the twenty-first century as for the sixteenth. Shakespeare was one of those Catholics who 'reacted against the suicidal violence of the fanatics with a project of freedom of conscience and mutual toleration, ... [a] programme which has lessons for our age of religious terrorism and sectarian hatred' (ix). However, in his more recent book on *Shakespeare in French Theory: King of Shadows* (2007), Wilson expresses the opinion that in *Hamlet*, which was first published at the very point when James VI of Scotland became James I of England, Shakespeare's silence is somewhat silenced, for the play's Catholic and apocalyptic language and imagery reflect 'a rising apprehension, as the new age dawns, of the disaster of Stuart rule' (237).

The whole issue of the extent to which Shakespeare was 'religious' would appear to have caught the interest of a number of other writers and scholars. In 2003 the Catholic writer Peter Milward published a study on *Shakespeare's Meta-drama: 'Hamlet' and 'Macbeth'*, in which he argued that '*Hamlet* is a deeply religious play' (7), whereas in his *Godless Shakespeare* of 2007, Eric S. Mallin sets out to suggest some of the ways in which Shakespeare's beliefs, in so far as they can be inferred, show 'a mind and a spirit uncontained by orthodoxy' (3). John E. Curran's *Hamlet, Protestantism, and the Mourning of Contingency* of 2006 denies that Shakespeare was necessarily himself a Catholic, but sees him as Catholic-minded, and finds that in *Hamlet* he struggled unsuccessfully to apply such a world view to a Calvinist universe in which all human action is predetermined. Brian Cummings's *Mortal Thoughts: Religion, Secularity and Identity in Shakespeare and Early Modern Culture*, published in 2014, argues that creeping secularism did not prevent Shakespeare's presentation of 'selfhood', both in his use of soliloquy and in his treatment of topics such as conscience and suicide, from being conducted within a framework of religious thinking.

And in 2005 Philip Edwards, having produced a major edition of *Hamlet* in 1985, published a study of *Pilgrimage and Literary Tradition*, in which he included a stimulating chapter on the play. In it he took his cue from scene 4.5, where Ophelia enters and begins to sing a version of the old Walsingham ballad: 'How should I your true love know / From another one? / By his cockle hat and staff / And his sandal shoon' (lines 23–6). The woman's lover has forsaken her, and we can tell by his appearance that he has done so because he has taken vows to become a pilgrim. Edwards distinguishes between two types of pilgrim. There are those who travel to a shrine seeking communication with higher powers, and there are those who have already received illumination and now travel on in order to deepen and spread that illumination. Hamlet is the first type, except that it is the higher power (his father's ghost) that has come in search of communication with him. However, at the same time, and more importantly, he is also the second, missionary type. Hamlet goes beyond what the Ghost requires of him. He takes the path of celibacy, demands the same of Ophelia and sets out to cleanse society at large. Further complicating and intensifying the tragedy of the role he has taken on, Hamlet both accepts and rejects the authenticity of the Ghost and its message, which means 'he feels he has a commission to change the world, and he wishes to leave the world altogether; he is both a person under divine instruction and a person creating his own instructions' (202). He is, in consequence, 'alienated and doomed' (44).

In *Shakespeare and Impure Aesthetics* (2009) Hugh Grady sees *Hamlet* as a collection of ambiguous 'signifying objects' in a melancholy world empty of intrinsic meaning. The most emotionally powerful of these objects are the graveyard and Yorick's skull. The clowns' gallows humour forces Hamlet, and us, to think anew about death, recognising that here in this world outside the court death is both commonplace and 'a moment of life which continues in the community as it is extinguished in the individual' (179). Published in the same year, Paul A. Kottman's *Tragic Conditions in Shakespeare* also examines emotion in the graveyard scene: prompted by Hamlet's disgust at the smell of a skull, Kottman recalls the old argument that societies are founded on the imperative to bury one's dead before they rot. In Hamlet's case, he can only bury his father at this late stage by avenging his death, thereby fulfilling his duty as a social being. But in the process of fulfilling that duty, he has tragically helped reduce his immediate society to a heap of corpses. Tragedy's social function lies in the spontaneous emotional bond which such an outcome forges with a theatre audience.

Those who write about that bond describe it in different ways. Kottman talks of 'a collective shiver of the spine' (77). Harold Bloom's approach to Hamlet in *Hamlet: Poem Unlimited*, his 2003 follow-up to the earlier *Shakespeare: The Invention of the Human*, is highly personal: 'Hamlet bewilders me', he confesses (109). As for his readers, Bloom looks to establish a bond with them by again being personal: 'Hamlet is more intelligent than you are, whoever you are' (86). He is nevertheless at his most personal when he discusses the bond that the play forges with him in the theatre. He confesses that 'every time I have managed to get through an entire performance of *Hamlet* – increasingly difficult these days – I have to admit that even my most intense rereadings of the play do not prepare me for the cognitive and aesthetic effect of Hamlet's death upon me' (94). For Bloom that effect is Apotheosis – 'an extraordinary challenge even to Shakespeare's powers of representation: how can you dramatize the exaltation of a human being to a seeming transcendence?' (94).

Shakespeare achieves that. At least he does for Bloom. We feel, he tells us, 'augmented, rather than diminished' by the death of this 'charismatic eminence' (95, 109). Greenblatt's reading of *Hamlet* is similarly informed by an intense responsiveness to the play's emotional power, and he communicates that involvement and excitement to his readers with immense skill. The same is true of Bloom. You feel augmented, rather than diminished, by his extraordinary reading -- and by his writing.

Margreta de Grazia and an old Hamlet within *Hamlet*

For Harold Bloom, *Hamlet* is a play about Hamlet. But he goes further. 'The foreground to Shakespeare's tragedy is Hamlet's consciousness of his own consciousness' (86). This narrow focus on one character and on one aspect of that character, his mind, can also be found in Marvin W. Hunt's *Looking for Hamlet* (2007), another book aimed at the general reader but skilfully and intelligently argued. Hunt finds in the play 'a radical new belief – or fear: that what goes on inside our heads is what is ultimately real' (80). Indeed, he describes it as 'the single most important work in constructing who we are, especially how we understand our psychological, intellectual and emotional beings' (7-8), for 'the resulting sense of a palpable interiority has reflected and shaped the intellectual history of the West' (7).

This focus on inwardness, on Hamlet's internal mental and emotional life, is what we have been encouraged to recognize as *Hamlet*'s distinctive feature. Indeed it is, according to Greenblatt, 'the principal cause of its astonishing, worldwide renown' (208). But we have also been encouraged to diagnose the unusual, even pathological, features of that mind. I only quoted part of Bloom's sentence at the start of this section. The full sentence runs, 'The foreground to Shakespeare's tragedy is Hamlet's consciousness of his own consciousness, unlimited yet at war with itself' (86).

In other words, *Hamlet* is a play not merely about a brilliant mind, but about a messed up brilliant mind. The state of health of that mind has been a source of fascination for amateur psychologists for years. And not just amateurs. As John Lee makes clear in his chapter on 'The Critical Background' earlier in this volume (34–8), twentieth-century criticism of the play, and twentieth-century productions on the stage and on screen, were frequently influenced by ideas deriving directly or indirectly from Freudian psychoanalysis. Today's actors, ultimately influenced by the Method school's approach to characterization, still attempt to understand their parts by creating fictional psychological backstories, and they will probably continue to do so (see, for example, Neil Taylor, 'An Actress Prepares', 2012). Meanwhile, Hamlet's psyche continues to dominate directors' approach to the play. Indeed, the production starring Michael Sheen as Hamlet at London's Young Vic theatre in 2011 was set in a psychiatric institution, part-hospital, part-prison, and the audience was presented with what the *Guardian* described as 'the Freudian dream of a disturbed in-patient' (9 November).

Similarly, but to a much lesser extent, psychoanalytic thinking continues to feed into some recent literary studies (see, for example, Christopher Pye's *The Vanishing:*

Shakespeare, the Subject, and Early Modern Culture [2000], Linda Charnes's *Hamlet's Heirs: Shakespeare and the Politics of a New Millennium* [2006], David Hillman's *Shakespeare's Entrails: Belief, Scepticism and the Interior of the Body* [2007], and Simon Critchley and Jamieson Webster's *The Shakespeare Doctrine* [2013]). But on the whole, criticism in the final decades of the twentieth century tended to be dominated by readings of Shakespeare based on the theories of the New Historicist and Cultural Materialist critics.

There has been some evidence of a reaction against what Daphne Patai and Will H. Corral called 'Theory's Empire' (their title for an 'Anthology of Dissent' which they edited in 2005). Richard Meek, in *Narrating the Visual in Shakespeare* (2009) quotes approvingly Russ McDonald's sense in 2001 that New Historicist and Cultural Materialist criticism might be beginning to give way to 'a new formalism, and even a new aestheticism' (*Shakespeare and the Arts of Language*: 7). John Lee's study of *Shakespeare's 'Hamlet' and the Controversies of Self*, which was published at the turn of the new century, describes the New Historicist and Cultural Materialist theoretical position as assuming that characters in Renaissance drama lacked a sense of interiority – or, as he puts it, 'a self-constituted sense of self' (1). Lee disagrees with them strongly, arguing that, despite the fact that *Hamlet*, for example, cannot employ 'the modern vocabulary of meaning through which interiority is described' (2), Hamlet's self-constituting sense of self is central to his tragedy. What is more, Lee believes that in the process of revising his play (as Lee, along with many others, believes he did between the texts that appeared in 1604 and in 1623), Shakespeare altered his presentation of Hamlet's interiority in certain respects: the Folio's Prince is quieter than the Quarto Prince, less given to rely on external theories of the self, less willing to think via 'normative systems' (239).

However, *'Hamlet' Without Hamlet*, which Margreta de Grazia brought out in 2007, sets out to resist what she regards as the post-Romantic reading of the play, the reading that sees it as above all a revolutionary exploration of an individual's inner life. Like Greenblatt, de Grazia would have us go forward by going back. 'The Hamlet this book would do without is the modern Hamlet, the one distinguished by an inner being so transcendent that it barely comes into contact with the play from which it emerges.' Instead, she would have us return to an earlier reading of the play, for 'Hamlet's deep and complex inwardness was not perceived as the play's salient feature until around 1800' (1).

De Grazia insists that Hamlet's delay only became seen as 'psychological' once Coleridge began to use the term to describe Shakespeare's insight into character and Hamlet became associated with things 'modern'. The earliest quarto texts of *Hamlet* may differ radically in terms of language and even some aspects of plot, but they agree on one thing at least, for all five describe the play as a 'Tragicall Historie'. It is not until 1623, seven years after Shakespeare's death, that the First Folio classifies the play as a Tragedy and the word History is dropped.

The play, she reminds us, is full of references to 'the stuff of history – the fall of states, kingdoms, and empires', beginning with the threat of invasion and ending with a foreign occupation (48). After 1660 Fortinbras went missing, with the result that there was no foreign takeover at the end and no threat of such a thing at the beginning. Everything that signifies the play's involvement in the history of governments and nations got abbreviated or removed. Even after Fortinbras had reappeared on the London stage at the very end of the nineteenth century, A. C. Bradley's lectures on Shakespearean Tragedy (*Hamlet*, *King Lear*, *Macbeth* and *Othello*), which were published in 1904, defined the form as concentrating on the suffering of great individuals.

This meant that Bradley ignored *Hamlet*'s preoccupation with 'the process of history, the alternations of state that punctuate world history, as one kingdom gives way to another in what might be called a pre-modern imperial schema that assumes the eventual fall of all kingdoms and their final subsumption by the apocalyptic kingdom-to-come' (65). De

Grazia reckons the play has a fairly precise historical setting somewhere within the fifty-year period in which Britain fell first to the Danes and then to the Normans. At the same time, within the text there are verbal references, not only to the famous imperial falls of ancient history (Troy, Greece, Carthage and Rome), but also to 'the two great modern threats to Christendom: the standoff between Luther and Charles V that split Christendom in two and the hovering threat of the Turks who in the sixteenth century had made their way to the very gates of Vienna, the seat of the Holy Roman Empire' (80).

She argues – carefully, subtly, forcefully – that if we try to ignore the modern obsession with *Hamlet*'s 'modernity' and examine scrupulously the plot and the play's language, we can recover a play that is conceived as history as much as tragedy and that is very much about the ownership and conquest of land. She reads the prince's supposed madness and delay as functions of a plot in which his behaviour is largely determined by his uncle's and mother's conspiracy to dispossess him of his inheritance. 'The future of both Hamlet and Laertes has been despoiled by their fathers' sudden and shady passing. One departs intestate, the other in "hugger-mugger" fashion (4.5.84). ... In both families, the father's irregular death blocks the son's birthright and drives him to extremes ... / ... both men are pushed over the edge by the blasted image of their patrilineal dream, their outrageous behaviour symptomatic of a society deeply invested in land' (144–5).

De Grazia is at her most brilliant and absorbing when she digs deeper into the play's verbal texture to unearth its 'worldly preoccupations' (204). For example, this:

Hamlet explains, 'My wit's diseased' (3.2.313). With that adjective, he both describes his condition and names its cause. Until the eighteenth century, *diseased* shared both spelling and pronunciation with *diseized*: to be illegitimately dispossessed of lands ... The pun epitomizes not only the relation between human and humus so central to this book, but also a sedimentation in language so deep as to be almost beyond retrieval, at least for modern sensibilities which have turned to less worldly matters to explain Hamlet's unwholesomeness or 'insanity'. (157)

Fortinbras may have made his way back onstage by the beginning of the twentieth century, but Ralph Berry in 2008 complained that, after the fall of the Berlin Wall, most of the productions of *Hamlet* which he had seen suggested that his journey had not really been necessary. The political dimension of the play was increasingly underplayed as it became 'contracted to the domestic, the private even' (43). Fortinbras's lines were once again either severely reduced or completely eliminated in a series of high-profile productions. Berry cited a number of examples, including Matthew Warchus's production for the Royal Shakespeare Company in 1998 and John Caird's at the National Theatre in 2000. (This process of depoliticization has continued since the essay was published. One thinks of Greg Doran's 2008 production for the Royal Shakespeare Company, starring David Tennant, which was broadcast on BBC television in 2009 and then widely distributed as a DVD.) Berry adds that the edition of the play published by the Oxford University Press in 1987 (and he might now add the Royal Shakespeare Company in 2007), which was based on the Folio rather than the Second Quarto, has also given the downplaying of Fortinbras the authority of textual scholarship.

Of course, there are other characters in the play apart from Hamlet and Fortinbras and the Ghost. Recent scholarship has shown some interest in at least two. In 2012, Kaara L. Peterson and Deanne Williams edited a collection of essays on *The Afterlife of Ophelia*, and Marguerite Tassi's book on *Women and Revenge*, which discusses Ophelia's and Gertrude's role in the revenge action, has already been mentioned. But the one character who might be said to have edged into the limelight is Horatio.

He turns out to have some interesting features. Bloom points out that Horatio is the only person at Elsinore whom

Claudius doesn't try to suborn (15). The 2006 Arden edition of the play notes another peculiarity of Horatio's part, namely that his is the only role that cannot be doubled (Appendix 2). Christopher Warley, in a 2009 *ELH* article on 'Specters of Horatio', explores the personal and political ambiguity of Horatio's role: to Hamlet he is reliable, being a disinterested outsider, whereas to Marcellus he is reliable because he is an interested insider. In *Distant Reading* (2009) Franco Moretti has conducted a visual analysis of the plot of *Hamlet*. He does this by drawing lines between any characters who communicate orally with one another. What he discovers is that if Hamlet is removed from the network (i.e. *Hamlet* literally without Hamlet), two camps begin to emerge: the Court and the others. He then suggests that Horatio heralds the coming of a new political reality, namely the replacement of the Court by the State, for the network of impersonal, bureaucratic 'others' disintegrates if Horatio is also removed (*Hamlet* without either Hamlet or Horatio). Bloom explores another scenario, retaining Hamlet but removing Horatio, and concludes that Horatio is the most important figure in the tragedy apart from Hamlet, for, ironically, 'without Horatio we are too distanced from Hamlet' (16).

Zachary Lesser and the 'new (old) play'

An interesting feature of Margreta de Grazia's book, and one which is shared with other studies of *Hamlet* that have been published in the new century, is the eclectic approach it has to the play's multiple texts. Despite deliberately choosing as the source of her quotations 'the edition most saturated with the modern critical tradition' (xii) – Harold Jenkins's modernized Arden edition of 1982 – de Grazia is happy to mine any or all of the early texts for material to support her readings. Her justification is that the three texts, although separate, are not discrete, and she wants 'to open up possibilities limited or foreclosed by the modern edition' (xii). The result is that 'Hamlet' has become not so much a text as a bank of resource material, from which readers can select a play of their choosing.

So what are the early texts? *Hamlet* exists in three distinct early printed versions, the First Quarto of 1603 (Q1), the Second Quarto of 1604/5 (Q2) and the text printed in the First Folio of 1623 (F). However, editors of the play have traditionally printed a single text, basing it on whichever of Q2 or F they believed to be closer to Shakespeare's intentions, but introducing readings from one or more of the other texts where they have felt that they completed or corrected the reading in their chosen control text. Q1 was regarded as being corrupt, although possibly reflecting early performances of the play, and was therefore rarely employed as a source of readings. Thus, Harold Jenkins based his 1982 Arden edition on Q2, but introduced some readings from F, whereas G. R. Hibbard based his 1987 Oxford edition on F and, while correcting some of F's readings with reference to Q2, included as Appendix A, i–xviii, 'Passages Peculiar to the Second Quarto' (355–69).

In the latter stages of the twentieth century, the practice of producing a single, conflated text began to be challenged. Just as the growth of continental and American literary theory in universities undermined conventional assumptions about the unity and stability of the human subject, the value of value-judgements, and role of the author, so the theory of editing began to be rigorously explored and conventional assumptions rethought. The popularity of Theatre and Performance Studies had an impact too, as editors were encouraged by their publishers to give increased attention to their play's stage and screen history; meanwhile, some editors at least (Stanley Wells and Gary Taylor, for example, in their Oxford Shakespeare of 1986) decided that their role was to establish not what Shakespeare wrote (or intended to write), but what got performed by his acting company. Unfortunately, we do not have more than one, brief example of a Shakespeare manuscript of a play-text (the Hand D additions to *The Book of Sir Thomas More* by Thomas Munday and others), and even that is disputed, and, equally unfortunately, we have precious little evidence of how Shakespeare's plays were performed during his lifetime. An editor can only work from the early printed texts of the plays, and develop hypotheses or draw inferences from them. But we do not know how much authority to attribute to these printed texts. We cannot be sure of the route by which they came to be printed, they all contain manifest errors which we cannot be sure how to correct, and, anyway, more than half of the plays usually attributed to Shakespeare have come down to us in at least two (and sometimes more) printed versions.

The General Introduction which Graham Holderness and Bryan Loughrey attached to their *Shakespearean Originals* series in 1992 declared that their editors 'reject the claim that it is possible to construct a rehabilitated text reflecting a form approximating Shakespeare's artistic vision. Instead we prefer to embrace the early printed texts as authentic material objects, the concrete forms from which all subsequent editions ultimately derive' (8). They went on to explain that there is 'no philosophical justification for emendation', and 'The worst form of emendation is conflation' (9).

The *Oxford Complete Works*, which Stanley Wells and Gary Taylor had edited in 1986, broke new ground by printing two versions of *King Lear* – a *History of King Lear*, based on the 1608 Quarto, and a *Tragedy of King Lear*, based on the text printed in the 1623 First Folio – and in 1993 René Weis printed the Quarto and Folio *Lear*s in a 'Parallel Text Edition', with the Quarto on the left-hand page and the Folio on the right, so that the reader could compare the texts line by line.

Multiple-text editions began to multiply. While modern scholarly editions had normally been in the habit of informing their readers of the existence of variants between texts as footnotes to the edited text, the general editors of the third series Arden Shakespeare decided in 1995 that photographic facsimiles of any 'bad quartos' (i.e. texts which were heavily adapted, or reconstructed from memory, or both) would be included as appendices to editions. However, in the case of *King Lear*, the Quarto is not normally regarded as 'bad', so, in an attempt to provide readers with a sense of what distinguishes the Quarto and Folio texts, R. A. Foakes's 1997 conflated *King Lear* framed passages found only in the Quarto with a superscript Q and passages found only in the Folio with a superscript F.

What, then, of *Hamlet*? In 1991 Paul Bertram and Bernice W. Kliman produced diplomatic facsimiles of Q1, Q2 and F. Each text was printed in a separate column (the procedure which Weis copied in his parallel-text *King Lear*). However, Kliman's 'enfolded *Hamlet*' appeared in 1996, and, in 2002, Jesús Tronch-Pérez produced what he called a '*reading critical edition*' (58), *A Synoptic 'Hamlet'* which printed his modern spelling editions of both Q2 and F, with the quarto variants superimposed on the folio variants (rather as if they were sleeping in bunk-beds!). Most recently, in 2006, Ann Thompson and Neil Taylor edited all three early texts, Q1, Q2 and F, for the third series of the Arden Shakespeare.

The previous year, 2005, James Shapiro had written 'Soon – in a generation or two, I suspect – only scholars interested in the history of the play's reception will be reading a conflated *Hamlet*' (Shapiro 2005: 357). More recently Janet Clare has expressed the view that 'It is now editorial orthodoxy that the three variant texts of *Hamlet* each have distinctive features, and it is difficult to imagine in the current bibliographical climate the production of a scholarly conflated edition' (Clare 2014: 166).

Paul Werstine commented in 2002 that 'textual critics and editors have come to realise that they neither can know nor need to know what kind of manuscripts served as printer's copy for the earliest printings of Shakespeare's plays' (Werstine 2002: 131). Nevertheless, Jonathan Bate and Eric Rasmussen based their 2007 edition of *Hamlet* in the RSC *Complete Works* on F, in the belief that the text established by John Heminges and Henry Condell (the editors of the 1623 First Folio) was the one contained in the *Hamlet* playbook held by the King's Men, the acting company for which they, and Shakespeare himself, worked (Bate 2007).

Meanwhile, Q1 has come in for considerable scrutiny. Lene Petersen, for example, in her 2013 book on *Shakespeare's Errant Texts: Textual Form and Linguistic Style in Shakespearean 'Bad' Quartos and Co-authored Plays*, adopts what became in the twentieth century the conventional view of the temporal relationship between the texts – namely that the text behind Q1 comes later than those behind Q2 and F, and argues that its shaping of the plot reflects a process of streamlining consistent with that sequence of events. But others have begun to revive some older theories and revisited the idea that Q1 was not just the first to be printed, but the first to be written.

Before turning to that development, the well-established theory that Q1 was a 'bootleg' version, poorly put together by disaffected actors, has come to be questioned. Charles Adams Kelly, for example, has argued since 2007 that the text of Q1 could not have been derived by memorial reconstruction from either the Q2 or the F text. Q1 omits ten Q2 passages which are not in F, and three F passages which are not in Q2. The statistical probability of the author of Q1 not remembering *any* of these 259 lines is so tiny that Kelly concludes that they cannot have existed. Q1's text therefore predates both Q2 and F. Paul Menzer's 2008 *The 'Hamlets': Cues, Qs, and Remembered Texts* also challenges the theory that Q1 is a memorial reconstruction. Actors were supplied with their own parts along with the briefest of cues. Since Q2 and F have most of their cues in common, whereas Q1's are largely very different, Menzer finds it hard to believe that even a group of the company's minor actors could have reconstructed the entire play from memory. He concludes that Q1 is 'a separate Hamlet project – an independent act of creation by a person or persons unknown.'

Menzer calls Q1 'the most "literary" of the early *Hamlets*', believing that the manuscript behind it was solely intended for publication (20–1). Zachary Lesser and Peter Stallybrass, in an essay written in the same year as Menzer's book (2008), also argued (but for different reasons) that Q1 could be regarded as 'literary'. They point out that, for all that it is usually regarded as recording an early moment in the performance history of Shakespeare's play, certain typographical details in the printed text reproduce 'a feature central to early seventeenth century attempts to forge a culture of literary drama or poesy in the vernacular' (376). They don't attribute these marks to Shakespeare himself but think the publisher introduced them to appeal to readers' taste for literary texts. Meanwhile, Tiffany Stern, writing on 'Sermons, plays and note-takers: *Hamlet* Q1 as a "noted" text' (Stern, 2013b), has revived the largely discarded old theory that Q1 is the result, not of memorial reconstruction, but of one or more members of the audience attempting to take the text down in a mixture of shorthand and longhand during one or more performances.

In *Owning William Shakespeare: the King's Men and their Intellectual Property* (2011), James J. Marino argues for a *Hamlet* that was evolving continuously for at least thirty-five years (i.e. from the earliest references to a Hamlet play on the English stage to the version that appeared in the First Folio), as Shakespeare's acting company worked on it, while nevertheless identifying the results with his increasingly marketable name. The act of revision, Marino insists, 'should not be imagined as a single, easily confined moment of rewriting, in which a hypothetical *ur-Hamlet* is discarded for a new, distinct and "Shakespearean *Hamlet*"'. No, 'the three existing texts of *Hamlet* are results of a competitive revision process, reiterated over many years of repertory existence' (105). Like Menzer, Marino is indebted to Simon Palfrey's and Tiffany Stern's *Shakespeare in Parts* (2007), which argues that Shakespeare's actors would have learnt their lines, not from the complete text of the play, but from a scribe's transcription of just their own speeches along with their cues. If a play text had to be revised during rehearsal or during a run, it would be important to leave the cues intact so that they would not have to be relearned. Ironically, therefore, 'The cue is in some senses the most "fixed" bit of the part' (Palfrey and Stern 2011: 93). Marino reflects on the long-held theory that the actor playing Marcellus was at least largely responsible for establishing the text of the 'Bad Quarto' of *Hamlet*.

> The memorial reconstruction hypothesis for First Quarto *Hamlet* presumes that Marcellus's part would be altered in any general rewriting of the play, but there seems little clear advantage in improving this minor character's role. Conversely, once substantial changes have been introduced to a major character's part, requiring a scribe to make a new copy, the reviser incurs no further expense by making improvements to that part as come to mind, as long as the changes don't alter other players' cues or the sequence of the plot ... More interesting perhaps than the 'goodness' of Marcellus's part in the First Quarto is the 'badness' of Hamlet's part, the one role in the 1603 text that is marred not only by pedestrian verse but by garbled syntax ... [So] somewhere behind the First Quarto may lie a text cobbled together from actors' parts of varying quality. (93–4)

In the end Marino considers Q1 to be 'an unexplained and perhaps inexplicable text, full of useful information about stage practice but offering no easy key to its identity' (94).

However, in 2014, Margrethe Jolly's *The First Two Quartos of 'Hamlet': a New View of the Origins and Relationships of the Texts* and Terri Bourus's *Young Shakespeare's Young Hamlet: Print, Piracy and Performance* have each gone back to the very earliest theory of Q1, arguing that it is based on the text of an original play by Shakespeare. Indeed, they are prepared to say that it was written at least as early as 1589 (the year in which Thomas Nashe alluded to 'whole Hamlets, I should say handfuls, of tragical speeches'). Bourus thinks Shakespeare revised this play twice, F being a revision of the Q1 text, and Q2 being a revision of the F text.

Q1 is not the only one of the early texts to have prompted a radical rethink. Lukas Erne, in *Shakespeare as Literary Dramatist* (2003), argues that the Q2 and F texts of *Hamlet* are simply too long to have been performed. Uncut, Q2 lasts more than four hours, whereas there is quite a bit of evidence to suggest plays were expected to last around two hours. Why would authors write more than they needed and then be required to see it cut down for performance? Surely they were looking to print as the medium by which their ideas could be communicated to readers. Erne feels that the texts of Q2 and F are reading texts, and that they 'invite us to inquire into a character who conveys a strong sense of interiority and psychological complexity. In Q1, in contrast, the Prince's character is more easily understandable and therefore can recede behind the intrigue and action which the stage play is most interested in' (236). Q1 represents an attempted record of the play as it was delivered orally on stage, whereas the noticeably longer and more literary Q2 corresponds to 'what an emergent dramatic author wrote for readers in an attempt to raise the literary respectability of playtexts' (220).

Erne finds support for this theory in the late Giorgio Melchiori's assertions in 1992 that 'behind Q2 there is a play for the closet, not for the stage' and that Shakespeare would have conceived of it 'as a new form of literary work' (Melchiori: 200, 196). He concludes that 'Shakespeare became a dramatic author during his own lifetime, writing drama for the stage *and* the page, to be published in performance *and* in print', with the literariness of the long texts and the theatricality of the short texts reflecting 'an emergent culture of increasing literacy and an enduring culture of orality' (Erne 2003: 244).

In 2006 the American journalist and cultural historian, Ron Rosenbaum, brought out his book *The Shakespeare Wars: Clashing Scholars, Public Fiascos, Palace Coups*, in which he set out to 'make the seductions of Shakespearean textual scholarship apparent' (xiv). In a chapter entitled 'One *Hamlet* or Three?', Rosenbaum drew on interviews he had conducted with a number of editors of *Hamlet*, beginning with Harold Jenkins, whose Arden edition was published in 1982, and culminating with Ann Thompson, whose Arden edition which she had edited with Neil Taylor came out just as *The Shakespeare Wars* hit the bookstalls in 2006. For Rosenbaum, the debate over the authority of each of the three texts, and the cases for and against conflation, had amounted to 'Civil Wars Among the Textual Scholars', to quote his title for the section in which his account of the debate occurred.

Rosenbaum's very readable chapter is essentially directed at the general reader. Another fascinating treatment of the history of editing these texts (this time aimed at a more specialized audience) is to be found in the Introduction and Conclusion of Zachary Lesser's brilliant *'Hamlet' After Q1: An Uncanny History of the Shakespearean Text* (2015), a book in which he describes the far-reaching, and sometimes most surprising, effects of the rediscovery in 1823 of the first quarto of *Hamlet* – 'this (new old) Play' as the *Literary Gazette* described it (59; quoted in Lesser: 10). As Lesser convincingly demonstrates, that influence has shown up, not just in scholarly theories of the status of the other two texts, but in mainstream interpretations of *Hamlet* by both literary critics and theatre directors.

The three central chapters of Lesser's book give him the opportunity to present three fascinating examples of ways in which Q1's impact on scholars, readers and audiences has been both subtle and perverse. A chapter on 'Contrary Matters: The Power of the Gloss and the History of an Obscenity' shows how Q1 helped to entrench a particular reading of just one of Hamlet's lines in Q2/F – a reading which remains universally accepted today (Q2 3.2.110, F 3.2.113). Within three years of Q1's discovery, Samuel Weller Singer had emended 'country matters' with a reading from Q1 – 'contrary matters' (9.82; in fact, he mistakenly printed it as 'contray matters'). Editors and readers were relieved that an obscenity had been removed (and even managed to persuade themselves that, in this respect at least, Q1 was more authoritative than either Q2 or F1). However, 'before Q1 returned from its purgatory, there seems to have been no widespread consensus that country matters was obscene. The discovery of Q1 did not create this interpretation of the phrase, but by presenting a seemingly innocent alternative, it reinforced the perceived vulgarity of Q2/F and thereby ensured the dominance of this reading' (89).

Another case study involves a line from Hamlet's 'To be or not to be' soliloquy. Lesser argues that when, in its version, Q1 (re)introduced the world to the line, 'O, this conscience makes cowards of us all' (7.136), it completely transformed how this line was understood in its familiar versions ('Thus conscience does make cowards' at Q2 3.1.82; 'Thus conscience does make cowards of us all' at F 3.1.83). Those who believed that Q1 reflected Shakespeare's early thoughts or an element in the process whereby he revised an earlier play about Hamlet, wished to find in Q2 and F a more developed, more sceptical, more agnostic Hamlet, and Q1's 'conscience' allowed them to relegate that version of the play to a less developed status. It thus became necessary to assert that 'conscience' here did not mean moral sense, but consciousness. This reading became orthodoxy until acceptance of G. I. Duthie's mid-twentieth-century theory that Q1 post-dated Q2's text, being the result of memorial reconstruction, allowed most recent editors and critics to revert to the more obvious, 'modern' interpretation of the word 'conscience'.

Lesser's interest is not restricted to the impact of Q1 on readers: he engages with theatre practice as well. In a chapter on 'Enter the Ghost in his Night Gowne: Behind Gertrude's Bed', he demonstrates by reference to an engraving in the 1714 edition of Rowe's Shakespeare that the idea of introducing a bed into the closet scene (4.3) is not, as is frequently asserted, a twentieth-century innovation by directors under the influence of Freud. However, when Q1 in 1823 introduced a ghost, not clad in armour but *in his night gowne* (11.57), Hamlet's father was transformed from a military commander on his way to battle into an ordinary husband on his way to bed. And Lesser argues that this tiny stage direction strongly affected nineteenth-century understandings of the relationships within Hamlet's nuclear family, informing, for example, Henry Irving's famous 1874 production at the Lyceum Theatre which 'located the heart of Hamlet's mystery firmly within the domestic family; the drama centred on the Ghost's revelation of domestic secrets and Hamlet's purification of his contaminated family through the reformation of his fallen mother' (135). Thus, Q1 'signals a faulty or perverted inheritance, not the Oedipal crisis of a son who wants to inhabit his father's bed, but an early modern crisis in which the son has not properly assumed his father's noble identity, just as the Ghost's armour signifies precisely that Hamlet himself has *not* inherited that armour' (153–4).

Finally, Lesser's Introduction and Conclusion concentrate on the impact on editors of *Hamlet*. He begins with Charles Knight and John Payne Collier in the mid-nineteenth century and ends with the editors of the Arden third series multiple-text edition of the play, which was published in 2006. This Arden edition, he finds, crystallizes the postmodern approach to the Shakespearean text, 'the movement to unedit Shakespeare' (209). This *Hamlet*, he judges, represents 'the culmination and, I believe, the exhaustion of the dominant approach of its moment' (207).

Another dead end, then? If it really is, then I suppose it's time for someone to go back and find another route forward.

4

New Directions:
Hamlet and Gender

Catherine Belsey

In 2014 the Royal Exchange Theatre in Manchester put on *Hamlet* with Maxine Peake in the title role. There was a good deal of cross-casting in this production, set in the 1970s. The text was adapted to accommodate Polonia as the mother of Laertes and Ophelia; the gravediggers were women, as were Rosencrantz, Marcella and the Player. But Peake's Hamlet was male – or perhaps closer to the ambiguity of the young David Bowie, whose haircut he also modelled. Her prince was angry, courteous, agonized, calculating and comic by turns, but always clear-headed and absorbed in the moment, a Hamlet in all respects for the twenty-first century.

It is increasingly common to see women play men. Shakespeare, who wrote for an all-male theatre, offered his boy actors complex and demanding parts as Rosalind, Viola, Juliet or Cleopatra. But sexual politics have now opened the grand male roles to women too and Peake met the challenge with conviction. What many of her audience would not have known without recourse to the programme note was that, although modern women in the role had been relatively uncommon, the tradition of actresses as Hamlet goes back to the late eighteenth century, when Sarah Siddons took the part. Some of the most famous Victorian Hamlets were women. There was then, as now, some resistance, if for slightly different reasons, but the Hamlets of Charlotte Cushman, Alice Marriott and Sarah Bernhardt were highly regarded by most critics.

The part was held to benefit from an injection of femininity. That view evolved from an understanding of the tragedy developed by the Romantics and still in evidence now, if only residually. Meanwhile, a new flexibility in our own understanding of gender roles expands the possibilities for *Hamlet*. In 2009 Blanca Portillo played the prince in modern dress in Madrid. Her androgynous Hamlet was athletic and vengeful, but torn between masculine and feminine identities. In this experimental production, Portillo delivered 'To be or not to be' naked, as she contemplated her own image in the water that formed a crucial part of the design (González 2014: 281). The story of *Hamlet*'s interpretation unfolds in line with the history of gender relations. Sarah Frankcom's production of Maxine Peake's Hamlet has its place in a continuing narrative that has also had implications for the perception of Gertrude and Ophelia, as well as Horatio.

Hamlet's beard

Shakespeare's Hamlet wears a beard. So, in common with most of his male contemporaries, did Richard Burbage, who played the part. Hamlet mentions his own in defence of his courage: 'Am I a coward? / Who calls me villain, breaks my pate across, / Plucks off my beard and blows it in my face?' (2.2.506–8). No one gets away with insulting him in these ways, he insists, although he has still not killed Claudius.

To early modern audiences facial hair signified adult masculinity. It is a standing joke in the comedies that a youth in possession of a good disposition must be in want of whiskers. When the cross-dressed Viola tips Feste to avoid becoming the butt of the clown's foolery, he replies, 'Now Jove in his next commodity of hair send thee a beard'. She longs for one, Viola reflects, but not on her own chin (*Twelfth Night*, 3.1.42–6). Poor Slender in *The Merry Wives of Windsor* can only muster a little yellow beard (1.4.20). But beards gradually went out of favour and by the mid-seventeenth century men were increasingly clean-shaven. Thomas Betterton played Hamlet from 1661 and in his acting edition of the play the prince's reference to his beard was deleted. Eighteenth-century Hamlets, including David Garrick, were clean-shaven and the cut stayed in place.[1] Although the Victorians brought beards back, they did not generally ascribe one to Hamlet. In the second half of the nineteenth century Henry Irving played the prince clean-shaven, as did the American Edwin Booth and the Austrian Josef Kainz. Ronald Gower's bronze Hamlet on the Shakespeare Memorial in Stratford-upon-Avon is beardless in 1888.

Perhaps the student from Wittenberg was now seen as too young for a beard. Hamlet's age is one of the play's many inconsistencies. Early modern boys completed their grammar-school education at the age of fourteen or so and then went on to the university. In introducing Hamlet and Horatio as students, Shakespeare seems to have made them teenagers. Moreover, Rosencrantz and Guildenstern grew up with the prince, and must belong, therefore, to the same generation (2.2.11–12); the First Quarto of 1603 calls them his 'school-fellows' from Wittenberg (7.237–9). Youth would account for Hamlet's hesitation, the malleability of Rosencrantz and Guildenstern, and the ease with which Claudius bypasses Hamlet's hopes of inheriting the throne (5.2.64). On the other hand, in Q2 (and the Folio, although not in Q1) the Gravedigger goes out of his way to explain that he has been at his trade thirty years, ever since the day Hamlet was born (5.1.135–53). Has a longer time elapsed since Act 1 than we realized? Possibly, but that doesn't solve the problem, since it's in Act 2 that Hamlet names his beard, less than twice two months after his father's death (3.2.121).

Instead, this loose end, one of many, suggests that it would be a mistake to treat the play as if it were a novel, a soap opera or a Hollywood movie, where continuity is of the essence. On Shakespeare's stage, perhaps it didn't much matter how old the hero was. One of the problems with the length of the play as we have it is that cuts are virtually inevitable, but deletions have implications for meaning. If in 1601 Hamlet's beard would have conveyed adult masculinity, his Victorian beard-lessness carries connotations of adolescence or femininity, or a combination of the two.

But by now a conception of Hamlet determined his image. Horatio is as explicitly a student as Hamlet and yet Viktor Müller's painting of *Hamlet and Horatio at the Grave of Ophelia* (1868) shows a strong, bearded Horatio giving heart to a slight, impressible, clean-shaven Hamlet. Eugène Delacroix's version of the same scene in 1839 depicted an equally bearded, muscular Horatio, while the model for his Hamlet was a woman. Laertes evidently belongs to the same generation and is, perhaps, a student in Paris, still subject to moral instruction by his father, but in 1899 Sarah Bernhardt as Hamlet fought a duel with a whiskered Laertes.[2] Selective emphasis does as much work as cuts. Post-Romantic *Hamlets* in general emphasized the references to Wittenberg at the expense of the Gravedigger's arithmetic, but only when it came to Hamlet. Women could legitimately play the prince because he was not fully a man. Instead, he was too young, or too effeminate, or both.

Revenge sanitized

No one plucks off his beard, and yet Hamlet berates himself for cowardice because he has not yet 'fatted all the region kites / With this slave's offal' (2.2.514–15). Instead, he just talks, he says – and curses like a prostitute (520–1). No wonder the Victorians found the protagonist's hesitation feminine: at this moment of self-reproach he evidently does too. It might seem odd to us that real men should be defined by their readiness to feed human entrails to birds of prey but, in the course of time, other cuts had done much to sanitize the play's account of revenge and in the process to modify the perception of Hamlet's problem. When revenge is seen as right, Hamlet's hesitation becomes inadequate, unmanly.

We do not know exactly how much of this long play was performed on Shakespeare's stage but the acting editions of later productions tell a story of erasures that redefined what audiences saw and heard. Cuts were introduced not only to bring the play within the time limits of conventional performance but also to preserve decorum. The Restoration theatres that reopened after the Commonwealth of 1649–60 were dedicated to propriety; Shakespeare's wild genius now seemed to belong to a more barbarous age and the plays needed to be brought into line with the canons of decency and good taste. Tragedy ought to be consistently grand and heroic, confined to an elevated manner. Stylistically, therefore, as well as to save time, much of the speech about Pyrrhus, for instance, was best eliminated. From Betterton on through the eighteenth century, Shakespeare's parody of an earlier manner was regularly reduced: cuts removed the image of a revenger coated with blood, baked and 'impasted' (audible as em-pastied, enclosed in a pasty?) with the dust of the streets, 'roasted in wrath and fire' as he makes his way to Priam's palace to avenge the death of his father, Achilles. Hecuba's grief remained in place but not the sight of Pyrrhus as he makes 'malicious sport / In mincing with his sword her husband's limbs' (2.2.390–456).

In excising Hamlet's portrait of '*the hellish Pyrrhus*', these actor-editors removed an image that defines, by contrast with the speaker himself, the revenger's violence as he advances through the burning city to kill the Trojan king. Further cuts also diminished the remorselessness of revenge. Although the prayer scene presents the perfect opportunity to carry out the

Ghost's command, since Claudius is alone and undefended, Hamlet does not seize the moment for fear of sending the king to heaven: 'And am I then revenged / To take him in the purging of his soul?' (3.3.84–5). Instead, his uncle must die in the enjoyment of his pleasures, 'that his soul may be as damned and black / As hell whereto it goes' (94–5). Damnation, however, was not a fit term for the Enlightenment stage. After the Restoration these lines were cut as unacceptable.

Their felt impropriety was not only a matter of vocabulary. In 1765 Samuel Johnson was appalled by the demand for vengeance beyond the grave:

> This speech, in which Hamlet, represented as a virtuous character, is not content with taking blood for blood, but contrives damnation for the man that he would punish, is too horrible to be read or to be uttered. (Johnson 1989: 242)

David Garrick, the definitive Hamlet from 1742 to 1776, for most of his career erased this soliloquy in its entirety, initiating a tradition that survived well into the nineteenth century. Bell's acting edition of 1773 annotated its own cut: 'A long speech of *Hamlet's* is here commendably thrown aside, first, as being unnecessary, and next, as tending to vitiate and degrade his character, much.'

On an alternative reading, what the speech degrades is the revenge ethic, which finds itself in conflict with morality elsewhere too. When Laertes, like Hamlet a 'noble youth' (5.1.213, 1.5.37), seeks to avenge the death of *his* father, he explicitly casts aside virtue for the purpose: 'To hell allegiance, vows to the blackest devil.' The eighteenth century editions retained this line but cut the next two: 'Conscience and grace to the profoundest pit. / I dare damnation' (4.5.130–2). Removing the words reshapes the meaning. It begins to seem that what the actor-editors found indecorous, whether consciously or not, was revenge itself as the play defines it. But by excising the terms that specified its horror, they encouraged their audiences, whether consciously or not, to mistake it for justice.

As a lover of the theatre, Shakespeare's Hamlet would know the difference. In the 1580s Thomas Kyd's Hieronimo begs loudly for justice; only when it is denied does he become a revenger. One of Hamlet's own Shakespearean predecessors remains 'so just that he will not revenge' (*Titus Andronicus*, 4.1.128), until, driven beyond endurance, he cooks the perpetrators and feeds them in a pie to their mother. In revisiting the genre up to ten years later, the playwright has not given up on the excesses of revenge but he now pays more attention to the thought processes of a man anxious to do what is noble. Once eighteenth-century decorum has modified the excesses of revenge, however, Hamlet's problem gradually transfers itself from morality to psychology – and specifically to gender.

Conscience

As a revenger, Laertes, another virtuous character in Dr Johnson's terms, does not plan to accomplish his task in a fair fight but poisons his sword to be sure. Even so, he hesitates in the act: 'And yet it is almost against my conscience' (5.2.279). On similar grounds, Hamlet too hesitates: 'conscience does make cowards' (3.1.82). But would it be better to leave the situation to take care of itself? The question he confronts is which is nobler, to bear the injuries fortune inflicts or to take arms against a sea of troubles and expect to be overwhelmed in the process: to die, and risk damnation.

On this reading, from the moment he undertakes to set things right (1.5.187), Shakespeare's Hamlet is caught in an ethical dilemma. Filial love demands action, which must be bloodthirsty; conscience counsels caution, which looks weak. The post-Restoration cuts, however, make his obligations much more straightforward. One small emendation, not obviously motivated by either decorum or the desire to save time, registers how the Enlightenment reframed Hamlet's choice. In Shakespeare's version 'the native hue of resolution / Is sicklied o'er with the pale cast of thought' (3.1.83–4). There is room for doubt about the exact terms of this figurative distinction between one complexion and another. Resolution personified is born red (sanguine, bloody) and the contrast with the sickly pallor of thought retains from the beginning of the speech a degree of ambivalence about whether it is 'nobler' to oppose or to suffer, to let blood or bear wrongs. Alternatively, we might construe that Hamlet's native, instinctive anger, his natural impulse to avenge his father ('If thou hast nature in thee bear it not' [1.5.81]) turns pale when he thinks the problem through. Pallor, sickness, cowardice are all, ironically, brought on by conscience, with the effect of inhibiting heroism – or should that be heroics? From the 1660s onwards, however, the 'native hue' of resolution became its 'healthful face', which loads the dice in favour of resolution. Revenge, we are now to suppose, is wholesome; only inaction is aberrant.

Inheriting this stage tradition, the next generation would engage with the question why Hamlet takes so long to carry out what has now become his duty – and would find the solution in his character. Hamlet was not up to the task because he was not a proper man. In the mid-eighteenth century it was a matter for criticism that some felt Garrick feminized Hamlet's grief (Howard 2007: 20), but already the plates were shifting. In the same year as Garrick first took on the role, Fanny Furnival performed as Hamlet in Dublin. From 1775 Sarah Siddons was Hamlet in the English provincial cities and in 1796 Jane Powell played the prince in London.

Vacillation

An interest in individual psychology also influenced the rise of the novel and the emergence of the psy-disciplines. In due course, Hamlet's hesitation would be ascribed to a particular weakness of will or a specific mental disorder; he was constitutionally indecisive, depressive, or just plain mad, conditions thought commoner among women than men.

This was new. Medieval moral plays called their heroes Mankind or Everyman and traced the temptations and threats that befall representative human beings. Shakespeare's contemporaries gave their protagonists names and contexts but remained more interested in human behaviour in general than in treating personality as destiny. There were at this time fictional social types: obsessive misers, jealous husbands, braggart soldiers, but tragic heroes were precisely not such caricatures. Instead, they were tested by confrontation with the ills that all flesh is heir to. What Partridge in 1749 dismisses, to the amusement of his fellow playgoers in Henry Fielding's *Tom Jones*, as the failure to act is Garrick's skill in portraying what anyone might feel: '"I am sure if I had seen a ghost, I should have looked in the very same manner, and done just as he did"' (bk 16, Ch. 5). Dr Johnson was adamant that 'Nothing can please many, and please long, but just representations of general nature'. For him Shakespeare stands out because his figures are driven by the same impulses as other people's. 'In the writings of other poets a character is too often an individual; in those of Shakespeare it is commonly a species' (Johnson 1989: 122).

In this context there was no strong call to query Hamlet's masculinity. The Romantics, however, reversed these values. This was when 'To be or not to be' became a contemplation of suicide. In rewriting 'the native hue' as 'the healthful face' of resolution, the eighteenth century made clear that, whatever the imperative that conscience deflected, it was not Hamlet's desire to kill himself. Even the most antique Roman would not have given suicide a healthy complexion. On the contrary, in 1765 Dr Johnson had explained the speech as grappling with the desire *not* to die. Hamlet's options were to bear the outrages of fortune patiently or to oppose them, risking his life in the process. If, he continued, to die were no more than to sleep, it would surely be a welcome relief from the vexations of life, but the cause of anxiety was what happened after death (Johnson 1989: 240–1).

As a playgoer, Shakespeare's Hamlet would know that in killing the king he would hazard his own life. On the early modern stage revengers never prosper: like Laertes, they are in one way or another justly caught in their own treachery (5.2.291–2); as John Ford would later reiterate, '*Revenge proves its own executioner*' (*The Broken Heart*, 4.1.139, 152; 5.2.147). When the decisive moment comes, Hamlet knows that he must be ready to leave this life (5.2. 200–2). And as a prince seeking to define the 'nobler' course, he would also know that by obeying the Ghost's injunction to repeat the crime of regicide he risked the fate of his immortal soul, the damnation the eighteenth century banished from the hearing of the audience.

When John Philip Kemble, who played the part repeatedly between 1783 and 1817, restored 'the native hue of resolution', however, he also introduced an ambiguity about the value of the resolve that is overcome by conscience. The new emphasis on character led actors to make Hamlet consistent and Kemble himself laid the stress on melancholy. By 1814 it was self-evident to a reviewer of Edmund Kean's performance that 'To be or not to be' was about the case for and against suicide. Charles Fechter, the Hamlet of the 1860s, brought on an unsheathed sword for the purpose (Hapgood 1999: 179n.). The assumption survives in Laurence Olivier's film version of 1948, perhaps the last of the great Romantic *Hamlet*s. In this black and white Gothic realization of the play, 'To be' is taken out of its context as overheard by the king and Polonius: Olivier's soulful Hamlet delivers the set piece on 'the dreadful summit of the cliff' (1.4.70), overlooking a turbulent sea that figures his own troubled psyche and, at 'by opposing end them', he turns his bare bodkin towards his own heart.

In 1904 A. C. Bradley, perhaps the most influential Shakespeare critic of all time, rewrote the tragedies as if they were novels, the prevailing genre in his time. Bradley's commentary on 'To be or not to be' illustrates Hamlet's metamorphosis into a ditherer. In the previous soliloquy, Bradley explains, Hamlet has lashed himself into a fury of revenge, only to make an excuse for delay in a sudden doubt about the honesty of the Ghost. *The Mousetrap* will put this to the test. 'A night passes', Bradley calculates, and then Hamlet is sent for. And what is he thinking of? *The Murder of Gonzago*? 'Not at all. He is meditating on suicide.' For one thing, this issue is irrelevant to his duty to avenge his father; it is evidently no more than another piece of procrastination. Worse, Hamlet had already considered this possibility two months earlier (1.2.129–32) before he encountered the Ghost and took on the sacred duty of revenge. In short, half-way through the play Hamlet is precisely where he was at the beginning (Bradley 1957: 105).

As Olivier's film opens, the voiceover intones 'This is the tragedy of a man who could not make up his mind'.[3] By this time, criticism had gone a long way towards turning the play inside out. Once the problem of *Hamlet* was seen as Hamlet's indecisiveness, what he said was longer to be trusted. His public display of an 'antic disposition' (1.5.170), the moments when he is 'idle' (3.2.87) or 'mad in craft' (3.4.184) were widely taken to provide evidence of his true state of mind, while his private or solitary utterances were no more than so much talk, designed to defer action. 'Conscience' no longer meant conscience; in the prayer scene Hamlet did not mean to damn Claudius but was merely dredging up another excuse for delay. And when the Ghost visibly doubles as Claudius, as in the Royal Shakespeare Company production of 2008,[4] Hamlet's contrast between his father and his uncle (1.2.140; 3.4.51–65) looks delusional.

Bradley did not see Hamlet's vacillation as feminine; instead, he ascribed it to a melancholy so deep as to amount to clinical depression. But others did. Kean's cry resembling 'the stifled sob of a fainting woman' met with approval (Howard 2007: 20); Charles Fechter's performance in 1861 was praised for its refinement and 'feminine delicacy' (Lewes 1875: 136); Edwin

Booth was admired for the 'feminine qualities in his style' (Foakes 1993: 24). 'I doubt if ever a robust and masculine treatment of the character will be accepted so generally as the more womanly and refined interpretation', Booth argued in 1882 (Hapgood 1999: 36). This emphasis on delicacy and refinement goes back to Wolfgang von Goethe's influential verdict on Hamlet in *Wilhelm Meister's Apprenticeship*: 'A lovely, pure, noble and most moral nature, without the strength of nerve which forms a hero, sinks beneath a burden which it cannot bear and must not cast away' (Bate 1992: 306).

Meanwhile, the new habit of reading Shakespeare compounded doubts about Hamlet's masculinity. While critics now pondered the texts, families read the plays round the fire and, in 1807, Harriet and Thomas Bowdler published the first edition of their best-selling expurgated Shakespeare for the purpose. Since character was the pressing issue, the soliloquies elicited special attention from readers, and the last of these now came newly into prominence. The eighteenth-century acting editions generally deleted the Fortinbras story, along with the self-castigation prompted by Hamlet's sight of his army as it faced death with equanimity (4.4.31–65).[5] Although this soliloquy was generally omitted on the nineteenth-century stage too (Bradley 1957: 112), from Bradley's perspective it was crucial to unlocking Hamlet's character. While the self-reproach is reformulated in the speech, it is fair to say that Hamlet's account of his situation has not developed noticeably since Act 2: he is still ashamed that has not killed the king. And Bradley concludes that 'he has learnt little or nothing from his delay'. In the course of the play, Hamlet has repeatedly insisted that he must act, but 'why, we ask ourselves in despair, should the bloody thoughts he now resolves to cherish ever pass beyond the realm of thought?' (Bradley 1957: 113). We might add, although Bradley doesn't, that only in the final Act does a new resignation come to stand in for resolution: now conscience is surely justified in urging action (5.2.62–6);[6] in this changed spirit, 'the readiness is all' (200).

If it is the rarely staged last soliloquy that best justifies the vacillating prince, however, it is also worth noting the possibility that Burbage too left it out. There is no suggestion that Shakespeare did not write it; the question is whether it was performed. The speech does not appear either in the First Quarto of 1603 or in the Folio text of 1623, put together by the Shakespeare theatre company after the playwright's death. The authority for its inclusion is the longest of the three early modern versions, the Second Quarto of 1604–5, and debate continues about whether elements of the play that appear only in this fuller version were ever staged. Since that question is unlikely to be resolved to universal satisfaction, we shall probably never have definitive access to the Hamlet early modern audiences saw.

We can, however, be much more confident about the widespread nineteenth-century verdict on Hamlet: he was generally irresolute, indecisive, inadequate, unequal to his task and unfit to carry out his obligation to kill Claudius. These negative prefixes tell their own story – or lead to their own false syllogism: Hamlet lacked resolve; women also lacked resolve; women therefore appropriately played Hamlet. The Parisian Mme Judith, who appeared in a revised version of the play in 1867, recorded a comment that 'my sex really helped me to express the melancholy and indecision of the character' (Howard 2007: 98).

Female Hamlets

This was offered as praise but it might strike us as faint enough to damn not only Hamlet but women too. Ironically, however, women who played the part often challenged the prevailing orthodoxy. The American Charlotte Cushman, among the most highly regarded actors of her time, made Hamlet intelligent, dignified and vigorous. Her mid-century version of the prince was understated by contemporary standards and attentive to the varying moods depicted by the text (Howard 2007: 45–56, Potter in this volume [71]).

It was as if the female voice and body on the stage acknowledged what the period found feminine in Hamlet, releasing the player to develop a more subtle and flexible interpretation of the role. In Germany Felicita von Vestvali allowed Hamlet to be a dreamer but also stressed his heroic energy (Howard 2007: 57). Other female Hamlets were involved offstage in the movement for women's suffrage (Howard 2007: 86–91). Sarah Bernhardt played the prince as a revenger, with no trace of languid soul-sickness, and in 1899 a reviewer asserted that she 'has undoubtedly rendered a great service to the interpretation of Shakespeare's play, for she has restored to Hamlet the strong character which Goethe took away from him' (Taranow 1996: 58). A century later Angela Carter would salute the Victorian tradition in an allusion to a publicity photograph of the fictional nineteenth-century actress Estella Hazard: 'here she is in drag as, famously, Hamlet. Black tights. Tremendous legs'. Later, it will emerge that Estella's actor-son Melchior, 'Our greatest living Shakespearean', has never played Hamlet: 'perhaps he was nervous the critics might think he wasn't half the man his mother had been' (Carter 1992: 12, 89).

Meanwhile, the apotheosis of the female Hamlet was in preparation in America when in 1881 Edward P. Vining investigated *The Mystery of Hamlet*. How, Vining wondered, can we explain the popularity of this unheroic hero? Weak and vacillating Hamlet is, and yet his refinement draws us to him. The answer must be that he possesses all the qualities of woman, including delicacy, fear, impulsiveness, a tendency to dissimulate and an inclination to hysteria. It follows that, although Shakespeare may not have realized fully what he was doing, in the move from Q1, with its blunt revenger, to Q2, with its shrinking protagonist, the playwright rewrote *Hamlet* as the story of a woman. And in evidence Vining adduces the backstory. Hamlet was born on the day Old Hamlet overcame Fortinbras (5.1.135–53) and, no doubt, in this hard fight the king was wounded. His prolonged absence left the throne undefended and Gertrude, disappointed to have given birth to a girl, let it be known, in the interests of stability, that the kingdom now had a male heir. Princess Hamlet was sent out into the world cross-dressed, only to fall in love with Horatio, so that, when Horatio was drawn to Ophelia, it was no surprise that the jealous Hamlet subjected the young woman to such scorn.

This ingenious interpretation might have sunk without trace but for two repercussions. James Joyce immortalized it, however scathingly, in *Ulysses*: 'I hear that an actress played Hamlet for the fourhundredandeighth time last night in Dublin. Vining held that the prince was a woman. Has no-one made him out to be an Irishman?' (1993: 190). A parallel thought has already occurred to Leopold Bloom as he catches sight of a poster advertising Millicent Bandmann Palmer's appearance at the Gaiety Theatre. '*Hamlet* she played last night. Male impersonator. Perhaps he was a woman. Why Ophelia committed suicide?' (73).

The second – and this time triumphant – consequence of Vining's book was Asta Nielsen's role in *Hamlet: The Drama of Revenge*, a silent film made in 1920. Nielsen played Hamlet as a woman masquerading as a man, possessed of all the masculine skills and lacking only the instinct to kill. Suspecting foul play, she sets resolutely about the task of finding proof. When she contemplates suicide in 'To be or not to be', it is for love of Horatio, not out of weakness or world-weariness. Nielsen's Princess Hamlet is resourceful, subtle, self-disciplined and entirely sane. The problem she confronts is her father's murderer, not her own soul-sickness.[7]

Paradoxically, it was partly thanks to the performances of these women that in the twentieth century Hamlet gradually regained his beard and his vigour. There was an alternative, they demonstrated, to Hamlet the ineffectual dreamer. In the meantime, our understanding of masculinity no longer privileges action over reflection: real men are now permitted to think. Richard Burton's energetic, mid-century Hamlet did not wear a beard but Mel Gibson's did in Franco Zeffirelli's filmed *Hamlet* in 1990. If by now the beard evokes something different (an outsider? an intellectual?), it also distances this Hamlet from the old effeminacy: Gibson's performance is distinguished by its drive, as well as its intelligence. Zeffirelli chose him for the part on the basis of his previous record as an action hero – and cut twenty lines of 'O, what a rogue and peasant slave am I!', as well as the last soliloquy, thus excluding much of Hamlet's self-reproach. In 1996 Kenneth Branagh, in his film set in nineteenth-century Denmark, wears a dapper 'soul patch' – and does justice to the wide range of moods the text allows the prince. These versions did much to set the pace for modern Hamlets. David Tennant in Gregory Doran's production at the Royal Shakespeare Company in 2008 made him at least as witty, charming and athletic as he was capable of reflection and grief. When Maxine Peake approached the part in 2014, she had a new tradition to draw on. It would be gratifying to think that the more mercurial Hamlet is closer to Burbage's version than the tortured depressive, characterized as feminine, of mainstream Victorian interpretation.[8]

Gertrude and Hamlet

Hamlet himself does not think highly of women. After his initial disgust at his mother's precipitate remarriage – 'Frailty, thy name is Woman' (1.2.146) – most of his references to the other sex are disparaging. While his scorn for their 'paintings' (3.1.141) is designed for public consumption ('It hath made me mad', 145–6), there is no one to delude in the graveyard. Even so, the topic recurs in his address to Yorick's skull: 'Now get you to my lady's table and tell her, let her paint an inch thick, to this favour she must come' (5.1.182–4). And he despises what he finds effeminate in his own behaviour (2.2.520–1); his fear of the fencing match is 'foolery', 'such a kind of gaingiving as would perhaps trouble a woman' (5.2.193–4).

Meanwhile, it has to be conceded that the women in the play do very little to challenge this misogyny. Gertrude submits to Claudius, and then to Hamlet; Ophelia submits to her father. Shakespeare notably depicts independent women elsewhere but not in this play.[9] Gertrude herself presents something of a puzzle. Was she involved in an adulterous liaison with Claudius before Old Hamlet's death, as the Ghost seems to imply (1.5.42–57)? Was she complicit with the murder or is she surprised by the accusation (3.4.28)? Does she realize that her marriage to her husband's brother is incestuous, within the forbidden degrees of kinship (1.2.157; 1.5.42, 3.3.90), or does she recognize its impropriety only as 'hasty' (2.2.57) ('o'er hasty' in F 2.2.56)? In Q1 she promises to help Hamlet secure his revenge (11.95–100) but this undertaking, which seems to lead nowhere, does not appear in the other editions.

Determined to base a character on these uncertainties, the nineteenth century delivered a range of moral verdicts. In 1832 Anna Jameson finds Gertrude's affection for Ophelia a redeeming touch in this 'wicked queen' (1836: 257). Bradley, more forgiving, concludes that Gertrude, who apparently suspects nothing and no one, must be stupid. He compares her to a sheep (1957: 135), a reference jubilantly exploited in Angela Carter's repeated allusions to the sheep-like appearance of Melchior's first wife, whose fortune funds his theatrical 'royalty'.

Conversely, the play allots some of its most lyrical lines to Gertrude, among them, 'all that lives must die / Passing through nature to eternity' (1.2.72–3), and the account of Ophelia's death (4.7.164–81). On the basis of such incon- sistencies, it has been open to actors to make of the part what they choose. Stage Gertrudes have ranged from naïve to sexually voracious, clinging to Claudius in the way Hamlet claims she hung on his father, 'As if increase of appetite had grown / By what it fed on' (1.2.144–5).

In New York in 1922 John Barrymore played an Oedipal Hamlet, whose caresses in the closet scene were explicitly sexual

(Hapgood 1999: 61). And indeed, this solitary encounter with Gertrude often licences a quasi-sexual violence, a possibility reinforced by the tendency to transform the text's 'closet' (3.2.323; 3.3.27) into a bedroom. Early modern closets were personal spaces, effectively studies. When Gertrude's chair gives way to satin sheets, however, it is hard to avoid a sexual undercurrent in this scene. Sometimes the initiative comes from Gertrude herself, most notably in Zeffirelli's film version (where Glenn Close was forty-three and Gibson thirty-four). Are there no bounds to this woman's desires? In Olivier's film Eileen Herlie (then twenty-seven to Olivier's forty) also seems more affectionate towards Hamlet than motherhood strictly requires. And yet she comes good in the end, testing the drink she suspects is poisoned to warn Hamlet.

With most onstage business compounding her short-comings, however, Gertrude has tended to rely for sympathy on her afterlife in subsequent fiction. John Updike's *Gertrude and Claudius* shows her at the mercy of an arranged and unsatisfying marriage to Hamlet's father, escaping from boredom into medieval romance, and eventually turning to her brother-in-law for the thrill of forbidden, if 'reechy' sex (2000: 118, cf. 3.4.182). The murder, of which she knows nothing, while intended to bring the couple closer, has the effect of driving them further apart in a plot twist that owes something to *Macbeth*. And yet, despite such postmodern ironies, the Gertrude of Updike's novel strikingly resembles Bradley's novelistic character: 'The Queen was not a bad-hearted woman, not at all the woman to think little of murder. But she had a soft animal nature, and was very dull and very shallow. She loved to be happy, like a sheep in the sun' (Bradley 1957: 135).

My personal favourite reinscription is Margaret Atwood's closet scene in 'Gertrude Talks Back'. Here the queen is not wringing her hands: she's drying her nails. Old Hamlet, honourable as he was, just wasn't much fun. And in the end, 'It wasn't Claudius, darling. It was me' (Atwood 1992: 19). Better a monster, surely, than a sheep?

Ophelia and Hamlet

There has been, to my knowledge, no such option for Ophelia, although there have been modern apologists for this curiously uncharacteristic Shakespearean heroine. Juliet, Hermia, Desdemona all defy their fathers for love but, after a momentary self-justification (1.3.109–10, 112–13), Ophelia goes on to obey hers to the letter. She is apparently the first victim of Hamlet's antic disposition, when he appears in her closet with doublet undone and stockings round his ankles (2.1.74–97).

And yet, as so often in this play, it is hard to be sure whether the prince's assumed madness includes a kernel of truth. The sigh, 'so piteous and profound', might well represent his genuine feelings as he parts from the young woman who now has no place in his future. Revenge is obsessional; it wipes away 'all trivial fond records' to survive alone in the mind of the revenger (1.5.98–104); revengers do not expect to marry and have children. In Jacques Lacan's psychoanalytic reading of the play, Hamlet gives up on his desire for Ophelia to enter a world of death. Knowing that he has bound himself to another Law, to meet his fate at a time determined by others, he plays the fool to fend off that awareness and Ophelia becomes the butt of a sexual wordplay that takes the place of desire (Lacan 1982).

Sometimes adapters make the most astute readers. Hamlet loves the protagonist of Lisa Klein's novel *Ophelia*, but the revenge ethic drives them apart. Akira Kurosawa inventively reverses the process in his film *The Bad Sleep Well*. There the central figure marries to advance the plan to avenge his father's death but wavers when he unexpectedly falls in love with his new wife. Intense love and hate cannot easily coexist in a single mind.

Out of obedience, Shakespeare's Ophelia collaborates with Hamlet's enemies. Grigori Kozintsev's film, made in the Soviet Union in 1964, gives her compliance the emblematic form of an iron cage that supports her mourning garments; in her madness, she dances like a marionette. Does Hamlet know she is a decoy? An older generation of critics allowed such questions to preoccupy them. John Dover Wilson explained that if a stage direction were moved back nine lines in 2.2, Hamlet could be made to overhear the plot to eavesdrop in the lobby (1934: lvi–lix). Since alteration and adaptation have been the fate of *Hamlet* since the seventeenth century, some directors have taken up this suggestion, including Olivier. In Kenneth Branagh's film, the auditors give themselves away, fuelling his repudiation of Ophelia; Michael Almereyda's film, set in contemporary New York, shows Hamlet uncovering the wire Ophelia wears to waylay him in 3.1.

Does it matter whether the play shows Hamlet learning what the audience knows? And would the knowledge account for Hamlet's cruelty here and in the play scene? The best we can say, perhaps, is that Ophelia's fate – madness and death – demonstrates the truth of Hamlet's comment on the deaths of the equally compliant Rosencrantz and Guildenstern: ''Tis dangerous when the baser nature comes / Between the pass and fell incensed points / Of mighty opposites' (5.2.59–61).

Since nothing touched Victorian heartstrings like a victimized virgin, the nineteenth century loved Ophelia. Adjectives that recur in the period are 'innocent', 'pure', 'fresh', 'spotless', 'diffident', 'guileless', 'childlike'. Visual artists, however, perhaps diagnosing repression in the bawdry released by Ophelia's delirium, seem drawn to the paradoxes of virgin sexuality. Her madness and death became favourite subjects for Romantic and Victorian painters. Among them, Benjamin West's painting of the mad scene survives only as an engraving of 1802. It shows a dishevelled, barefoot Ophelia, with the light falling on a body delineated under the flimsy fabric of her white dress, dancing wildly before a court both fascinated by her performance and in various ways as distraught as she is (Pape and Burwick 1996: 286). Later in the century, John William Waterhouse would portray the mad Ophelia three times. In his first version in 1889, she once again wears white and lies on her back in a meadow in a pose suggesting sexual abandon. But perhaps the most striking of his images belongs to 1910, where the anguish is fully internalized. Ophelia stands with her back to the stream; wild flowers in her hair and her hands, she stares desperately back at the viewer. The look in her eyes might be read as frenzy – or desire.

Alternatively, virginity is treated as supremely vulnerable. The thin, white-clad figure with reeds in her hair portrayed by Arthur Hughes in 1852 is barely more than a child. This Ophelia stares into the river, surrounded by an eerie, menacing landscape. Here the connotations of childhood are not innocence so much as defencelessness against an unnamed threat. The context is as different as could be, however, in the exactly contemporary representation of her death by John Everett Millais, where Ophelia drifts with the stream, surrounded by green, growing things. Here the arc of the vegetation seems to welcome her head and shoulders into its sombre embrace. Apart from the brightly coloured garlands she has made, the flowers, faithfully depicted, are predominantly white, as is the dress that spreads wide to bear her up. Ophelia's mouth is open, evidently chanting snatches of song, and she lies at full length, with her palms upwards, as if surrendering herself to the water. This is the moment before death, when the frail mutability of spring blossom matches the fragile transience of virginity.

While an etching gave the image wide circulation at the time (Sillars 2012: 75), it might be hoped that Millais's image of ultimate female passivity, however perfectly executed, would have lost some of its appeal in the twenty-first century. This *Ophelia* remains, however, the most popular of the postcards sold by the Tate Gallery. In the meantime, such exceptional actors as Ellen Terry and Julia Marlowe had allowed her a degree of force and independence (Hapgood 1999: 50–2); many twentieth-century productions stressed her sexuality.[10] In print Lisa Klein's Ophelia is independent and resourceful: like Juliet, she mimics death, after taking a potion she herself has concocted; like Rosalind and Viola, she cross-dresses to fool predators.

But the prize for rescue must surely go to Angela Carter, whose Hamlet does not deserve Ophelia. Tristram Hazard, grandson of the Estella who played Hamlet in drag, seduces the beautiful, innocent, virginal, mixed-race Tiffany, only to humiliate her when she appears on his television game-show, her clothes awry, flowers in her hair, singing snatches of lewd music-hall song. As Melchior covers her nakedness, he calls her 'Pretty, pretty lady' (Carter 1992: 46, cf. *Hamlet*, 4.5.41). That night the pregnant Tiffany is reported drowned and it is her mother who does physical battle on her behalf with Tristram. *Wise Children* is a comedy, told from the point of view not of the Hazards but of the Chances, women who have consistently faced the music and danced. In the event, their favourite Tiffany resurfaces as a feminist and repudiates the repentant Tristram: '"Pull yourself together and be a man, or try to," said Tiffany sharply. "You've not got what it takes to be a father"' (Carter 1992: 211).

Horatio and Hamlet

While Hamlet does not think much of women, he values Horatio highly. Is this cordiality homoerotic? Personally, I think that to sexualize the relationship is to ignore the high value placed on same-sex friendships in the period, as well as the humanist regard for the poor scholar whose fidelity to virtue is not driven by political or financial gain. Horatio represents Hamlet's confidant, his only ally and his touchstone. It is Horatio who tells him about the apparition on the battlements, so improbable and yet so insistent; Hamlet asks Horatio to confirm the king's reaction to the play; he turns to Horatio for confirmation that the mounting evidence against Claudius now justifies his death (5.2.62–6). The value of Horatio's friendship resides in its unmotivated character: precisely because there is nothing *else* at stake in his support, he has the effect of anchoring the turbulence of the action in a version of sanity.

And yet it is not clear what exactly constitutes this sanity. If Horatio's responses are not evasive, they are, even so, inconclusive. Did he observe the king's reaction to the play? 'I did very well note him' (3.2.282). Is it not now perfect conscience [to even the score]? In Q2 Horatio makes no answer; in the Folio he confines himself to the practicalities of Hamlet's current situation (5.2.71–2). His continued allegiance, however, seems to vindicate Hamlet's provisional conclusions in this inconclusive play. If Horatio's is the voice of sanity, sanity does not reside in knowing the answers.

Q1 establishes an alliance between Horatio and Gertrude, confirming that she keeps faith with Hamlet after the closet scene (14). In the more familiar versions of the play, however, Horatio does little to forward the plot. Indeed, from the perspective of the play's opposition between endurance and resolution, Hamlet's praise of Horatio, coming so soon after 'To be or not to be', can be seen as offering a model of the alternative to action. If the choice is between suffering the outrages of fortune or opposing them, bearing the situation or intervening in it, Horatio represents stoical endurance: 'A man that Fortune's buffets and rewards / Hast ta'en with equal thanks' (3.2.63–4). He is not a slave to passion (68) but one in whom 'blood' (or resolution) and 'judgement' maintain a perfect balance (65). And for exactly that reason, he is best understood as a support for the hero, and not as the protagonist of a separate, unwritten, sexual drama.

It is one of the peculiarities of *Hamlet* that the figures who surround the prince barely have their own, independent stories. Horatio's includes as many loose ends as the others. If he was there for the funeral (1.2.175), how did Hamlet fail to notice? He speaks of 'our' King Hamlet (1.1.79, 83, 90) and 'our state' (100), but Hamlet greets him as a visitor (1.2.164, 173). Hamlet's fellow-student, he nevertheless appears to recognize the armour Old Hamlet wore in a battle that, it turns out, took place thirty years earlier (1.1.59–60).

In my view, none of this matters on the stage, where the attention of the audience is engaged by quite other concerns.

However far interpretations differ, they centre on Hamlet or on Hamlet's dilemma. While the problem of revenge is obsessive for the son called to avenge his father, while it wipes away all other considerations for Hamlet, it is as if rewriting the revenge genre is obsessive for the playwright too. In other tragedies, different stories intersect; in *Hamlet*, by contrast, despite its extraordinary length, the questions at the heart of the play have the effect of driving other people's stories to the margins.

No wonder, then, that so many actors, directors, film directors, critics, artists and writers have been impelled to supplement Shakespeare's text with stage business, readings, explanations and reinscriptions. At the same time, perhaps what draws us back to the play is the degree to which its central issues, including its treatment of gender, not only change in the course of cultural history but remain open to revision and reinterpretation.

5

New Directions:
Hamlet, Cinema, the World

Mark Thornton Burnett

Of all of Shakespeare's works, *Hamlet* is the play that has most frequently been adapted to the cinematic medium. More significantly, screen versions of the play are characteristic of the majority of the world's filmmaking traditions. In film, *Hamlet* has been granted a global exposure. When we turn the lens away from the better known examples, it becomes clear that almost every country has crafted an individual film engagement with *Hamlet* at some stage, and often more than once. In world *Hamlet* films, the play operates as a creative hub and a transnational touchstone, a primary characteristic being the ingenious identification of alternative habitats for Shakespeare's work. Wherever it is transposed to, *Hamlet* speaks in and to a variety of locales. Exposed to *Hamlet* in world cinema, audiences find ratified the play's manoeuvrability – its capacity for commenting on local situations and ideologies that run along divergent lines. Through film, multiple constituencies have claimed the play as their own, testifying to a vital part of the *Hamlet* story and pointing up the crucial importance accorded

Shakespeare's most celebrated hero in the international imaginary.

In this chapter, world *Hamlet* films are explored by way of a three-part approach: political critique, regionalization, and gender/agency. Under the first approach, I discuss the complementary political inflections of Akira Kurosawa's *The Bad Sleep Well* (1960), a lesser-known Japanese *Hamlet* adaptation, and Michael Almereyda's *Hamlet* (2000). For the second approach, I compare and contrast two recent Chinese adaptations, *Prince of the Himalayas* (dir. Sherwood Hu 2006) and *The Banquet* (dir. Xiaogang Feng 2006). Pursuing the third approach, I identify as a meaningful element the varying constructions, shaped by time and genre, of the Ophelia character in Grigori Kozintsev's Russian *Gamlet* (1964) and a recent Iranian adaptation of the play, *Tardid* (dir. Varuzh Karim Masihi 2009). These three approaches are not distinctive; rather, they cross-fertilize and interlock, offering complementary ways of coming to terms with the significance of *Hamlet* on screen as a global phenomenon. In some instances, as this discussion suggests, there is a direct connection, a cause-and-effect relation as one filmmaker, across national borders, responds to another, reworking and readjusting an earlier adaptation model for new audiences and publics. In other instances, the connection is less obvious and inheres in a coincident or accidental relation, two filmmakers gravitating to the play simultaneously so as to address a specific social and cultural situation at a particular historical juncture. Whatever the relation, world *Hamlet* films form part of a continuum which illuminates a range and depth of creative engagement and a fascination with the play's enduring applications and relevancies.

Corporate cityscapes

Akira Kurosawa's *The Bad Sleep Well* (1960) belongs to the *gendai-mono* or modern story genre; the action is firmly rooted in the twentieth century, with *Hamlet* appearing in the narrative in revealing reversals, echoes and citations. Central to the situation of Nishi/Hamlet is the loss of his father, Furuya/ Old Hamlet, an official at the Public Corporation for Land Development. Part of the trauma of the Nishi/Hamlet character is his father's apparent suicide; he allegedly jumps to his death from a seventh-floor window. Subsequently, Nishi/Hamlet becomes a secretary in the Public Corporation and marries Yoshiko/Ophelia, daughter to the company's boss, Iwabuchi/ Claudius, as part of a plan to expose the latter's involvement in his father's demise. Taking place in post-occupation Tokyo, the film sees as synonymous the murder of the father and corporate corruption. Throughout, we are confronted with the seamy, underlying realities of mutually profitable alliances between business and government: 'Something' is indeed 'rotten' in the 'state' of modern Japan (1.4.90), as reflected in the ways in which political and corporate spheres are imagined as mutually reinforcing and venally entangled.[1] (Underpinning the operations of the Public Corporation is a consistent policy of rigging bids for building work that is put out to tender.) Corruption in *The Bad Sleep Well* is visually intimated in news footage of a worried-looking *mama-san* descending a stairwell (in this sense, 'hospitality' is transacted around women's bodies) or through wide-screen exterior location shots of vacant lots; in particular, the pan past a notice stating 'Public Corporation for Land Development: Site Three', with a subsequent focus on a wasteland, identifies and indicts the company for a continuing failure to execute its mandate productively. Corruption in *The Bad Sleep Well* is also a matter of secrecy. Here, the film avails itself of a perennial Japanese double code involving the *omote* (face) and *ura* (back); as Yoshio Sugimoto says of the pairing, '*omote* represents the correct surface or front [...] whereas *ura* connotes the wrong, dark, concealed side which is ... unacceptable or even illegal'.[2] The difficulty of displaying the *ura* behind the *omote* is reflected in *The Bad Sleep Well* in the omnipresent smoke, a constitutive part of the film's *mise-en-scène*; whether from Nishi/Hamlet's cigarettes or Iwabuchi/Claudius' cigars, a foggy obfuscation casts a haze over events, suggesting a general condition of impenetrability and indistinctness. In this sense, Kurosawa shows himself delighting in intertextuality, playing with some of the American film types to which he was indebted, including the thriller and *film noir*.

Addressing systemic corruption, Kurosawa felt he had to tread carefully. The director describes wanting 'to make a film of some social significance [...] But even while we were making it, I knew that it wasn't working out [...] I was simply not telling and showing enough.'[3] The disclaimer is surprising for, in fact, one of the director's notable achievements in *The Bad Sleep Well* is appropriating the interrogative and dystopian aspects of *film noir* – the genre's capacity cynically to analogize 'a felt mutation in the structures of power' – to effect an unnerving reflection on post-war Japanese society.[4] Over the course of the film, there are no less than four real or apparent suicides – those of Furuya, Nishi's father, Miura, the accountant who throws himself in front of a truck to safeguard his superiors, Wada, another accountant who attempts to launch himself into a volcano to avoid the consequences of a police enquiry (both may be seen as the film's realizations of Rosencrantz and Guildenstern) and Nishi/Hamlet himself. In these episodes (versions of samurai-style acts of ritualistic suicide) is a powerful registration of the film's acerbic treatment of the kinds of obedience and protectorship that ostensibly support traditional Japanese company attachments.

If *The Bad Sleep Well* is critically responsive to notions of obligation, conformity and duty, then it also engages with broader seams of political discontent. In 1960, when the film was released, writes Rachael Hutchinson, 'the renewal of the US-Japan Security Treaty was set to ensure Japan's status as a shield for the US against East Asian communism in the Cold War, and protest was widespread.'[5] Finally released on 19 September, it is possible that Kurosawa's film takes some of its radical energy from the spirit of the riots which took place in the period May to June of the same year. Crucially, the demonstrations, and the general strike, resulted in the desperate attempts of the then Prime Minister, Nobusuke Kishi, to force American policy through in the Japanese Diet. Such was the volume of discontent precipitated that Kishi, popularly seen as the practitioner of grotesquely 'autocratic methods', resigned shortly afterwards, leading one historian to dub the unrest 'a turning-point in Japan's post-war political history'.[6] Part of the crisis facing post-war Japan was the collision of different kinds of cultural attachment. *The Bad Sleep Well* can be read as receptive to the notion that, at this moment, the country was divided in its loyalties. At the bombed-out munitions factory (recalling the graveyard in *Hamlet*) that is their hideout, Nishi/Hamlet and Itakura/ Horatio, his friend, reflect on what their lives were like in the war's immediate aftermath. Widescreen shots of twisted metal, amputated structures and piles of debris, about which swirl wind and dust, recall the firestorms of 1944 and 1945 that laid waste to Tokyo, leaving 75,000 to 200,000 dead and destroying up to fifty per cent of the metropolis. The setting is horrifically suggestive, a reminder, if any is needed, that, as in *Hamlet*, a revenge motif resides at the film's heart. Recalling that they, too, were once involved in racketing, Nishi/Hamlet and Itakura/Horatio are able to draw lessons from the hellish scene and resolve to move on from their previous lives.

But such a progression is continually bedevilled by the bifurcated state in which Nishi/Hamlet finds himself. As the film reveals, Nishi/Hamlet has, in fact, exchanged identities with Itakura/Horatio so as the more effectively to execute revenge. *The Bad Sleep Well* extrapolates the Shakespearean motif of the 'antic disposition' (1.5.170) in an extreme sense in that Nishi/Hamlet occupies Itakura/Horatio's place: legally, the protagonist is not what he appears to be and, once the impersonation has been exposed, he can no longer maintain the fantasy of his *alter ego*. The shaky foundations of Nishi/Hamlet's identity are spotlighted in the moment of his death. In contradistinction to *Hamlet*, Nishi's actual death – organized by Iwabuchi/Claudius – occurs off-stage. We are told he was injected with alcohol (the reference to the poison plot of the duel scene again reminds us of the film's preoccupation with revenge), made unconscious and placed in a car with which a train collided. It is a sombre dénouement to an even more sombre parable. As Stephen Prince states, 'The intensity of Nishi's protest has not even bruised the institutions of power ... individual heroism is an inadequate form of protest against the corporate state.'[7] Closing, as it does, with another apparent suicide, *The Bad Sleep Well* comes full circle, linking the deaths of father and son. The effect is to underline not only the extent to which *Hamlet* continues to circulate in the filmic narrative but also the overarching power of corporate culture. In keeping with a *film noir* aesthetic, Nishi/Hamlet fails in his mission; his is imagined as a courageous but ultimately doomed endeavour that illuminates the tensions and the challenges, the ambitions and the contradictions, of Japan's relation to modernity.

When American director Michael Almeredya was in the planning stages for his millennial, dystopian and New York-set *Hamlet* (2000), his first thought was to go back to *The Bad Sleep Well*, with its simultaneously 'poignant' and 'dingy' evocation of a 'corrupt ... world'.[8] In fact, the connection goes further, Kurosawa's film functioning, in many ways, as a palimpsest for the later director's intervention. For, at every turn, Almereyda reads Shakespeare's play through the lens of a late-capitalist mindset. Elsinore is figured as the Denmark Corporation, a global empire in turn-of-the-century New York; the city scene is stamped with all the signs of corporate anonymity; and brand names and surfaces communicate a vision of human interaction in thrall to technology. At the same time, Almereyda offers alternatives to this dystopian perspective by investing in images of countermovements that throw into relief the seeming dominance of a soulless metropolis. Crucially, it is through the protagonist's filmmaking – a self-conscious representational practice – that Hamlet is allowed to achieve his tragic integrity, a form of felt autonomy.

Forms of corporate capitalism are everywhere apparent. For example, Hamlet is seen striding past a supermarket displaying discounted goods, while Claudius is perceived against the backdrop of neon share indexes: the contrast points up both the physical distance between the two men and the prevalence of a monetary imperative. More generally, the film abounds in logos and advertisements, with the prominence of 'Boss', 'Karlsberg', 'Key Food', 'Marlboro' and 'Panasonic' functioning to indicate a cultural moment defined by the need for product placement. Even the Ghost is implicated in this process of commodification. When he appears before Hamlet to reveal the 'truth' of the skulduggery behind the throne, a TV monitor in the background reveals images of oilfields burning. The televised conflagration activates recollections of the Gulf War, a global conflict precipitated by the disputed ownership of one of the most precious commodities in a capitalist economy, and an apocalyptic realization of capitalist implosion. If the Ghost is caught up in late capitalism at his appearance, he is also defined by it at his disappearance. Fading into a machine dispensing 'Pepsi One Calorie', the Ghost is deployed to make more than a brand-name joke. The implication is that his dissolution is also a consumption: Hamlet's father is engulfed by the very energies that, as president of the Denmark Corporation, he had earlier commanded.

In such a universe, it is perhaps not surprising that the individual subject should appear as disoriented. Fredric Jameson notes that, in postmodernity, the 'human body' is unable 'to organize its immediate surroundings perceptually, and cognitively to map its position in a mappable external world'.[9] This is also a predicament common to Almereyda's *Hamlet* in which floating signifiers, simulations and imitations feature (*faux* architectural symbols continually intrude into the filmic frame) and in which Hamlet himself is imagined as a decentred soul striving for a subjective coherence. Part of Hamlet's difficulty is his incarcerated status. Picking up on the 'Denmark's a prison' analogy from the Folio version

of *Hamlet*, the film elaborates New York as a type of gaol
(albeit of a metaphorical and corporate kind).[10] Plate-glass
apartments, the aisles of a video store, and the first-class
compartment of an aeroplane – all are made legible through
a cinematic grammar of confinement. In addition, Hamlet is
made prisoner by members of his own family. In the encounter
with the Ghost, he is asked, in a tone of aggressive reprimand
by the spirit of his father, to lend his 'serious hearing' to
the imminent revelations. Even as they are seen as in thrall
to expressions of corporate capitalism, so are the film's
players belittled and infantilized by the unflinching face of
postmodern patriarchy.

For Hamlet, an opportunity for release presents itself
in technology. As filmmaker and, in some senses, screenwriter, Hamlet cognitively maps a personal script, either
fast-forwarding or rewinding (endlessly rehearsing) on his
pixelvision video diary the traces of a lived experience. So it is
that Almereyda's camera dwells repeatedly on Hamlet's eyes,
as if reminding us of the film's internal auteur. Hamlet's directorial undertakings also have a dissident dimension, and it is
in his film-within-a-film, a witty reinvention of Shakespeare's
play-within-a-play, that the protagonist's critical method
comes to the fore. In the opening, we see footage from the
1950s of an idyllic family at leisure; because this is presented
as a home movie, the implication is that there is no equivalent example of a functional familial unit in the Elsinore of
the millennium. Then, among other extracts severed from
their contexts, *The Mousetrap* yields up a section from an
army training film (a militaristic Denmark Corporation, it
is suggested, has produced similarly faceless recruits) and
a scene from Gerard Damiano's infamous pornographic
film, *Deep Throat* (1972). Partly because the 'star', Linda
Marchiano (known as Linda Lovelace), described how she
was bullied and coerced into appearing in the film, *Deep
Throat* was seen as a prime example of cinematic terrorism
whose net effect was to oppress women's minds and bodies.
Notions of repression and exploitation are thus inscribed in

the *Deep Throat* citation, helping to bolster the construction of Claudius as an obscene man who is enslaving his wife (and, more generally, as a tyrannical business mogul). Unmoored from their original points of reference, Hamlet's filmic snippets become a collage with which he challenges Elsinore's power at the level of its public disciplinary regimes and its covert body politics.

The critical edge displayed in *The Mousetrap* forms a bridge to numerous related sites of transgressive energy. Typically, although these forces are communicated only in piecemeal, they occupy a privileged niche because of their anti-capitalist flavour. First, visual flashes of Che Guevara and Malcolm X (their images are glimpsed in the photo montage on the wall of Hamlet's apartment) work to implicate the protagonist in revolutionary discourses and to liken him to a liberating yet doom-laden saviour. Second, aural snatches of the song, 'All Along the Watchtower', as sung by the Gravedigger, recall its composer and first performer, Bob Dylan, and his involvement with the burgeoning civil rights movement; again, Hamlet is vitalized by the association. Kurosawa's *The Bad Sleep Well* closes with a gloomy sense of Nishi/Hamlet's anti-establishment undertaking; by contrast, Almereyda's *Hamlet* reverses the dynamic, affirmatively realizing the moment at which Hamlet reviews in his mind the key events of both the film and his life. Through the action of revenge, the protagonist is able cognitively to 'map' the story that he inaugurated with the film-within-a-film. Now that Hamlet has found in himself and his autobiography a personalized role model, there is no need for iconic equivalents, suggesting that at the close he assumes adulthood, recuperates the dispersal of his subjectivity (speaking visually as an 'I'), and claims a final auteurial authority.

Asian worlds

The Bad Sleep Well and Almereyda's *Hamlet* invite comparison because of the ways in which a pattern of cross-references highlights a shared response to issues of moral accountability, corporate responsibility and government. *Prince of the Himalayas* (dir. Sherwood Hu 2006) and *The Banquet* (dir. Xiaogang Feng 2006)[11] were conceived of and produced independently (that is, they do not echo each other directly). Nevertheless, they consort with each other as adaptations of *Hamlet* in that each looks to an ancient world as part of a confrontation with the contemporary and each uses Shakespeare to reflect upon 'Asia', broadly conceived and multiply understood, at a key stage of its recent global emergence. In this sense, *The Banquet* and *Prince of the Himalayas* bear witness to the interpretative virtues of a regionalizing interpretative procedure. In *The Banquet*, epic generic affiliations are quickly established through the evocation of a bloody moment in Chinese history: an on-screen announcement informs us that the action is set in 'China, 907 B.C. [...] the period [of ...] the "Five Dynasties and Ten Kingdoms" [...] an era plagued by widespread turmoil [...] and a bitter struggle for power within the imperial family'. Within these contexts, the Gertrude figure is situated at the centre and female sexuality is constructed as the linchpin or underlying spur to the narrative. Thus, in the film, Empress Wan/Gertrude is involved in a love affair with her stepson, Wu Luan/Hamlet, despite her power-brokering marriage to Emperor Li/Claudius: the authority she wields stems from her combined roles as stepmother and ruler. In contrast to *The Banquet*, *Prince of the Himalayas* is set in ancient Tibet. The work of the US-trained Chinese director and screenwriter, Sherwood Hu, and the Tibetan screenwriters Trashidawa and Dorje Tsering or Jangbu, the film constitutes a specific species of transnationalism. Equally, *Prince of the Himalayas* is of interest for the ways in which it turns and develops the

Shakespearean story: in this adaptation, the Ghost of King Tsanpo/Old Hamlet is a malevolent force that stands in the way of the sympathetically discovered lovers, Queen Nanm/Gertrude and King Kulo-ngam/Claudius. Reorienting the play in this fashion, *Prince of the Himalayas*, as in *The Banquet*, reconfigures the Shakespearean family so as to highlight culture-specific questions about female agency.

Both films establish themselves as adaptations of *Hamlet* by rehearsing some of the key questions and motifs associated with the play. *Prince of the Himalayas*, for instance, builds upon ambiguities already present in *Hamlet*, pursuing rather than bypassing narrative tensions and difficulties. Specifically, it separates out King Tsanpo/the Ghost's revelation – 'O denizens of heaven, do not let me die wizened of a broken heart! [...] I was poisoned ... Take revenge' – into multiple units spread over the course of the film, the effect of which is to forestall explanation and to keep an audience in a state of heightened expectancy. In a film which self-consciously plays upon ideas of delay, this drip-feed of information means that the precise circumstances surrounding the death of King Tsanpo are revealed only via a slowly retrospective movement. The most dramatic use of partial discourse is the gradual revelation that Lhamoklodan/Hamlet is the product of the relationship between Kulo-ngam/Claudius and Queen Nanm/Gertrude, a plot twist that helps to explain the protagonist's tense relation to filial duty. Similarly, *The Banquet*'s engagement with *Hamlet* is suggested in the highlighting of readings or images that have gained widespread critical currency. Hence, whenever Qing Nu/Ophelia appears, the sound of running water is heard: this diegetic signature is picked up in the song associated with her about the boat girl and stamps the character (who dies via poisoning rather than drowning) with the memory of her counterpart's means of death in Shakespeare's 'original'. At the same time, *The Banquet* prioritizes *Hamlet*'s Oedipal dimension: because Wu Luan/Hamlet is figured as having lost not only his father but also his former lover (Empress Wan/Gertrude), an obvious

rationale is offered for his melancholy and subsequent reification of paternal bereavement. 'Who' or 'what inhabits the
armour of the dead Hamlet?', one critic asks; *The Banquet*
answers the question by figuring the Ghost as a chain-mailed
carapace that is empathetically occupied.[12] In the scene where
Wu Luan/Hamlet investigates his father's armour, a point-
of-view shot from inside the casing's eyeholes suggests a still
sentient presence, while an accompanying glimpse of blood
trickling from the sockets points up the idea of harm or injury.
These episodes are largely wordless, yet they have the virtue
of communicating in an economic way the richness of the text
and a powerful history of Shakespearean interpretation and
debate.

Emerging from an encounter with Shakespeare defined
in self-conscious terms is a concentration on the local. At
the start of *The Banquet*, Wu Luan/Hamlet meditates in an
outdoor theatre, 'under the protection of the Crown Prince',
in the 'southern heartlands'. Inside his retreat, Wu Luan/
Hamlet, seeking 'solace in the art of music and dance', acts
out through mime impressions of sufferings and disappoint-
ments, suggesting theatre as recuperative and physicality
as a way of coming to terms with romantic rejection. The
stillness of his body in these sequences, coupled with the
care with which he performs individual gestures, bespeaks a
conjunction of body, mind and spirit: as Sheng-mei Ma states,
in Asian chivalric stories 'the protagonist's arduous apprenticeship and later combat is predicated upon a philosophy
of stringent self-discipline'.[13] Skilfulness in music and dance
prepares the way for the discovery of Wu Luan/Hamlet's
proficiency in calligraphy. Because this form of writing was
thought to define masculine strength, Wu Luan/Hamlet is
thus envisaged as particularly empowered. Brush strokes in
calligraphy imitated parts of the bamboo plant, and following
hard upon orange-filtered battle scenes comes the introduction
of Wu Luan/Hamlet in a swaying bamboo grove: the juxta-
position analogizes the ways in which families can be pushed
by politics and fortunes fluctuate in times of war. Flexibility,

probity and righteousness, qualities which bamboo is said to incarnate, are also, of course, the distinguishing markers of a Wu Luan/Hamlet who, dressed in white and consummately executing expertise in martial arts, outwits his dark armoured opponents and acrobatically avoids injury: body and plant are imagined as one. *The Banquet* commences, to adopt a formulation of Gary G. Xu, with a 'poetic sense' of *'yiying* [...] the harmony between the human mind and ... surrounding nature'.[14] Yet such a balance is upset in the spectacle of the armed assassins sent against Wu Luan/Hamlet by his conspiratorial uncle: here, the Confucian virtues of loyalty and camaraderie (*zhong* and *yi*), which were commonly tied to the bamboo, are conspicuous by their absence. A conjuration of the local visualizes a Shakespearean preoccupation; at the same time, such a procedure is key to establishing the moral polarities of the particular filmic universe.

The equivalent investment in the local suggests itself in *Prince of the Himalayas* in the use of costuming, custom and setting. Intricately layered costumes comprised of leathers, snow leopard hides and wolf furs suggest a court weighed down with a legacy of burdens, while interwoven images of turbulent rivers approximate a disturbed psychic state. Glimpses of monks, yaks and rotating drums, and shots of flags and trumpets, summon a vital sense of Tibetan traditions or, at least, reference a Tibetan cultural imaginary. Wide-angle pans of the holy mountains of 'Lianbao Yeze' reinforce these associations and indicate human actions dwarfed by larger processes and unbridgeable emotional distances. Such landscapes – often, like the lakes and rivers, circular or winding in appearance – evoke, within a Buddhist schema of interpretation, the operations of *karma*, the notion that whatever we do will have a corresponding effect. Certainly, in the film, there are frequent circular movements and returns, as when Lhamoklodan/Hamlet elects to 'quit Jiabo [his country] in all haste', 'comes back' and is, in fact, represented as never leaving the country. 'How I have shamed myself', he states, adding, 'I flee abroad and have abandoned my quest for justice', a formulation that spotlights a reconsideration of priorities. With these latter scenes, in particular, the structuring convention is that a negative *karma* might be replaced by one of a more positive orientation. Here, as elsewhere, *Prince of the Himalayas* draws upon memories of the Chinese invasion of Tibet in 1950, and the Dalai Lama's flight into exile of 1959, elaborating Lhamoklodan/Hamlet as committed to a heroic return. The Himalayas, of course, specify an area rather than a nation. In this connection, it is striking that the original title for the film, *King of Tibet*, was not approved by the Chinese film authorities and that a new title was necessitated. Presumably, 'Tibet' was deemed to connote a separate entity and 'King' was seen to suggest a majority royal rule; by contrast, the 'Himalayas' as a designator points to extraordinary natural phenomena and to a vaguer set of regional meanings. Against a current background of deadlock and volatility in Chinese–Tibetan relations, the fact that Tibet is nowhere referred to in the dialogue of *Prince of the Himalayas* is arresting. No less significant, and possibly politically expedient, is the way in which the film favours an older historical moment when Tibet was not so much a unified nation as a looser collection of principalities. *Prince of the Himalayas* finds virtues in local colouring and frames of reference; at the same time, it avoids pressing at the local too forcefully, drawing back from the topical or the immediate.

Lhamoklodan/Hamlet courses through *Prince of the Himalayas* on horseback (he even rides a horse naked during a dream sequence); having chosen to be unfaithful and to keep a secret, however, Queen Nanm/Gertrude is, for much of the film, imagined as constricted in her mobility. Only in the concluding sequences where Queen Nanm/Gertrude joins forces with the Wolf-Woman, a folkloric figure who mediates the spirit world, to tell Lhamoklodan/Hamlet of his origins is she given a more responsive prominence. In this regard, the Wolf-Woman tells the story that Queen Nanm/Gertrude is mostly prevented from disclosing and, in so doing, points up a contrasting model of speaking female action. Linda Charnes writes that, in *Hamlet*, the 'individual bloodline' is erased; 'existence' is cancelled 'in both the literary and symbolic realms'.[15] This is not the case in *Prince of the Himalayas*, as the scene of Odsaluyang/Ophelia's demise suggests. Although taking place in water, this core episode from Shakespeare's play is accompanied in the film by the delivery of Lhamoklodan and Odsaluyang's son, which implies not so much suicide as death in childbirth: the heroine does not, it seems, elect to dispatch herself. The *mise-en-scène* places mother and infant side-by-side in the river (with a subsequent tracking shot tracing the journey of the child downstream). The identity of the princely babe is immediately recognized by the Wolf-Woman in a sequence which undergirds the notion of the preservation of the royal lineage by mobilizing Buddhist practices of the acknowledgement of the reincarnation of religious leaders. As the dying Lhamoklodan/Hamlet is introduced to his son, the precious child is cradled by the Wolf-Woman and Ajisuji/Fortinbras, who, represented in this adaptation as a courageous and 'graceful' Subi nation warrior woman, is also used to highlight Queen Nanm/Gertrude's retirement from the world. The coming together of the Jiabo and Subi nations at the close marks the emergence of a new dynastic partnership even as it celebrates the birth of a child who will rule in minority.

The Banquet elaborates its comparable women characters via more obviously foregrounded efforts at female emancipation. Hence, remodelled as a villainous Claudius, Empress Wan/Gertrude is discovered as a proactive and scheming aspirant in a *Hamlet* that places her, and not her male counterparts, at centre stage. Contests for privilege are at work in the scene where Empress Wan/Gertrude and Emperor Li/Claudius play, half-threateningly, half-erotically, with each other's ties and titles: relational terms are bandied in tit-for-tat fashion, while the mutual insistence on the 'correct' forms of 'address' being employed ('Your Majesty' and 'Empress') suggests a jockeying for advantage. On a later occasion, Empress Wan/Gertrude reflects on her titular trajectory: 'Little Wan ...

Empress ... Her Majesty, the Emperor,' she intones, tracing a historical journey from child to adult, from dependent to independent, from female to male. Simultaneously stated is an identification with the Chinese phoenix or *fenghuang*, a mythical creature embodying an empress's powers and abilities. 'I shall rise,' exclaims Empress Wan/Gertrude in a promise that is as arresting for its glorification of singleness as it is for its exclusion of the male Chinese dragon with which the female phoenix was conventionally allied.

Ultimately, however, *The Banquet* offers an essentially dispassionate picture of the woman's quest for a greater autonomy. Stabbed by an anonymous assassin as snow falls, Empress Wan/Gertrude fails in her political endeavour, the cold of the snow symbolically blanketing and changing the heated temperature of her 'desire'. White covers red (the spirit of Wu Luan/Hamlet returns) and effaces Empress Wan/Gertrude's 'flame' of ambition. Writes Molly Hand of *The Banquet*: 'chaos and death, darkness and despair, there is little hope for renewal or rebirth'.[16] Yet the closing montage is not as definitive as this assessment allows. As the knife blade is seen being dropped into a mossy pool, a glimpse is afforded of koi carp swimming together beneath. Beyond the 'unweeded garden' (1.2.135) of the court, it is implied, and past the knotty entanglement of mystery and motive, the beautiful and the rare are still discernible. Linked in Chinese mythology to love and friendship, and associated with a state of bliss, the koi carp indexes an as yet unrealized world of harmonious interaction that belies surface appearances.

There is, then, an ameliorative turn at the end of *The Banquet*, one which, typically, is characterized by the utilization of a local aesthetic. *Prince of the Himalayas* is even more distinctive in its rewriting of the play's tragic conclusion. Because introduced to his son and assured of what lies beyond, Lhamoklodan/Hamlet is realized as ready to embrace his own destiny, and confidence in succession means that he can finally lay the spirit of King Tsanpo to rest. Rejecting the Ghost's claims, Lhamoklodan/Hamlet refuses to 'raise his sword' against his biological father and, hence, turns his back on a paternal–filial relation expressed as a reverence for authority. Instead, an inflexible and male-defined doctrine of violence is replaced by an open and female-shaped pacific philosophy: as the Wolf-Woman asserts in the closing montage, 'Love, all-embracing love' is what is ultimately important. Here, *Prince of the Himalayas* openly recasts itself as a parable of forgiveness rather than a narrative of revenge. If *Hamlet* is a play perennially associated with questions about identity, moreover, then these are addressed in the reformative plans for Lhamoklodan/Hamlet's offspring's future development. The protagonist's question, 'Who am I?' (a version of 'To be, or not to be'), does not remain unanswered, with the film's generic reimagining working to enshrine a new cycle of reconciled relations that bridges generations, genders and nations.

Envisioning Ophelia

Invariably in world cinema adaptations of *Hamlet,* alterations to the tragic emphasis revolve around the fate of the protagonist himself. A pairing of two seemingly unrelated *Hamlet* adaptations, however, is an exception to the rule, for, with these examples (the Russian *Gamlet* [dir. Grigori Kozintsev 1964] and the Iranian *Tardid* [dir. Varuzh Karim Masihi 2009]), we see how the Ophelia figure, limned in the earlier film as physically and ideologically restrained, becomes, in the later film, an independent agent, thereby shifting the play's orientations and effects. At once in *Gamlet,* Ophelia is portrayed as a familial possession, as in training for a public appearance. In the cramped and low-ceilinged rooms of the family quarters in which she first appears (the architecture of the environs bespeaks reduction), a portrait of Polonius stares down from the walls, sensitizing us to where the disposition of power resides. The camera rests on Ophelia, unadorned and with hair scraped back, sitting at her father's feet, and, because of a high angle shot that privileges Polonius's perspective, his daughter appears correspondingly diminished in size and scale. 'Elsinore chains [Ophelia] to a lifeless ceremonial,' notes director Kozintsev, and nowhere is this more apparent than in the scene in which, to twanging music played on a lute by a black-robed crone, she dances a mechanistic measure.[17] On the one hand, this interlude references the First Quarto's stage direction, '*Enter Ofelia playing on a lute*', intertextually preparing the way for her madness; on the other hand, it undergirds the construction of a character who is discovered primarily as an object of instruction, as lacking in freedom of movement because still in tutelage.[18] At these moments the domination of Ophelia is writ large; at the same time, as befits the vision of a director raised under the shadow of a repressive Soviet regime, there is a political component to the representation. To cite John Collick on *Gamlet*, we are continually made aware of 'the inescapable and implacable weight of history'.[19]

Ophelia, in fact, and here *Gamlet* offers an extended extrapolation of the First Folio metaphor, is realized as her system's prisoner. Not accidentally is Polonius pictured jangling the keys of the trunks on which Ophelia perches herself; too, shots of a parrot in a cage, of a stifling black collar and of a balustrade behind which she shelters point up the idea that, throughout, she is hemmed in by custom and convention. The most forceful expression of Ophelia's incarceration is reserved for the scene in which she is dressed in an iron farthingale as a preparation for her donning a funereal black dress; the metallic structure suggests hardness and rigidity, while the heaviness of the dress points up a sense of suffocation and engulfment. In the play, Hamlet is accused of 'bar[ring] the door upon [his] own liberty' (3.2.329–30); in his film, Kozintsev inverts and executes the suggestion, making of Ophelia an example par excellence of an inmate moulded according to institutional praxes. More tellingly, Ophelia's condition is symptomatic. It mirrors the situation of identically dressed female courtiers, who move in unison; it chimes with the scene in which Hamlet, too, is made small by the massive corpus of the Ghost; and it brings to mind the cognate circumstances of the workers who labour on a wheel to close the castle portcullis. As Courtney Lehmann states, in *Gamlet* the 'well-hidden strings of a totalizing power activate their human functionaries'.[20] What happens beyond Ophelia is replicated in the minutiae of her own predicament.

This is a predicament that affects body as well as mind. *Gamlet* is a Shakespearean adaptation in which the details of setting are consistently thematically communicative. For instance, Claudius's saturnine appearance and phallic traits have an analogue in the sculpture of the bare-breasted maidens that decorate his bedroom's fireplace: if only implicitly, an audience is made aware of the exploitative treatment meted out to women under his regime. Similarly, the tapestries that decorate the quarters of Polonius's family show satyrs, wild men, dragons and beasts; this is a world of heightened sexuality from which Ophelia, in her training to be a court lady, is actively excluded. Her distance from such a world is highlighted when a masque-like entertainment featuring a Minotaur and maidens is staged during the wedding celebrations – it is as if the tapestry has come alive. Within this context, the use of Ophelia as bait to draw out the distracted Hamlet takes on additional resonances; in particular, Polonius's statement that he will 'loose' (2.2.159) his daughter suggests a reification of her body and a manipulation of her sexual allure. The subsequent ostracization of Ophelia by Polonius here is returned to in the scenes of her public appearance. At the play-within-the-play, for instance, Ophelia is attired in a sumptuous dress; this, it is implied, is the occasion of public importance for which she has been preparing. But, as Polonius's brusque movement past her during the post-performance chaos suggests, her entry into the wider world is accompanied by rejection and humiliation. Indeed, for the remainder of the film, Ophelia appears only in public, but in such a way as to emphasize her status as victim and casualty. Shot as a minuscule figure within a lofty arch during the mad scenes, she registers as even more fragile and vulnerable. In addition, the circular movements she traces evoke the dance steps she was earlier rehearsing, suggesting a sad parody of her education. The injunctions Ophelia launches at the court during these sequences, including 'You must sing "a-down a-down"' (4.5.165), sound, therefore, as pathetic echoes of requirements for performance, adding to the impression of taught behaviours gone awry. In a creative reworking of the living herbs and flowers of the play, the film has Ophelia handling the dead twigs and branches from the fire, signs of a spent energy. And, because, at her last appearance, she is, for once, unaccompanied by her black-robed crones, an idea of abandonment is forcefully conveyed.

There are just two indications of an attempt to break the mould, to resist the castle's confines. The first is when, in an invented interlude, Ophelia is pictured in her bedroom reading aloud Hamlet's poem, 'Doubt thou the stars are fire, / Doubt that the sun doth move' (2.2.114–15). In the play, the words are not hers, yet, in Kozintsev's adaptation, the transposition of the lines to Ophelia hints at other dimensions to her sensibility and at a voice. Second, as this scene establishes, Ophelia's bedroom is draped with tapestries showing a unicorn, a peacock, deer and doves. This fantastical and pastoral landscape paves the way for the symbolically freighted sequence that ensues directly upon Ophelia's suicide. Recalling Kozintsev's concept of 'winged realism', and arguably also bringing to mind the acrobatic excesses of the players (and, beyond them, the 'agitational forms' of revolutionary Russian popular culture), the camera tracks a seagull's flight from left to right, and from right to left.[21] Here, in this conjuration of a departing spirit, is an idea of unshackled movement, of a journey that court expectations prohibited, and of a force rising inexorably upwards. In such a reconfiguration of Ophelia we find, to summarize Kozintsev, an effort to 'increase the altitude of *Hamlet* ... to rest the tragedy on contemporary reality, the air of our time'.[22]

The registration of Ophelia as a soul-in-transition perhaps worked as an imaginative prompt for Iranian director, Varuzh

Karim Masihi, when he came to his *Hamlet* adaptation, *Tardid* (2009). *Tardid* relocates the action of the play to modern Tehran, as established in shots of traffic-choked roads, deserted rooftops and palatial residences (a creamy mansion in a wealthy suburb stands in for Elsinore). The film conceives of the Hamlet figure, Siavash, as a type of artist, a photojournalist whose interest in culture and representation reveals itself in the images, puppets and African masks that adorn his apartment's walls, and it is distinctive for the way in which it presents the protagonist as slowly waking up to the fact that his life and that of Shakespeare's Hamlet run along parallel lines. In this connection, Masihi's adaptation is highly self-conscious, the narrative thrust centring on various efforts to prevent *Hamlet* repeating itself. This much might suggest Almereyda's *Hamlet* as the point of departure, but, in fact, as Masihi states in interview, 'I haven't seen this film [...] in my case, you have to turn the clock back to Kozintsev's film (his Ophelia I continue to be greatly struck by)'.[23] *Gamlet* and *Tardid*, I suggest, are in implicit dialogue with each other; the latter answers back to the former and, in so doing, establishes itself as an adaptation of an adaptation. The connection is not necessarily surprising, for, as Margaret Litvin has shown, Kozintsev's *Gamlet* has long served as a port of call for artists and practitioners in the Middle Eastern world.[24] At an immediate level, Kozintsev's film is adumbrated in *Tardid* in a shot of Siavash/Hamlet reclining on a sofa in a ruined cinema; behind him can be discerned a poster for *Gamlet*, suggesting a model for the adaptive process. Contextual parallels assist in the elaboration of connections. Within four months of the release of *Gamlet*, Leonid Brezhnev 'led a coup against Krushchev and abruptly reversed his policies'; the thaw came to a close and, as Courtney Lehmann notes, Soviet culture was again placed under state control.[25] *Tardid*, too, anticipates a moment of radical political upset. From 2009 to 2010, Iranian cities were shaken by a series of violent protests objecting to irregularities in the presidential elections. Labelled the 'Green Movement', these protests constituted a demand not only for

improved citizens' rights but also for women to be treated
with greater equity and, as such, represented a 'defiance', in
Fatemeh Sadeghi's words, of 'the systematic gender discrimination of the post-revolutionary Islamic apparatus'.[26] Posed
on the cusp of the electoral discontent, *Tardid* debates
women's roles inside a constraining system, and, in so doing,
makes a contribution to larger questions about national
self-determination. It mounts its case through reversing and
extending Kozintsev's Ophelia; Mahtab/Ophelia, Masihi's
realization of the character, is granted an agency beyond the
constrictions of her Shakespearean equivalent and functions
to voice mixed hopes for future reconstitution and reform.

Tardid deploys metaphors of water and images of ponds
to suggest corruption's manifold manifestations. Functioning
as an amalgam of the gravedigger and Yorick, the family
company archivist describes Tehran's business world as a
'stagnant pool' with a 'dirty stink'. 'Money' is the 'slave of
[... the] pool's rules,' Siavash/Hamlet is informed, the archivist
continuing, 'somebody will eventually stand on your shoulders
[...] and you will drown'. Emerging from these formulations
is a vivid sense of moral besmirching and unnatural pollution
that owes its genesis to *Hamlet*'s 'unweeded garden / That
grows to seed' (1.2.135–6). Specifically, the archivist's warning
brings back into the film's consciousness the river in which we
glimpse the corpse of Hemmatollah/Old Hamlet; choked with
detritus and the froth of effluent, this slow-moving waterway
is used to suggest something 'rank and gross' (1.2.136) in the
'state' (1.4.90) of modern-day Iran. Yet, for Siavash, despite
his photojournalism, his family's corrupt affairs remain as
murky as the water in which his father meets his demise. As
a result, he is characterized by inaction, and his 'doubt' (one
translation of the film's title) cements his paralysis.

Interestingly, within such a situation, it is women who are
envisaged as possessing a greater capability, their qualities
of self-assurance and conviction throwing characters such
as Siavash/Hamlet into sharp relief. Important extra-textual
female characters in *Tardid* include Anna, Garo/Horatio's

mother, a theatre director, but woman as independent agent finds its most complete statement in Mahtab/Ophelia, who is possessed of an immediately identifiable capability and acumen. Despite the changes that have overtaken women's roles in contemporary Iran, types of 'discrimination and segregation', notes David Waines, continue.[27] The idea is illustrated in *Tardid* in the ways in which, when men and women gather in the family mansion, they are grouped in separate areas; Mahtab/Ophelia refuses these distinctions, forging a route through demarcated spaces and traversing forbidden boundaries. Her athleticism (despite the restrictions of the *hijab*), and the busy and lively score that characterizes her, register a capacity for action and sense of purpose. Like Siavash/Hamlet, Mahtab/Ophelia is immersed in the arts; she aids Siavash/Hamlet in his eavesdropping activities and acts as prompter during the play-within-the-play, suggesting not only support for the plan to have Roozbehan/Claudius exposed but also an alliance with women theatrical practitioners. Elsewhere, Mahtab/Ophelia emerges as distinctive in Shakespearean adaptations of *Hamlet* in that she is represented as caring for her stepbrother, Danial/Laertes, who has Down syndrome, arranging driving lessons for him and generally ensuring his welfare; here, by foregrounding disability, *Tardid* reverses a film and stage tradition of a brother–sister dynamic based on the former's domination of the latter.

Crucially, once the parallels between the unfolding action and Shakespeare's *Hamlet* are pointed out to her, Mahtab/Ophelia is quick to resist the momentum that threatens to shape events according to a seemingly inexorable Shakespearean dramatic logic. On the starry rooftop of the ruined cinema, strewn with rubbish and bathed in an eerie blue light, she balks at seeing an exhausted Siavash/Hamlet supine on a coffin-like box. Extinguishing the candle, she exclaims, 'I'll prevent this tragedy [...] from happening [...] I'll make your uncle drink that poisoned chalice!', a statement that underscores her defiance of fate and espousal of agency. A similar moment occurs in the same sequence when 'To be, or not to be' is referenced; as Siavash/Hamlet lies down to sleep, Garo/ Horatio, whose mind is running on the theme of slumber, intones, 'to die: to sleep' (3.1.59), only to be interrupted by Mahtab/Ophelia, who exclaims, 'Now I see why Hamlet gets killed; because he too has a pessimistic friend like you!' Her note of reprimand and bathetic deflation of Garo/Horatio's pseudo-philosophizing, as well as the fact that, contrary to expectation, the famous soliloquy is removed from Siavash/ Hamlet's discursive ownership, clarify the nature of *Tardid*'s appropriation of the play – in part irreverent, in part deferential, wittily invoking assumptions in order to undermine them, sculpting new traditions out of old.

The *dénouement* revolves around Roozbehan/Claudius's plot to convince Danial/Laertes to shoot Siavash/Hamlet at Ansari/Polonius's memorial service. However, Danial/Laertes wounds rather than kills Siavash/Hamlet, gunning down instead Roozbehan/Claudius, one of his aides and a passing guest. Profusely bleeding, Siavash/Hamlet is incapable of saving Danial/Laertes, who is spirited away by Roozbehan/ Claudius's henchmen, dying in a rigged car crash on the Elsinore estate's grounds. The film climaxes, then, with 'casual slaughters [...] deaths put on by cunning, and for no cause [...] purposes mistook' (5.2.366–8), and any revenge achieved is meted out accidentally. In keeping with the Shakespearean idea of tragic contingency, we do not witness Siavash/Hamlet's death within the film proper; fatally injured, he is pictured bleeding on the bench next to the estate's ornamental pool. Having freed himself of the corrupt constrictions of family, and now confirmed in the loyalties between lovers and friends, his doubts, it is suggested, are finally resolved. But the still image on which we come to rest in the concluding montage is Mahtab/Ophelia's; she assumes the film's thematic focus and stands as the action's inheritrix. Her position at the edge of the pool shows her once again resisting both the thrust of *Hamlet* and the film's association of water with corruption. As the camera pans from head to toe, resting finally on Mahtab/Ophelia's upside-down reflection in the pond, the film showcases the fact that, in contradistinction to the John Everett Millais portrait, which we have seen earlier in a dream inset, this Ophelia does not – will not – drown (the body in the water is an illusion only, a product of the camera's self-conscious playfulness) and will not succumb to madness. The moment, in fact, recalls *Tardid*'s opening scene (where the camera pans in the reverse direction from toe to head to suggest the drowned body of Hemmatollah/Old Hamlet) and points up how Mahtab/Ophelia reserves the right to change the course of her Shakespearean destiny.

Conclusions

This chapter has mapped three routes into an understanding of *Hamlet* on screen around the world. But it needs emphasizing that these approaches are not mutually exclusive. That is, they have the capacity to cross-fertilize and commingle. For example, *Prince of the Himalayas*, as much as it trades on a local aesthetic, constitutes a political vision about Chinese–Tibetan relations in a late capitalist historical moment. *The Banquet*, too, by means of its eloquent rendering of places, colours and things, might be seen as negotiating questions about Asia's engagement with late capitalist modernity. *Tardid*, similarly, is not limited in its relation to *Hamlet*; the film draws on a number of local traditions, such as a *zar* ritual to approximate the visitation of the Ghost, so as to reflect on how Shakespeare signifies in contemporary contexts. We do well to bear in mind, then, when approaching *Hamlet* on film around the world, that the play is not straitjacketed in its imaginative reach, investments and uses. The films discussed here, and others of their ilk, form an intertextual nexus that reveals, whether by accident or design, a rich array of activities. In many instances, the points of connection go further than the immediately obvious, pointing up how film adaptations of the play can move in unexpected directions. As a corpus of interpretation, these works indicate how debate continues to be conducted around questions of agency, action, responsibility, duty and freedom of expression. And, if the films invite comparison in their shared concern with countries or cultures in transition, then they also differ from each other in operating in particular, local and sometimes contradictory ways. Crucially, in world cinema's commerce with *Hamlet*, we apprehend new *Hamlet*s that not only showcase the vitality of the play's afterlives but represent imaginative creations in their own right.

6

New Directions:
Being Hamlet Not
Being Hamlet

Frank McGuinness

In Greek Theatre the gods believe in humanity. They have to. That is the source of their power. Without our stories of their cruelty, their capriciousness, their infinite ability to deny and defy our attempts to control our destinies, what are they? Mere manifestations of breath, or else spoilt children stamping like brats on the universe, showing who is boss to those who give a damn about them. In the greatest of Greek plays man transcends the gods in the power of our complexity, in our stamina and endless capacity for suffering, and in our determination to tell the tale as we would tell it. Oedipus is more worthy of admiration than Apollo, the god who dances to see the blind man in agony. Andromeda and Hecuba in *Women of Troy* embody a strength and stoical wisdom that put Pallas Athena to shame, revealing the whims of her spite. Roles are then reversed in this subversive space. Its cry may not quite be the gods are dead – but they are certainly diminished. We go

to this theatre to meet ourselves transformed. It is then a most
unpredictable place. And the play of *Hamlet* continues that
ancient tradition. So who is it that we set out to meet there?
Where will the meeting happen?

A castle, Elsinore. A country, Denmark. A castle, a country,
a stage. And all three announce one thing about themselves.
These spaces are haunted. In this Denmark, through this
Elsinore, on this stage, ghosts may rise from their grave. These
dead awaken to encounter the living, imparting messages full
of danger, of warning, danger and warning tinged perhaps
by envy. So here is one property associated with these places
– the power of transformation. As they can appear, so these
spectres, these shadows of past selves, they may disappear.
As they vanish, those who succeeded in pomp and majesty
now make their presence felt, in all their power opposing
the powerless phantoms, in all their living vigour replacing
dead souls. This castle, this country, this stage are primarily
set up as sites where connections can be made, most theatrically threatening, connections between the quick and the
dead, the living and the lost. Transformations on this stage,
connections in this place – they seriously affect its measures of
time. When boundaries between past and present existences
blur themselves, when meetings of the dead and living melt
them into one, time might be said to declare it is a law unto
itself, refuting linearity, asserting itself to be free of any order
but that which events in the play choose to impose upon its
code of chronology. This gives to time in *Hamlet* not means
of control – that is not what time desires – but instead a
contributory power that plot shall release information only
as it chooses to reveal it, thereby ensuring the business of the
play is then revelation, and the great revelation exposed in
this theatre is the man himself, Prince Hamlet. It is not the
audience who ultimately will choose how and when to meet
him. He will choose to meet us when Shakespeare feels the
occasion good and ready, and not until then. With customary
caution, masquerading as always as chaos, Shakespeare delays
the entry of his protagonist, whetting the collective appetite,

democratizing theatrical procedure, sharing the status of unknown quantity between Hamlet and those gathered here to witness his progress through his play, here being that strange space where all is connected, all is transformed, most revolutionary in the way theatre itself conducts its art, making actors of its audience, audience of its actors, radicalizing the way a play – a part – embodies itself.

The most cursory glance at the whole text displays the debt *Hamlet*'s metaphors owe to the trade of the theatre itself. The crucial act of revelation in this play of revelations is a play within a play in Act 3, Scene 2, *The Murder of Gonzago*, also called *The Mouse Trap*. King Claudius is confronted by his own guilt as he watches the players dramatize the story of this Gonzago, poisoned by his blood relation and rival for the love of a woman, as Hamlet's father is poisoned by Claudius. The obvious explanation for this is Shakespeare's exploitation of his own trade for narrative ends. And yet is this sufficient? Why does Claudius react to the play by demanding 'Give me some light, away', Polonius repeating the command three times, 'Lights! Lights! Lights!'. This emphasis on illumination adds to the question of who observes who in *Hamlet*? Audience or actor? If it is the latter, has *Hamlet* turned on its head the basis of dramatic performance? And if that basis is reversed, who then stands in the lights? If the corrupt king screams for light, is the audience, bringing the light of interpretation, also corrupted, stained by what happens, on a theatrical and metatheatrical level, in *Hamlet*? Do we observe ourselves as he observes himself, and, through that observation, ourselves? In *The Love Song of J. Alfred Prufrock*, T. S. Eliot reminds us we are not Prince Hamlet, but then neither is he, since he is not innocent of what is rotten in Denmark, subjected as he is to its time and place, its incessant questions. Where? How? When? Then? Time knows no limits in *Hamlet* but what events impose on themselves. Meeting him in this time, this place, the audience too must submit to these connections, these transformations. Audience meets actors, and the messages they bring are 'full of envy and danger', for they

speak in our languages verbal and visual, ethical and political,
remembering that politics – the manipulation of others and
of events for our own ends, good and bad – begin at home,
begins within the family.

Two families preoccupy the play of *Hamlet*; the royal
one of Claudius, Gertrude, Prince Hamlet and the ghost of
his dead father, King Hamlet; the noble family of the Lord
Chamberlain, Polonius, Laertes and Ophelia. To both families,
the father, one dead, one living, bring tragedy. Hamlet's father
sets in spiritual and physical motion the chain of events that
exterminate his blood, giving the kingdom of Denmark to
Norway's Prince Fortinbras. Polonius unwittingly involves,
through his daughter, his family in the blood bath and leads it
to annihilation. In both cases the spring for the father's action is
love. Selfless love? Or selfish love? For dead King Hamlet, that
father's selfless love might lie in his wish for his son's and for
his marriage's vindication. Claudius, the dead man's brother,
now occupies the royal throne. The same brother violates his
marriage bed. King Hamlet's wish for vindication might then
be rooted in his desire to see his son avenged through selfless
love. As servant to King Claudius, Polonius wishes to rid the
kingdom of Hamlet's dangerous, accusatory madness. He roots
it in love, Hamlet's for Ophelia. Polonius sacrifices his daughter's life, and his own life, to achieve that aim, acting selflessly
through loyal service to his master. But selfless love has its
selfish side. Hamlet's father wishes to avenge his own murder.
He rises from the grave bringing death as his accomplice, and
since he is himself dead, then that death must be intended for
others, his son included. Polonius is a servile man, but also an
ambitious one. He satisfies that ambition through heightening
the prospects of his daughter as the future Queen of Denmark.
Selfish and selfless aims mingle in *Hamlet*. Neither predom-
inate – neither can be separated. Fathers in the play share
moral ambiguity, and they bestow these ambiguities onto their
offspring and relatives. *Hamlet* is a play of lost innocence,
and the most pronounced, perhaps, is the audience's. Bearing
witness to all that happens, it stands back and lets it proceed,

in a position remarkably similar to Hamlet's father. Powerless and yet powerful, it waits for what happens next, in this most shifting world secure in the knowledge that it wills it to happen, as does Horatio, Hamlet's more than usually silent confidant, not interrupting the action, but urging it forward, as does its observers. A strange correspondence emerges between the characters of this place and the characters involved in the act of making theatre. If the audience, like Horatio, conspire to let things occur, then together with Polonius, the ghost of Hamlet's father stands as metaphor for the mind creating these occurrences. Their function then is authorial, their contrasting natures dual, one consciously devising, the other subconsciously, the conscious one ironically dead and buried, the subconscious one unaware he is on the verge of dying. And if they, in this scheme of things, are in their way embodiments of elements in the art of theatre, then Hamlet himself too is part and parcel of the process whereby his play takes definition from the workings of the craft of drama as Shakespeare now exposes that craft to most exacting and strenuous self-interrogation. The part of Hamlet is the ultimate test of acting, for Hamlet, in essence, consistently constructs and deconstructs, simultaneously constructs and deconstructs, the whole nature of performance. A supreme actor, brilliantly versed in directing and in playing, as his instructions to the Players in Act 3, Scene 2 accurately illustrate, Hamlet veers in character from one convincing extreme to another, his whole self resting for its semblance of coherence on its rapid choices of shifting personae. Eliot again in *The Love Song of J. Alfred Prufrock* speaks of 'time, time to prepare a face to meet the face that you meet', yet Prufrock is not, as stated, 'Prince Hamlet, but ... an attendant lord'. The attendant lords Rosencrantz and Guildenstern and, especially, Osric prepare faces for their meetings. Hamlet instead prepares meetings for these faces, and these meetings are meant to conflict, for in combat these faces will distort to reveal what lies behind the manners of their diplomacy – their true meanings, their treacherous intent, or is that too a fantasy of the Prince?

Unquestionably though, the ultimate opponent, the powerful enemy, the most threatening actor in this theatrical combat to the death is Claudius, aided and abetted by, in the play's scheme of favour and disfavour, his adopted son, Laertes. Between the opposite numbers in these male duels are the women, Gertrude and Ophelia. Shifting between the parties of Hamlet and Claudius, Gertrude truly belongs to neither. Neither does Ophelia, but in narrative terms Ophelia differs from the Queen. The younger woman dies before Gertrude dies. What's the reason for her early exit? Desiring Hamlet's love but fearing it, acknowledging Laertes's warnings yet returning them, obedient to her father and still sensible to the danger he places her and himself in, Ophelia moves through this perilous terrain aware of her confusion to a more marked degree than any other. It is not her weakness which impels her to her suicide, but her intelligence, an intelligence that cannot cope with the machinations of statecraft in Denmark, an intelligence that phrases itself exquisitely as the poetry of the mad scene, a madness Laertes diagnoses exactly, 'This nothing's more than matter', as being the only sane response to the events that have trapped his sister in her hapless position. Ophelia disappears then, and something disappears with her. That something is hope. She prefigures Cordelia in *King Lear*, for whom a more murderous end is coming. Ophelia's death is prophecy of the death in store for those implicated in her suicide. It is with savage irony Gertrude should witness and record so tenderly Ophelia's drowning. The Queen too will die from liquid, and just as Ophelia's mind is poisoned by intrigue, Gertrude's body shall consume the same poison of intrigue. Giving herself to water, Ophelia dies, and her drowning foreshadows the flow of blood that ends *Hamlet*. Is anyone innocent? Is anyone saved? Is Hamlet? Is 'the thing' – the play itself?

The play's innate theatricality underlines the drama's strong sense of self-consciousness, an all-pervading awareness of its status as a piece of dramatic action. If it consistently asserts that 'the play's the thing', is it possible to decipher what this thing is? Or who it is? And how did it come to be? The verb most readily identified with Hamlet is 'to be' itself. The text's most quoted line is 'To be or not to be, that is the question.' In choosing to be, Hamlet chooses to act. In choosing to act, the prince decides to live. His life leads, in Act 5, to his death, to his not being. The movement of the entire play rewrites its most famous line. 'To be or not to be' turns into 'to be and not to be'. The action of *Hamlet* sees existence not in terms of life opposed to death, but life in death and death in life. For this reason it should be stressed that the characters in Hamlet are haunted by the past and haunted by their own past. In this Denmark every dynasty counts its phantoms as equals to its flesh and blood. Throughout *Sailing to Byzantium* Yeats conjured a golden bird singing of what is past, present and to come. A same song informs the linguistic codes of *Hamlet*. Utterance acquires the nature of prophecy, since all that happens has already happened and will happen again. The inevitable in *Hamlet* has then, paradoxically, an unexpected quality, unexpected in that it bears within an unfinished quality, and who can finish this action off but its observers? And who do we observe most critically, most intimately, most lovingly? Who is the observed of all observers? The prince himself, the character called Hamlet. Why? To answer that, another question must be asked.

'To be or not to be, that is the question' – why pose this dilemma? Is it the consideration of a man who values life too highly or too lowly? Does Hamlet do both, a cautionary condition attendant on his split attitude to life in death, and death in life? The death of his father and its manner of execution familiarize Hamlet with the rotten state of man. The grief at his loss and the anger at this murder awake simultaneously in Hamlet the importance of family and the individual's prime relation to family. Caught between two poles of disgust and determination, Hamlet repels his mind frantically only to attract it powerfully towards the possibility of doing something or the possibility of doing nothing. This plan of action and inaction affects Hamlet's psychological entity. Since he is somebody who aspires to be nobody, his natural estate is a son not of a father but of a ghost. What implications does this carry for the play of *Hamlet*? It ensures that a definite sense of identity rarely hovers about this part. Whatever Hamlet says, so Hamlet becomes, and as he can say in his madness, assumed or actual, what he likes, so he can take what shape he likes – everything and nothing, somebody or nobody, Hamlet does not simply act his roles but is the incarnation of these roles. So diverse does the character appear, all singular forms, grammatical and lexical, seem inappropriate. His natural state is plurality. This more than double nature gives Hamlet licence to transform his selves into whatever person suits his purposes best. The licence thereby achieved removes the character from the sphere of conventional propriety – the standards by which those that surround him are judged – and places him in a shielded environment, a protected, feral species roaming loose through the jungle/court of Denmark, feared by his enemies, loved by the common crowd, for they sense in him a crowd of personalities changeable as the moods of the mob change rapidly. 'To be or not to be, that is the question', and the crowd answer, 'be'. Without his being, the play ceases to be, and the cessation of the play is the cessation of Hamlet's audience. As Hamlet loses his life, so does that audience lose its role. Fortinbras arrives, kept a nearly complete stranger till the very close of the drama. Elsinore is no place for strangers. The triumphant coming of Fortinbras signals it is time to leave, go from the theatre, out of place in this new dawn of a different, less tangled politics. Having watched Claudius, Gertrude, Laertes, Polonius and Hamlet himself die before the eyes of the audience, and Ophelia drowned, now with its entire cast of leading characters gone, it is time to surrender to our own death as participants in the complex web of this play. We enter the theatre to meet *Hamlet* as the living. We leave it as ghosts, drained, exhausted by the energy, the expense of spirit in a waste of shame happening in this text. A reversal of roles has occurred. Dramatic practice has violently altered from the norm. An average play demands it is watched passively from the stage. *Hamlet* demands we actively finish what is set in motion on its stage. That motion is the clearing – the annihilation of two houses, those of Polonius and King Hamlet – but the house is only truly scoured, the theatre left desolate when it is empty of its audience. 'The play's the thing' in *Hamlet* because in this play, more than in any other, every gesture, every ritual, every act onstage and referred to offstage, each is tightly controlled into possessing a secondary meaning or an imaginative weight. Nothing here is innocent of connotation. Just as the spurs to action within this family tragedy are fratricide and incest and the revenge that attends such crimes, so in its theatrical upheaval *Hamlet* affects relationships, well defined, highly structured relationships within theatre. Actor and audience change identities. Author and actor assume strange mutations. Audience and author evolve to place strange responsibilities on each other. To fulfil new roles perfectly it is necessary to defy assigned positions in the hierarchy of making theatre. And the most striking, perhaps most simple aspect about this thing we call the play in its defiance and brave manipulations is nowhere seen more powerfully than in the highly ambiguous yet effective character of Horatio.

Horatio accompanies Hamlet neither as guide nor accomplice but as a strange light shedding illumination on events through the act and art of confirming Hamlet's suspicions and plotting. He encourages Hamlet forward on his courses of action while attempting to maintain a crucial distance from events. That distance is of his own making, and it is ultimately the making and the saving of him for it allows him to escape the massacre at the play's conclusion, although who knows what plans Fortinbras has in mind for Hamlet's former allies? Still, Horatio remains the last observer, the judge who does not pass sentence. Friend to Hamlet, he must stand therefore as foe to Hamlet's foes, yet through the play at least he escapes their murderous attentions. Why? His worth to Hamlet is obvious, yet it is a worth that does not obviously threaten the power of Claudius, and so Horatio avoids the excesses of this most excessive man. While Hamlet delays his brief, Claudius goes beyond his. Claudius roots his judgements in his abruptness of ambition, abruptness most readily discernible in the brutal philosophy behind Claudius's politics: if a man threatens, eradicate him. His eradication of his brother, Hamlet's father; his sudden marriage to Hamlet's mother; his panicked manoeuvres through the helpless Rosencrantz and Guildenstern to be rid of Hamlet in England; his dangerous, desperate plot with Laertes; all contribute to indicate a man out of control of his destiny. Claudius is always and ever the victim of his own intrigues. A tragic Oliver Hardy with no blissful Laurel to blame, he constantly ends as the deserving dupe of his own arrogance. Winning the kingship and with it the queen, he loses credibility. As he prays, watched by Hamlet, Claudius laments the loss of his ability to speak to God, but more significantly, he has lost the ability to speak to himself, in marked contrast to Hamlet. Claudius will suffer for that existential silence when his nephew literally pours poisoned wine down his uncle's gullet, the king literally choking on his own stupidity. As Horatio would seem to be a born survivor, Claudius is a born loser, all the more pathetically so for appearing to have won it all. This victim Claudius takes as wife another victim, Gertrude, inheriting from her a most dangerous, most imaginative stepson, hell bent on destruction. The chronicle of his own career, however, illustrates that Claudius can be utterly trusted to destroy himself. But is Hamlet himself sufficiently self-destructive? The web of fatal circumstances Claudius weaves about himself contains Hamlet within its mesh. His killing of Polonius, prompting Ophelia's madness and suicide and the murderous return of Laertes, is due to an error, an accident – a mistaken belief he has killed the king and avenged his father. He cunningly sets the seal on the fates of Rosencrantz and Guildenstern. He provokes his mother with cruel but clever taunts. In his dealings Hamlet persistently displays imagination and intelligence, in the poetry of his soliloquies his powers of lyrical analysis are of breathtaking audacity, yet the fact remains this genius does not save him from Claudius nor from the curse of vengeance placed on him by his father. He is a man doomed to die existing in a world doomed to die, and that sense of universal doom beats at the tragic heart of Hamlet. The 'thing' that is 'the play' begins to explain itself, and its explanation rests on the ultimate failure of Prince Hamlet. Most driven, most dazzling as a performance, most convincing, most annihilating in exposition, Hamlet cannot transcend the limitations of the world he has inherited, cannot go beyond its bourns. So he will die there, a flawed, mortal man. The son of a ghost will turn into a ghost himself by his play's conclusion, leaving behind no son to avenge his murder, and leaving behind no one on whom that murder could be avenged, since all that matter in the shaping of the play's decisive events have by the end turned into ghosts themselves. Hamlet's father though has succeeded in his desire to be remembered – his desire for revenge, the synonym for his remembrance. He has reduced the world to less than rubble, reduced it to nothing. 'You are naught, you are naught', Ophelia chides the leering Hamlet. 'I'll mark the play', fulfilling her part in this play where punishment befalls all as consequence for the killing of King Hamlet, and all must die, guilty or innocent.

The play then has turned into one of passion, and this passion has no resurrection. The living space of the theatre transforms itself entirely into a field of graves, and those that rise to speak there speak of their dying lives. Everything about 'the thing' itself speaks of our mortality, reminds all on stage, all listening to what's said on stage, that they shall die:

> To be, or not to be – that is the question;
> Whether 'tis nobler in the mind to suffer
> The slings and arrows of outrageous fortune
> Or to take arms against a sea of troubles
> And by opposing end them; to die: to sleep –
> No more, and by a sleep to say we end
> The heartache and the thousand natural shocks
> That flesh is heir to: 'tis a consummation
> Devoutly to be wished – to die: to sleep –

To sleep, perchance to dream – ay, there's the rub,
For in that sleep of death what dreams may come
When we have shuffled off this mortal coil
Must give us pause: there's the respect
That makes calamity of so long life.
For who would bear the whips and scorns of time,
Th'oppressor's wrong, the proud man's contumely,
The pangs of despised love, the law's delay,
The insolence of office and the spurns
That patient merit of th'unworthy takes,
When he himself might his quietus make
With a bare bodkin. Who would fardels bear
To grunt and sweat under a weary life
But that the dread of something after death
(The undiscovered country from whose bourn
No traveller returns) puzzles the will
And makes us rather bear those ills we have
Than fly to others that we know not of.
Thus conscience does make cowards –
And thus the native hue of resolution
Is sicklied o'er with the pale cast of thought,
And enterprises of great pitch and moment
With this regard their currents turn awry
And lose the name of action. Soft you now,
The fair Ophelia! Nymph, in thy orisons
Be all my sins remembered.

The play takes us to the undiscovered country and leaves us there to find our way about it as best as we can. What comfort can it offer? Only that in this country we are not entirely strangers. Therefore we can follow the logic of this land which obeys an odd progression. Comparison turns to conjunction turns to equivalence: or is is to and as is is not to itself. In other words, to be or not to be is to be and not to be is to be is not to be, for in the final analysis Hamlet experiences the deepest paradox of human existence, one and the same being Hamlet not being Hamlet.

RESOURCES

Ann Thompson

Texts

The textual situation with *Hamlet* is complicated since three
early texts survive: the First Quarto (Q1) of 1603 (previously labelled a 'bad quarto' and widely thought to be a text
reported by actors or auditors), the Second Quarto (Q2) of
1604/5 (twice as long as the first Quarto and referred to as a
'good quarto', perhaps intended to replace the unreliable text
of Q1), and the Folio (F) of 1623 (very like Q2 but lacking
some 230 lines and adding some 70 lines). Debate continues
about the status of Q1, but scholars have accepted both Q2
and F as authorial versions, with some claiming that F is
Shakespeare's own revision of Q2.

Print editions (listed chronologically)

Hamlet, ed. Harold Jenkins, Arden Shakespeare, 2nd series
(London: Methuen, 1982)

This volume is one of the longest and fullest of the Arden
second series and contains extensive commentary and supplementary notes. Jenkins privileges Q2, although he takes
some readings from F. There is a long Introduction, concentrating mainly on the date, text and sources with a brief

critical introduction. There is no stage history, though the commentary often raises questions of staging.

Hamlet, ed. Philip Edwards, New Cambridge Shakespeare (Cambridge: Cambridge University Press, 1985)

Edwards privileges the Folio text, arguing that the Q2-only passages are authorial cuts; nevertheless, he prints them in their usual positions in square brackets. The introduction offers an interesting perspective on the difficulties experienced by modern readers and playgoers in sympathizing with Hamlet, as previous generations have done. Edwards objects to what he sees as the over-interpretation of twentieth-century 'directors' theatre'.

Hamlet, ed. G. R. Hibbard (Oxford: Oxford University Press, 1987)

Hibbard also privileges the Folio text, going further than Edwards by relegating the Q2-only passages to an appendix. He has more confidence in the appeal of the hero than Edwards, admiring him for his 'almost infallible capacity for recognizing and rejecting that which is not true'. His introductory essay 'From Stage to Study' provides a useful integration of the play's early stage history with its early editing history.

The Three-Text Hamlet: Parallel Texts of the First and Second Quartos and the First Folio, ed. Paul Bertram and Bernice W. Kliman (New York: AMS Press, 1991, 2nd edn 2003)

This large-format, original spelling edition does indeed provide all three texts in parallel, facing-page format (leading to some repetition and some blank pages). There is a very brief preface but no commentary notes.

Hamlet, ed. Barbara A. Mowat and Paul Werstine, Folger Shakespeare Library (New York: Washington Square Press, 1992)

Addressed primarily to undergraduate students, this edition provides scene-by-scene plot summaries and explanatory notes on pages facing the text. There is a general introduction on Shakespeare's life and theatre and an essay by Michael Neill provides 'A Modern Perspective' on the play. There is a brief annotated list of 'Further Reading'.

Hamlet, ed. Susanne L. Wofford, Case Studies in Contemporary Criticism (Boston and New York: Bedford Books of St Martin's Press, 1994)

Like others in its series, this volume provides the 1974 text of the play edited by G. Blakemore Evans for *The Riverside Shakespeare*, along with his brief commentary notes. It also includes useful essays on Feminist Criticism (by Elaine Showalter), Psychoanalytic Criticism (Janet Adelman), Deconstruction (Marjorie Garber), Marxist Criticism (Michael D. Bristol) and New Historicism (Karin S. Coddon). Each essay is accompanied by a Bibliography.

The First Quarto of Hamlet, ed. Kathleen O. Irace, The Early Quartos (Cambridge: Cambridge University Press, 1998)

This edition offers a modernized text of the First Quarto with extensive glossarial notes and a full introduction containing a lucid exposition of the textual complexities. It also has an extensive performance history, demonstrating how successful this text has been in the theatre.

Hamlet, ed. Robert Hapgood, Shakespeare in Production (Cambridge: Cambridge University Press, 1999)

Like others in its series, this volume uses the New Cambridge text (Edwards 1985) supplemented by a substantial introduction focusing on the play's history on stage and screen.

The extensive commentary offers line-by-line evidence of how actors and directors have interpreted particular moments, ranging from the earliest performances to Branagh's 1996 film.

Hamlet, ed. Ann Thompson and Neil Taylor, Arden Shakespeare, 3rd series (London: Thomson Learning/ Bloomsbury, 2006, rev. edn 2016)

Hamlet: The Texts of 1603 and 1623, eds Ann Thompson and Neil Taylor, Arden Shakespeare, 3rd series (London: Thomson Learning/Bloomsbury, 2006)

The two volumes of the Arden third series *Hamlet* provide all three texts in fully annotated form. The *Hamlet* volume is a self-contained, free-standing edition based on Q2, with the F-only passages in an appendix. It has a full introduction and numerous appendices on the texts, casting and other matters. It was revised in 2016. *The Texts of 1603 and 1623* is a supplementary volume which does not repeat material from the Q2 volume but offers detailed commentary on the texts of Q1 and F where they differ from Q2. It also contains a stage history of Q1.

Online resources

Googling strategies

Googling 'Shakespeare Resources' brings up a great number of links:

https://www.google.co.uk/search?q=Shakespeare+Resource s&gws_rd=cr&ei=h4qCVcnyNILkUanegrAO

For *Hamlet* resources more specifically, google 'Hamlet Resources': http://www.search.ask.com/web?l=dis&o=10000 0027cr&qsrc=2869&q=Hamlet+Resources&gct=kw

What follows is a list of sites that are worth exploring.

Royal Shakespeare Company

http://www.rsc.org.uk/education/online-resources/

This opens up extensive materials on all the RSC's productions and on the play itself.

Shakespeare's Globe Education

http://www.shakespearesglobe.com/education/library-research/library-archive/recommended-online-resources

The Globe divides its recommendations into seven sections: Text Resources: Shakespeare; Text Resources: General/Other Writers; Staging and Performance Projects; Online Historical Prompt Books; Online Journals; Online Databases and Indexes; Online Catalogues.

World Shakespeare Bibliography Online

http://www.worldshakesbib.org/

'… the most comprehensive record of Shakespeare-related scholarship and theatrical productions published or produced worldwide between 1960 and 2016.'

Old Variorum

Google have digitised the H. H. Furness Variorum (1877) at https://archive.org/details/anewvariorumedi20furngoog

Variorum editions aim to collect all the commentaries in Shakespeare editions down the years. Currently on-going is a New Variorum known as 'Hamlet Works', a huge set of resources (webmaster Jeffery A. Triggs), which can be found at http://triggs.djvu.org/global-language.com/ENFOLDED/index.php, or Hamletworks.org

Shakespeare Survey

http://universitypublishingonline.org/cambridge/shakespeare/about.jsf

Annual hardback book – no. 67 (2014) runs to 500 pages – featuring not only articles but review articles on the year's Shakespeare productions and round-ups of The Year's Contributions to Shakespeare Studies (Critical Studies, Shakespeare in Performance, Editions and Textual Studies). Naturally, much material on *Hamlet* is included.

Shakespeare Quarterly

https://muse.jhu.edu/journals/shakespeare_quarterly/

This leading academic journal features scholarly articles as well as an invaluable annual bibliography of publications on matters Shakespearean, including, naturally, the ever-growing *Hamlet* literature.

The British Library

http://www.bl.uk/
http://www.quartos.org/

The British Library's huge collections (by law, every book registered for copyright in the UK must have a copy deposited here) include scholarly (and other) books on *Hamlet*, listed in their on-line catalogue (accessed by the first site here). The second site is specifically *Hamlet*-oriented.

Folger Shakespeare Library

http://www.folgerdigitaltexts.org/?chapter=4
http://www.folger.edu/classroom-resources

https://folgereducation.wordpress.com/

Along with the Huntington Library, the Folger, sited in the centre of Washington DC and founded by a rich tycoon who turned book collector in his later years, is a major collection, complete with its own small theatre and changing exhibitions. It owns the largest collection of Shakespeare First Folios in the world.

The Huntington Library

http://www.huntington.org/WebAssets/Templates/general.aspx?id=17334

http://huntingtonblogs.org/

Sited in Los Angeles, and like the Folger based on the collecting flair of a rich man (Huntington and Folger were friendly rivals), the Huntington's sites are worth exploring with *Hamlet* in mind.

Shakespeare Newsletter

http://www.iona.edu/About/Iona-in-Community/The-Shakespeare-Newsletter.aspx

An American resource for news of publications on, and productions of, *Hamlet* and the rest of the canon.

Year's Work in English Studies

http://www.oxfordjournals.org/our_journals/ywes/about.html

This site also covers other abstracting/indexing links.

Theatre Record

http://www.theatrerecord.org/

This collects all reviews of theatre productions in the UK, so *Hamlet* features prominently. It requires a subscription.

Shakespeare sourcebooks

Google 'sourcebooks Shakespeare'

http://www.sourcebooks.com/blog/shakesperience-a-hands-on-shakespeare-experience.html

Pedagogically oriented materials on making Shakespeare accessible to students who begin by finding the texts off-putting.

Ophelia and popular culture

http://www.opheliapopularculture.com/

Alan Young's site is devoted to the place occupied by Ophelia in the popular imagination from the nineteenth century until now, with an especial concentration on visual images.

Cinematic resources (films are listed in chronological order)

Hamlet: the Drama of Vengeance, dir. Svend Gade and Heinz Schall, perf. Asta Nielsen (Hamlet), Eduard von Winterstein (Claudius), Mathilde Brandt (Gertrude), Lilli Jacobsson (Ophelia); (Art-Film, Germany, 1920)

This extraordinary and thought-provoking adaptation presents Hamlet as a woman, disguised as a male from birth in order to secure the succession, following a false report that Old Hamlet has been killed in battle. Nielsen (one of the biggest stars of the silent cinema) is brilliant in both comic and tragic modes. The film is discussed in detail by Tony Howard (see under 'Books' p. 187).

Hamlet, dir. Laurence Olivier, perf. Laurence Olivier, Basil Sydney, Eileen Herlie, Jean Simmons (Two Cities Films, UK, 1948)

Olivier gives an Oscar-winning performance in this film which explicitly presents the story as 'the tragedy of a man who could not make up his mind'. He jettisons the play's politics in favour of a psychoanalytical reading with a strong Oedipal focus (Herlie was just twenty-seven at the time, and Olivier was forty). The death of Ophelia is a careful animation of the 1851 painting by John Everett Millais.

Hamlet, dir. Grigori Kozintsev, perf. Innokenty Smoktunovsky, Mikhail Nazvanov, Elza Radzin, Anastasiya Vertinskaya (Lenfilm, USSR, 1964)

Kozintsev had staged Boris Pasternak's translation immediately after the death of Joseph Stalin in 1953 and his later film also presents Hamlet as an intellectual dissident in a totalitarian state. The text is heavily cut but there are some powerful visual effects as well as a soundtrack by Dmitri Shostakovich. Kozintsev discusses his film and provides notes on the production (see under 'Books' p. 187).

Hamlet, dir. Tony Richardson, perf. Nicol Williamson, Anthony Hopkins, Judy Parfitt, Marianne Faithfull (Woodfall Film Productions, UK, 1969)

Based on a theatrical production at the Round House, London, and shot on the stage there, this film is notable for its extensive use of close-ups, Williamson's brooding performance and the casting of Faithfull (better known at the time as a popular singer).

Hamlet, dir. Rodney Bennett, perf. Derek Jacobi, Patrick Stewart, Claire Bloom, Lalla Ward (BBC Television, UK, 1980)

Part of the BBC series of the entire Shakespeare canon, this film suffers from some of the aesthetic and economic constraints of the series (for example, mostly 'talking heads' in a studio-based set). Jacobi had come to the role after a long stint in a theatrical production (directed by Toby Robertson at the Old Vic) and his performance can seem 'stagey', but Stewart and Bloom are impressive.

Hamlet, dir. Franco Zeffirelli, perf. Mel Gibson, Alan Bates, Glenn Close, Helena Bonham-Carter (Warner Brothers, UK, 1990)

Gibson is perhaps surprisingly effective in an energetic interpretation of the central role. As in Olivier's film, the politics disappear and the relationship between Hamlet and Gertrude is sexualized (Gibson was thirty-four to Close's forty-three). The American stars are supported by some strong British actors, including Paul Scofield as the Ghost and Ian Holm as Polonius, but the overall effect, including a cut and rearranged text, is somewhat muted.

Hamlet, dir. Kenneth Branagh, perf. Kenneth Branagh, Derek Jacobi, Julie Christie, Kate Winslet (Castle Rock, UK, 1996)

Boasting a very full text and star performers in even minor roles (Judi Dench as Hecuba, Gerard Depardieu as Reynaldo, Ken Dodd as Yorick), this film updates *Hamlet* to the late nineteenth century and makes lavish use of Blenheim Palace as a setting. It received somewhat mixed reviews though the central performances are strong. The screenplay is available (London: Chatto and Windus, 1996).

Hamlet, dir. Michael Almereyda, perf. Ethan Hawke, Kyle MacLachlan, Diane Venora, Julia Stiles (Miramax, US, 2000)

Almereyda updates the play to a modern New York City

where the CEO of the Denmark Corporation has died. There are some ingenious moments: the Ghost is first seen on film shot by a security camera, Hamlet recites 'To be or not to be' in the 'action movies' aisle of a video store and he alters Claudius's message on Rosencrantz's laptop. Stiles is impressive and moving as Ophelia.

Hamlet, dir. Gregory Doran, perf. David Tennant, Patrick Stewart, Penny Downie, Mariah Gale (BBC, UK, 2008/9)

This television film is based closely on the Royal Shakespeare Company's stage production starring Tennant as a loose cannon, 'angry young man' Hamlet in a modern dress production. Strong supporting performances, especially from Penny Downie whose Gertrude was much admired by critics of the stage presentation, but who is less visible in the filmed version.

Adaptation and appropriation

Hamlet has probably been adapted and appropriated more than any other of Shakespeare's plays. It has inspired numerous prequels and sequels, it is quoted endlessly and it sometimes seems that every line in the play has been used as the title for another work. Stage adaptations since 1965 would include those by Charles Marowitz (*Hamlet Collage* (1965), *The Marowitz Hamlet* and *Ham-omlet* (both 1972)), as well as Heiner Muller's *Hamletmachine* (1979) and Peter Brook's *Qui est la?* (1996).

Atwood, Margaret, 'Gertrude talks back', in *Good Bones* (London: Virago, 1992)

Atwood's brisk four-page rewriting of the play's closet scene as a monologue from Gertrude's point of view provides brief back-stories for some of the leading characters and some surprising answers to questions that have troubled many critics.

Kurosawa, Akira, *The Bad Sleep Well* (Japan Kurosawa productions, 1960).

This is very different from Kurosawa's other Shakespeare films, *Throne of Blood* a.k.a. *Cobweb Castle* (based on *Macbeth*, 1957) and *Ran* (based on *King Lear*, 1985), both of which adapt Shakespeare's plays to Japanese historical settings. It is a very dark version set in the corrupt corporate world of post-World War Two Tokyo. The film can work quite independently of the play, but the parallels with *Hamlet* are extensive, including revenge for a murdered father, a 'ghost', poison and drugs. Toshiro Mifune stars as the Hamlet-figure.

Lavender, Andy, *'Hamlet' in Pieces: Shakespeare Reworked by Peter Brook, Robert Lepage, Robert Wilson* (London: Nick Hern Books, 2001).

As his title indicates, Lavender analyses the radical reworkings of *Hamlet* by Brook in *Qui est là?*, and the one-man shows by Lepage and Wilson. He includes extensive interview material from those who participated in all three productions, as well as sixteen pages of photographs. There is also a final chapter on Brook's (relatively) straight 2000 production in Paris which toured to London and New York in 2001, and an Appendix which gives the '48 French scenes' into which this version was divided.

Stoppard, Tom, *Rosencrantz and Guildenstern are Dead* (London: Faber, 1967)

In Stoppard's stage comedy (a big hit at the Edinburgh Fringe Festival in 1966) the two minor characters wander in and out of the play, not understanding what is going on. Stoppard later directed a film version (1990).

Thompson, Ann, '*Hamlet*: Looking Before and After; Why so Many Prequels and Sequels?' in *Reinventing the Renaissance: Shakespeare and his Contemporaries in Adaptation and Performance*, ed. Sarah Annes Brown, Robert I. Lublin and Lynsey McCulloch (Basingstoke: Palgrave Macmillan, 2013), 17–31

This essay discusses a range of re-imaginings of the *Hamlet* material from Q1 (if that can be seen as an adaptation) to 2000, and asks why the play is 'an itch we simply cannot stop scratching'. Lesser-known dramatic works included are Denton Jacques Snider's two-part sequel, *The Redemption of the Hamlets* (1923), St John Hankin's sequel, *The New Wing at Elsinore* (1925) and Percy MacKaye's four-part prequel, *The Mystery of Hamlet* (1950). The essay also considers prose fiction prequels by Mary Cowden Clarke and John Updike, and radio talks by Michael Innes.

Updike, John, *Gertrude and Claudius* (New York: Alfred A. Knopf, 2000)

The publishers claim on the dustjacket to Updike's novel that 'gaps and inconsistencies in the immortal play are … filled and explained by this prequel'. The pre-play relationships between Gertrude, her husband and her husband's brother are explored as well as Hamlet's youth and adolescence.

Books

Davies, Michael, *Character Studies: Hamlet* (London: Continuum, 2008)

This series offers a much-needed link between pre-degree level and undergraduate study. It builds on the focus on character (often seen as naïve or old-fashioned) to lead student readers to more diverse and sophisticated approaches. This is a considerable challenge in the case of *Hamlet*, but Davies offers a thoughtful and interesting close reading of the play.

Dawson, Anthony B., *Shakespeare in Performance: Hamlet* (Manchester: Manchester University Press, 1995)

Like others in its series, this book offers a chronological history of *Hamlet* on stage from the earliest performances up to 1992. There are also two chapters on film and television versions and an Appendix on translations which looks at some versions of *Hamlet* staged in Germany and in the Soviet Union.

De Grazia, Margreta, *'Hamlet' without Hamlet* (Cambridge: Cambridge University Press, 2007)

This book sets out to de-modernize *Hamlet* by resisting the post-Romantic emphasis on his interiority and to emphasize instead the extent to which the play is as much a history as it is a tragedy. The key motive of his behaviour becomes his dispossession of his inheritance by his uncle and his mother and the play is seen to revolve around man's relationship to the land and his affinity to dust.

Foakes, R. A., *Hamlet versus Lear: Cultural Politics and Shakespeare's Art* (Cambridge: Cambridge University Press, 1993)

Foakes traces how and why *Hamlet*, previously seen as Shakespeare's greatest tragedy, was apparently displaced by *King Lear* in the 1960s, at least in the Anglophone tradition. He analyses the reception of both plays since about 1800 and engages with the politics of the plays and the politics of literary criticism, especially the 'critical theory' of the 1980s.

Greenblatt, Stephen, *Hamlet in Purgatory* (Princeton, NJ: Princeton University Press, 2001)

The ghost of Hamlet's father clearly comes from Purgatory, but Protestants in Shakespeare's time had rejected the whole idea of Purgatory and the lucrative practices associated with it. Greenblatt explores a number of other stories of ghosts apparently returning from the dead, before embarking on a reading of *Hamlet* with a focus on memory as well as mourning.

Howard, Tony, *Women as Hamlet: Performance and Interpretation in Theatre, Film and Fiction* (Cambridge: Cambridge University Press, 2007)

Howard offers a richly detailed study of the numerous women (over 200) who have played the part of Hamlet on the professional stage and on screen from the eighteenth century to the present day. Most are from the Anglophone tradition but several are from the Soviet Union, Germany, Poland, Spain and Turkey. There are twenty illustrations and there is also a chapter on female Hamlets in prose fiction.

Kliman, Bernice W., *'Hamlet': Film, Television, and Radio Performance* (London and Toronto: Associated University Presses, 1988)

This book is in three parts: '*Hamlet* on Stage, Page and Screen', 'Setting in Television Productions', 'Silent Films and Sound Recordings'. The performances discussed are mainly in the Anglo-American tradition, but Kliman includes Kozintsev's Russian film, a Swedish television version (1984) and some European silent films.

Kozintsev, Grigori, *Shakespeare: Time and Conscience* (translated by Joyce Vining; London: Dobson Books, 1967)

The director of the 1964 film (see under 'Cinematic Resources' above) writes about his visits to London and Stratford-upon-Avon and the challenges of staging Shakespeare's plays (not just *Hamlet* but *King Lear* and the *Henry IV* plays), as well as providing a 65-page Appendix called 'Ten Years with *Hamlet*' which consists of notes from his diary during the genesis and production of the film.

Lee, John, *Shakespeare's 'Hamlet' and the Controversies of Self* (Oxford: Oxford University Press, 2000)

This book takes on the issue of Hamlet's sense of self ('that within') and the ways it has been discussed, for example by the New Historicist and Cultural Materialist critics of the 1980s and 1990s. Lee goes further back in the critical tradition to examine ideas about interiority from Montaigne to Hazlitt, as well as considering the relevance of modern theories from cognitive psychology and moral philosophy. He argues further that Shakespeare takes a different approach to Hamlet's subjectivity in the Folio from his approach in the Second Quarto.

Lesser, Zachary, *'Hamlet' After Q1: An Uncanny History of the Shakespearean Text* (Philadelphia, PA: Pennsylvania University Press, 2015)

Moving between the historical moment of the original publication of the First Quarto in 1603 and the moment of its rediscovery in 1823, Lesser discusses in detail the widespread effect of that rediscovery, not only on subsequent theories about the variant texts of *Hamlet* but on mainstream interpretations of the play by both literary critics and theatre directors.

Maher, Mary Z., *Modern Hamlets and Their Soliloquies*, expanded second edition (Iowa City: University of Iowa Press, 2003)

Using extensive interview material (where available) as well as written accounts and reviews, Maher examines how actors from John Gielgud to Simon Russell Beale performed Hamlet's soliloquies. The other actors are Alec Guinness, Laurence Olivier, Richard Burton, David Warner, Ben Kingsley, Derek Jacobi, Anton Lesser, David Rintoul, Randall Duk Kim, Kevin Kline and Kenneth Branagh.

Rosenberg, Marvin, *The Masks of 'Hamlet'* (Newark, DE: University of Delaware Press, 1992)

This book provides a detailed, scene-by-scene account of how *Hamlet* has been staged and performed from the earliest records to c. 1990. It also has chapters on each of the major characters. The focus is mainly on the Anglo-American tradition but some European productions are included, as well as several films.

Scofield, Martin, *The Ghosts of 'Hamlet': The Play and Modern Writers* (Cambridge: Cambridge University Press, 1980)

Scofield discusses how modern writers have responded to *Hamlet* and how they have drawn on it in their own work. Writers include Paul Claudel, T. S. Eliot, James Joyce, Franz Kafka, Søren Kierkegaard, Jules Laforgue, D. H. Lawrence, Stéphane Mallarmé and Paul Valéry.

Welsh, Alexander, *Hamlet in his Modern Guises* (Princeton, NJ and Oxford: Princeton University Press, 2001)

Welsh concentrates mainly on Hamlet's presence as a character in, and the more general influence of the play on, the nineteenth-century novel. He discusses works by Charles Dickens, Johann Wolfgang von Goethe, James Joyce, Herman Melville and Walter Scott.

Young, Alan, *'Hamlet' and the Visual Arts, 1709–1900* (Newark, DE and London: University of Delaware Press), 2002

Young analyses and illustrates how a selection from more than 2000 visual images of *Hamlet* 'both reflect the critical reception of the play and simultaneously possess a significant role in the ever-changing constructed cultural phenomenon that we refer to as Shakespeare'. His database of illustrations is now part of the Shakespeare Electronic Archive at the

Massachusetts Institute of technology (MIT) and is available to scholars at the Folger Shakespeare Library in Washington, DC and at the Shakespeare Institute in Stratford-upon-Avon.

Essay collections (listed alphabetically by editor)

Stage Directions in 'Hamlet'; New Essays and New Directions, ed. Hardin L. Aasand (Cranbury, NJ and London: Associated University Presses, 2003)

The fifteen essays in this collection use the stage directions in the three early texts of *Hamlet* to explore Early Modern theatrical practice. They also focus on how these directions have been interpreted (or ignored) by later editors, directors and actors on stage and screen.

New Essays on 'Hamlet', eds Mark Thornton Burnett and John Manning (New York: AMS Press, 1994)

This is the first volume of the publisher's ambitious 'Hamlet Collection' which also includes *'Hamlet' and Japan*, ed. Yoshiko Uéno (see p. 192). It contains seventeen essays grouped under the headings 'Sources and Symbologies', 'Politics and Performance', 'Psychoanalysis and Language', 'Renaissance Feminisms', 'Histories and Appropriations' and 'Nation and Culture'.

The 'Hamlet' First Published (Q1, 1603): Origins, Forms, Intertextualities, ed. Thomas Clayton (Newark, DE: University of Delaware Press, 1992)

The twelve essays in this collection offer a wide range of approaches to the First Quarto, including its status as a text, its reputation as an 'acting version', its impact on editorial and theatrical treatments of the other texts and its recent stage history.

Critical Essays on Shakespeare's 'Hamlet', ed. David Scott Kastan (New York: G. K. Hall, 1995)

Kastan puts together fourteen essays previously published in books and periodicals over the period from 1966 to 1991, including those by Jacqueline Rose (p. 195) and George T. Wright (p. 197). Topics include text, language, themes such as memory, ceremony, sexuality and revenge.

'Hamlet': New Critical Essays, ed. Arthur F. Kinney (New York and London: Routledge, 2002)

Kinney's lengthy introduction explores the diverse meanings of *Hamlet* from the earliest records we have up to the end of the twentieth century. Ten newly commissioned essays are grouped under the headings 'Tudor-Stuart *Hamlet*', 'Subsequent *Hamlet*s' and '*Hamlet* after Theory'.

'Hamlet' on Screen, Holger Klein and Dimiter Daphinoff, eds (New York: Edwin Mellen Press, 1997)

This collection was published as Volume 8 in the 'Shakespeare Yearbook' series. Its twenty-five essays offer wide-ranging and international perspectives on films and cinematic adaptations of *Hamlet* from 1913 (Johnston Forbes-Robertson) to 1996 (Kenneth Branagh).

The Afterlife of Ophelia, Kaara L. Peterson and Deanne Williams, eds (New York: Palgrave Macmillan, 2012)

This book offers a diverse collection of essays on the different ways in which Ophelia has been and is currently being represented in painting, film, social media, fiction and photography, as well as in the theatre. As the editors argue in their introduction, Ophelia continues to be 'a screen on which a culture projects its preoccupations and reflects its values back on itself'.

'Hamlet' and Japan, ed. Yoshiko Uéno (New York: AMS Press, 1995)

Like the collection edited by Burnett and Manning (see p. 190), this is part of the publisher's 'Hamlet Collection'. Toshio Kawatake maintained in his book, *Nihon no Hamuretto* (*Hamlet in Japan*) in 1972 that 'the history of importing *Hamlet* is nothing but an epitome of the modernization of Japan'. The sixteen essays included here comprise seven on thematic approaches, five on Gertrude and Ophelia, and four on Japanese adaptations, translations and productions. There is also a chronological overview of the reception of *Hamlet* in Japan from 1810 to 1992.

Shakespeare Survey 45: *'Hamlet' and its Afterlife,* ed. Stanley Wells (Cambridge: Cambridge University Press, 1993)

This issue of the periodical *Shakespeare Survey* contains seven essays on *Hamlet* including a useful retrospective essay on 'The Reception of *Hamlet*' by R. A. Foakes, an essay on 'Historical Criticism' by Paul N. Siegel, and two essays on *Hamlet* films.

Essays, chapters and articles

Adelman, Janet, 'Man and Wife is one Flesh: *Hamlet* and the Confrontation with the Maternal Body', in *Suffocating Mothers: Fantasies of Maternal Origin in Shakespeare's Plays, 'Hamlet' to 'The Tempest'* (New York and London: Routledge, 1992), 11–37

Starting from the observation that in *Hamlet* the figure of the mother returns to Shakespeare's dramatic world after a period of absence in the histories and romantic comedies, this is a psychoanalytical study exploring familial and sexual relation-ships in the play and the release of infantile fantasies and desires involving maternal malevolence and the submerged anxiety of the male regarding subjection to the female.

Aebischer, Pascale, '"Not Dead? Not Yet Quite Dead?"': *Hamlet*'s Unruly Corpses', in *Shakespeare's Violated Bodies: Stage and Screen Performance* (Cambridge: Cambridge University Press, 2004), 64–101

Aebischer discusses the importance of corpses, ghosts and revenants in the tragedy and how these not-quite-dead bodies are represented on stage and screen. Specific focus is on Old Hamlet's Ghost, the skull of Yorick, and the corpses of Polonius and Ophelia.

Catherine Belsey, 'Sibling Rivalry: *Hamlet* and the First Murder', in *Shakespeare and the Loss of Eden* (Basingstoke: Macmillan, 1999), 129–74

Belsey explores the representation of the family, not just in Shakespeare's plays but in early modern accounts of the stories of Adam and Eve, Cain and Abel, and in visual imagery of the period in furniture, tapestries and sculpture. She reads *Hamlet* as a kind of Dance of Death and shows how family values have always had negative effects as well as positive ones.

Garber, Marjorie, '*Hamlet*; Giving up the Ghost', in *Shakespeare's Ghost Writers: Literature as Uncanny Causality* (New York and London: Methuen, 1987), 124–76

Garber draws on Jacques Lacan as well as on Freud in a psychoanalytical reading which puts the focus on the father–son relationship; the Ghost becomes a marker of absence and a reminder of loss. She also analyses the role of *Hamlet* and Shakespeare more generally in the canon of Western literary study.

Gurr, Andrew and Mariko Ichikawa, 'The Early Staging of *Hamlet*', in *Staging in Shakespeare's Theatres* (Oxford; Oxford University Press, 2000), 121–62

The final chapter of this book on the ways in which Shakespeare's plays might have been staged originally in the different theatres of his time offers a scene-by-scene discussion of *Hamlet* as it might first have been staged at the Globe.

Holmes, Jonathan, 'Noble Memories: Playing Hamlet', in *Merely Players? Actors' Accounts of Performing Shakespeare* (New York and London: Routledge, 2004), 95–140

Holmes (a playwright and director as well as an academic) draws on actors' written reflections over the last 300 years, though the chapter on *Hamlet* concentrates mainly on the twentieth century, including John Gielgud, Laurence Olivier, Richard Burton, Derek Jacobi, Michael Pennington, Steven Berkoff, Ben Kingsley and Kenneth Branagh.

Mowat, Barbara, 'The Form of *Hamlet*'s Fortunes', *Renaissance Drama* 19 (1988): 97–125

Mowat traces how the text of *Hamlet* that was familiar to audiences and readers until the 1980s goes back to 1709 when Nicholas Rowe put together a 'conflated' text from the quarto of 1676 and the folio of 1685. She also explains how and why, after a period of textual stability from 1866 to 1980, the text became destabilized in modern editions.

Mullaney, Steven, 'Mourning and Misogyny: *Hamlet, The Revenger's Tragedy*, and the Final Progress of Elizabeth I, 1600–1607', *Shakespeare Quarterly* 45 (1994): 139–62

The problematic centrality of Gertrude in *Hamlet* is related here to a more general misogyny that anticipated the mourning for Queen Elizabeth I, whose death must have been expected at the time of the play's first performance, though it is not clear how easy it would have been for an Elizabethan audience to identify the 'incestuous' Gertrude, played by a boy, with their ageing Virgin Queen.

O'Brien, Ellen J., 'Revision by Excision: Rewriting Gertrude', *Shakespeare Survey* 45 (1993): 27–35

Through an examination of promptbooks used in the theatre in the nineteenth century, O'Brien establishes how the part of Gertrude was consistently rewritten so as to diminish and weaken her role, especially in the second half of the play. Moreover, this distorted representation continued, especially in films, into the twentieth century.

Rose, Jacqueline, 'Sexuality in the Reading of Shakespeare: *Hamlet* and *Measure for Measure*, in *Alternative Shakespeares* ed. John Drakakis (New York and London: Methuen, 1985), 95–118

This essay analyses how influential male readers of *Hamlet*, Ernest Jones (student and eventual biographer of Sigmund Freud) and T. S. Eliot, have echoed its hero's misogyny and blamed Gertrude for what they see as the aesthetic and moral failings of the play overall: femininity itself becomes *Hamlet*'s central problem.

Rutter, Carol Chillington, 'Snatched Bodies: Ophelia in the Grave', in *Enter the Body: Women and Representation on Shakespeare's Stage* (New York and London: Routledge, 2001), 27–56

Rutter analyses four films (Olivier, Kozintsev, Zeffirelli and Branagh; see 'Cinematic Resources' above for details) which all offer what she calls 'a resolutely masculinist *Hamlet*'. She pursues her interest in the 'countertext voiced by Ophelia' through a discussion of her role in each film and in particular the treatment of the graveyard scene and the handling of Ophelia's corpse.

Schiesari, Juliana, 'Mourning the Phallus? (Hamlet, Burton, Lacan and "Others")', in *The Gendering of Melancholia: Feminism, Psychoanalysis and the Symbolics of Loss in*

Renaissance Literature (Ithaca and London: Cornell University Press, 1992), 233–67

The concluding chapter of Schiesari's book reads *Hamlet* and the male tradition of *Hamlet* criticism from the point of view of Gertrude and Ophelia. Her overall argument is to 'displace the androcentric privilege of the psychoanalytic *and* Renaissance view of melancholia as creative lack by reading the disparaged practice of women's mourning as an alternative – and less narcissistic – expression of grief and loss' (xi).

Showalter, Elaine, 'Representing Ophelia: Women, Madness, and the Responsibilities of Feminist Criticism', in *Shakespeare and the Question of Theory*, Patricia Parker and Geoffrey Hartman, eds (New York and London: Methuen, 1985), 77–94

Showalter aims to tell Ophelia's story through the history of her representation in English and French painting, photography, psychiatry and literature. She points out that illustrations of Ophelia 'provide a manual of female insanity' and that 'the representation of Ophelia changes independently of theories of the meaning of the play or the prince, for it depends on attitudes to women and to madness'.

Stern, Tiffany, 'Sermons, Plays and Note-takers: *Hamlet* as a "Noted" Text', *Shakespeare Survey* 66 (2013): 1–23

This essay reviews the 'reported text' theory about Q1 *Hamlet*, using material taken from accounts of early modern note-taking during sermons and parliamentary speeches. She argues that if Q1 is indeed a 'pirated' text, the piracy was committed by members of the audience, not the actors.

Taylor, Gary, 'The Red Dragon in Sierra Leone' and '*Hamlet* in Africa 1607', in *Travel Knowledge: European 'Discoveries' in the Early Modern Period*, Ivo Kamps and Jyotsna Singh, eds (Basingstoke: Macmillan, 2001), 211–22, 223–48

The first performance of *Hamlet* of which we have a written record seems to have taken place on a ship, the *Red Dragon*, anchored off the coast of Africa in 1607, on its way to the East Indies. Taylor examines arguments about the authenticity of these records and the likelihood that English seafarers took books (including play-books) with them on their travels and might have put on plays for their own recreation and to entertain visitors from other cultures.

Wright, George T., 'Hendiadys and *Hamlet*', *PMLA* 96 (1981): 168–93

In an impressively detailed study of the play's language, Wright argues that hendiadys is a dominant figure or trope in *Hamlet* and that the basic pattern of doubling involved ('the gross and scope of my opinion', 'the dead vast and middle of the night', 'the perfume and suppliance of a minute') relates to larger patterns of doubling, division and mirroring in the play.

NOTES

Introduction

1   For further discussion of this issue, see R. A. Foakes, *Hamlet versus Lear* (Cambridge: Cambridge University Press, 1993).

2   The copy found in Suffolk, England, in 1823 lacked the last leaf; a second copy found in Dublin in 1856 lacked the title page. No other copies have yet been found.

3   For an extensive discussion of the discovery of the First Quarto and its impact on what we mean by *Hamlet*, see Zachary Lesser, '*Hamlet' After Q1* (Philadelphia: University of Pennsylvania Press, 2015).

4   See the Introduction to *Hamlet: The Texts of 1603 and 1623* in the Arden Shakespeare series, A. Thompson and N. Taylor, eds (London: Thomson Learning, 2006), 12–39.

5   Twenty-first-century productions in the UK include Trevor Nunn directing Ben Whishaw at the Old Vic and Michael Boyd directing Toby Stephens for the Royal Shakespeare Company, both in 2004, and Gregory Doran directing David Tennant for the Royal Shakespeare Company in 2008. In 2015, Lyndsey Turner, directing Benedict Cumberbatch at the Barbican, went further in performances early in the run by having the speech delivered at the very beginning of the play (and not repeated later).

6   For a full discussion of the development of the text(s) from 1709 to the late 1980s, see Barbara Mowat, 'The Form of *Hamlet*'s Fortunes', *Renaissance Drama* XIX (1988): 97–125.

7   George MacDonald, ed., *The Tragedie of Hamlet, Prince of Denmarke: A Study with the Text of the Folio of 1623* (London: Longmans, Green and Co., 1885), xi–xii.

8   Halliwell-Phillipps had written to thank MacDonald for

sending him a copy of the edition. MacDonald's reply is in the Folger Shakepeare Library (call no. W.b.83:61).

9   For a fuller account of MacDonald's edition, see Ann Thompson, 'George MacDonald's 1885 Folio-based Edition of *Hamlet*', *Shakespeare Quarterly* 51 (2000): 201–5.

10   See Ann Thompson, 'Teena Rochfort Smith, Frederick Furnivall, and the New Shakspere Society's Four-Text Edition of *Hamlet*', *Shakespeare Quarterly* 49 (1998): 125–39.

11   'Gamlet' is 'Hamlet' in Russian.

Chapter 1

1   For surveys of *Hamlet* criticism see Hunter 1959; Spencer 1963; Jenkins 1965; Weitz 1965; Conklin 1968; Vickers 1974–81; Watts 1988; Daniell 1990; Kerrigan 1994; Bevington 2011. For collections of mainly pre-twentieth century criticism and allusions see Munro 1932; Halliday 1949; Williamson 1950; Nichol Smith 1963; Vickers 1974–81; Farley-Hills 1997. For bibliographies of *Hamlet* criticism see Raven 1936; Robinson 1984; Dietrich 1992. Those wanting a history of the reception of the play should start with Scofield 1980 and see Lawrence 1916 for a particularly brilliant example. For a history of the importance of *Hamlet* within Russian literature see Rowe 1976.

2   Farren 1829 (an actuary); Halford 1833 [1829]; Bucknill (1860); *Shakespeare's Medical Knowledge* 1860; Kellogg 1866. For critical commentary on these and others see Bynum and Never 1986; Small 1996; Reiss 2005.

Chapter 2

1   From the anonymous 'Funeral Elegy on the Death of the famous Actor Richard Burbage who died on Saturday in Lent the 13th of March 1618' [1619], originally in an MS commonplace book, in G. Wickham, H. Berry and W. Ingram,

eds, *English Professional Theatre, 1530–1660* (Cambridge: Cambridge University Press, 2000), 182.

2   Marvin Rosenberg, *The Masks of Hamlet* (Newark: University of Delaware Press and London: AUP, 1992), xv, 823.

3   Michael Pennington, 'Hamlet', in *Players of Shakespeare* 1, ed. P. Brockbank (Cambridge: Cambridge University Press, 1985), 117.

4   This was Henry Irving's son, H. B. Irving, as described in Hesketh Pearson, *The Last Actor-Managers* (London: Methuen & Co. Ltd, 1950), 58.

5   Vanessa Cunningham, *Shakespeare and Garrick* (Cambridge: Cambridge University Press, 2008), 153. Cunningham notes also that Garrick apparently tried to get the comedian Woodward to play Polonius more seriously, but that the result was not appreciated.

6   See Cunningham, 147 and 155. This section is very much indebted to her analysis of the hard-to-interpret evidence about Garrick's *Hamlet* alterations (139–58).

7   Arthur Colby Sprague, *Shakespeare and the Actors: The Stage Business in His Plays (1660–1905)* (Cambridge, MA: Harvard University Press, 1944), 175–6.

8   William Shakespeare, *Hamlet*, New Variorum, ed. H. H. Furness (Philadelphia: J. B. Lippincott Company, 1877), I: xiv.

9   George Bernard Shaw, 'Hamlet', from *Our Theatres in the Nineties,* 3 vols, vol. 3 (London: Constable and Co. Ltd, 1932), 200. (Originally published in *The Saturday Review*, 2 October 1897.)

10 Fynes Morison, *Itinerary,* quoted in Ernest Brennecke, *Shakespeare in Germany 1590–1700, with translations of Five Early Plays* (Chicago: University of Chicago Press, 1964), 6.

11 See Brennecke, 291–2.

12 See Tiffany Stern, '"If I could see the Puppets Dallying": *Der Bestrafte Brudermord* and Hamlet's Encounters with the Puppets', *Shakespeare Bulletin* 31 (3) (Fall 2013): 337–52. A puppet version of the play, translated by Christine Schmidle and directed by Beth Burns, was performed by Hidden Room

Theatre at the Blackfriars, Staunton, Virginia, in 2013, and at the Wanamaker, London, in 2015.

13 Zdeněk Stříbrný, *Shakespeare in Eastern Europe* (Oxford: Oxford University Press, 2000), 19.

14 Christine Roger and Roger Paulin, 'August Wilhelm Schlegel', in *Great Shakespeareans,* vol. 3, ed. R. Paulin (London: Bloomsbury, 2010), 93–4.

15 Michèle Willems, 'The Mouse and the Urn: Versions of Shakespeare from Voltaire to Ducis', in *Shakespeare Survey* 60 (2007): 218.

16 Michèle Willems, 'Voltaire', in *Great Shakespeareans,* vol. 3, 30.

17 José Roberto O'Shea, 'Early Shakespearean Stars Performing on Brazilian Skies: João Caetano and National Theater', in *Latin American Shakespeares,* B. Kliman and R. J. Santos, eds (Madison: Fairleigh Dickinson Press, 2005), 29–30.

18 By 1886, Meurice had restored the tragic ending, which is also used in some versions of the opera. See Gerda Taranow, *The Bernhardt Hamlet: Culture and Context* (New York: Peter Lang, 1996), 5. Margaret Litvin was the first to identify this as the source of the 1902 musical version of *Hamlet,* successfully performed in Cairo for many years. See *Hamlet's Arab Journey: Shakespeare's Prince and Nasser's Ghost* (Princeton: Princeton University Press, 2011), 64–5. Early Turkish versions of the play were also based on French sources. See Talât S. Halman, 'Shakespeare Art in the Turkish Heart: The Bard in the Ottoman Empire and the Turkish Republic', in *Shakespeare 450,* ed. A. Deniz Bozer (Ankara: Hacettepe University, 2014), 11–27.

19 Henry Morley, *The Journal of a London Playgoer, with an Introduction by Michael Booth* (Leicester: Leicester University Press, 1974), 41–2.

20 Theodor Fontane, *Shakespeare in the London Theatre 1855–58,* trans. with an intro. and notes by R. Jackson (London: Society for Theatre Research, 1999), 61.

21 *Hamlet,* New Variorum, I: x.

22 Rodney Symington, *The Nazi Appropriation of Shakespeare:*

Cultural Politics in the Third Reich (Lewiston, NY: Edwin Mellen Press, 2005), 8.

23 Symington, 52. The same exception was made for Bernard Shaw, because Ireland was not considered an enemy country.

24 Nicole Fayard, *The Performance of Shakespeare in France Since the Second World War: Re-Imagining Shakespeare* (Lewiston, NY: Edwin Mellen Press, 2006), 279.

25 Keith Gregor, *Shakespeare in the Spanish Theatre: 1772 to the Present* (London: Continuum, 2010), 116–19.

26 See, e.g., Taranow, xvii; Keith Gregor, *Shakespeare in the Spanish Theatre* (London: Continuum, 2010), 73; Alexa C. Y. Huang, *Chinese Shakespeares: Two Centuries of Cultural Exchange* (New York: Columbia University Press, 2009), 88. Huang compares attacks on Chinese 'Hamletism' in the 1930s to those on German passivity in the early nineteenth century.

27 Martin Banham, Rashni Mooneeram and Jane Plastow, 'Shakespeare in Africa', in *The Cambridge Companion to Shakespeare on Stage*, S. Wells and S. Stanton, eds (Cambridge: Cambridge University Press, 2002), 298.

28 Poonam Trivedi, 'Introduction' to *India's Shakespeare: Translation, Interpretation, and Performance* (Newark: University of Delaware Press, 2005), 17.

29 Poonam Trivedi, '"Folk Shakespeare": The Performance of Shakespeare in Traditional Indian Theater Forms', in *India's Shakespeare*, 172–89.

30 Huang, 71–2.

31 Huang, 50.

32 Huang, 131.

33 James R. Brandon, 'Shakespeare in Kabuki', in *Performing Shakespeare in Japan*, M. Ryuta, I. Carruthers and J. Gillies, eds (Cambridge: Cambridge University Press, 2001), 43–4.

34 Kim Moran, 'The Stages "Occupied by Shakespeare": Intercultural Performances and the Search for "Korean-ness" in Postcolonial Korea', in P. Trivedi and M. Ryuta, eds, *Re-playing Shakespeare in Asia* (New York: Routledge, 2010), 202.

35 Poonam Trivedi, 'Introduction' to *India's Shakespeare*, 13.

36 Alexander Shurbanov and Boika Sokolova, *Painting Shakespeare Red: an East-European Appropriation* (Newark: University of Delaware Press, 2001), 16–18.

37 Kazuoko Matsuoka, 'Metamorphosis of *Hamlet* in Tokyo', in Y. Uéno, ed., '*Hamlet*' *and Japan* (New York: AMS Press, 1995), 232.

38 Litvin, 2.

39 See Shurbanov and Sokolova, 199; Stříbrný, *Eastern Europe*, 134 (plus personal experience); Symington, 20.

40 Marcel Reich-Ranicki, cited in Symington, 193–4.

41 Shurbanov and Sokolova, 204.

42 Lawrence Guntner, 'Brecht and Beyond: Shakespeare on the East German Stage', in D. Kennedy, ed., *Foreign Shakespeare: Contemporary Performance* (Cambridge: Cambridge University Press, 1993), 116–17.

43 Kate Flaherty, *Ours as We Play It: Australia Plays Shakespeare* (Crawley, Western Australia: UWA Publishing, 2011), 54.

44 Dennis Kennedy, 'Introduction' to Kennedy, ed., *Foreign Shakespeare*, 5.

45 Shaw, 204.

46 Michèle Willems, 'Voltaire', 37.

47 Barbara Hodgdon, 'The Visual Record: The Case of *Hamlet*', in D. Wiles and C. Dymkowski, eds, *The Cambridge Companion to Theatre History* (Cambridge: Cambridge University Press, 2013), 246–66.

48 John Gielgud, 'The Hamlet Tradition'. In J. Gielgud, with J. Miller, *Acting Shakespeare* (London: Pan Books, 1991, 1997), 137. First published in Rosamund Gilder, *John Gielgud as Hamlet* (London: Methuen, 1937).

49 Sprague, 169.

50 Samuel West, 'Hamlet', in M. Dobson, ed., *Performing Shakespeare's Tragedies Today: the Actor's Perspective* (Cambridge: Cambridge University Press, 2006), 42.

51 Alden T. Vaughan and Virginia Mason Vaughan, *Shakespeare in America* (Oxford: Oxford University Press, 2012), 29.

52 See Cunningham, 151, and Taranow, xviii–xix.

53 Hyon-u Lee, 'Dialectical Progress of Femininity in Korean Shakespeare since 1990', in *Shakespeare's World/World Shakespeares*, R. Fotheringham, C. Jansohn and R. S. White, eds (Newark: University of Delaware Press, 2008), 273–5.

54 Sprague, 155.

55 Jeremy Sims co-directed and played Hamlet in this Pork Chop Production; see Flaherty, 36–41.

56 Tony Church, 'Polonius', in *Players of Shakespeare* 1, 112.

57 Frances Barber, 'Ophelia in *Hamlet*', in *Players of Shakespeare 2: Further Essays in Shakespearean Performance,* R. Jackson and R. Smallwood, eds (Cambridge: Cambridge University Press, 1988), 139.

58 Ellen Terry, *The Story of My Life* (New York, 1909), 170–1, quoted in Anthony Dawson, *Hamlet* (Manchester: Manchester University Press, 1995), 63–4.

59 *Hamlet*, ed. A. Thompson and N. Taylor, 335.

60 Sprague, 166.

61 Imogen Stubbs, 'Gertrude', in M. Dobson, ed., *Performing Shakespeare's Tragedies*, 39.

62 Westland Marston, *Our Recent Actors*, 2 vols (1877: repr. Cambridge: Cambridge University Press, 2012), 2, 77.

63 Tony Howard, *Women as Hamlet: Performance and Interpretation in Theatre, Film and Fiction* (Cambridge: Cambridge University Press, 2007), 51.

64 Westland Marston, 1: 83.

65 Litvin, 73.

66 Howard, 119.

67 Howard, 122–3.

68 Howard, 207; Gregor, 96.

69 Howard, 201.

70 Howard, 200.

71 Steven Berkoff, *I am Hamlet* (London: Faber and Faber, 1989), 200.

72   Stříbrný, 'Recent Hamlets', 199.

73   *Laertes.* Ah! ... vous m'offrez, je croi [*sic*],
     Votre fleuret?

     Hamlet. (*avec un sourire courtois et railleur*) Sans doute, eh
     bien?

     Hamlet, Prince de Danemark, trans. P. Meurice and A. Dumas
     (Paris: Pagnerre, 1847, 1854), Part 10, scene 3, p. 139.

74   Jonathan Croall, *Hamlet Observed: The National Theatre at
     Work* (London: NT Publications, 2001), 12.

75   Dawson, *Hamlet,* 238.

76   Stříbrný, *Eastern Europe,* 134.

77   Stříbrný, *Eastern Europe,* 133, 100; Stříbrný, 'Recent Hamlets
     in Prague, and a Postscript', in Zdeněk Stříbrný, *The Whirligig
     of Time: Essays on Shakespeare and Czechoslovakia,* ed. L.
     Potter (Newark: University of Delaware Press, 2007), 196–8.
     This review was originally published in *Shakespeare Quarterly*
     35 (1984): 208–14; in *The Whirligig of Time,* Stříbrný adds a
     postscript (201–2) explaining the political warning given to the
     company at the Smetana theatre.

78   Brian Powell, 'One Man's *Hamlet* in 1911 Japan: The Bungei-
     Kyokai Production in the Imperial Theatre', in Takashi
     Sasayama, J. R. Mulryne and Margaret Shewring, eds,
     Shakespeare and the Japanese Stage (Cambridge: Cambridge
     University Press, 2010), 40.

79   Minami Ryuta '"What, has this thing appear'd again
     tonight?": Re-playing Shakespeare on the Japanese Stage', in P.
     Trivedi and M. Ryuta, eds, *Re-Playing Shakespeare,* 91.

80   Helena Buffery, *Shakespeare in Catalan: Translating
     Imperialism* (Cardiff: University of Wales Press, 2007), 121–2.

81   See Stříbrný, 'Recent Hamlets', 200.

82   Matsuoka, 'Metamorphosis of *Hamlet*', 228.

83   Croall, 14.

84   William Shakespeare, *Hamlet: Screenplay and Introduction
     by Kenneth Branagh* (New York: W. W. Norton & Co. Ltd,
     1996), xiv.

85   Rosenberg, 8.

86 For this last point, see Graham Holderness, '"I covet your skull": Death and Desire in *Hamlet*', in *Shakespeare Survey 60: Theatres for Shakespeare*, ed. P. Holland (Cambridge: Cambridge University Press, 2007), 223–36: esp. 229–30.

87 See Spencer Golub's moving account, 'Between the Curtain and the Grave: The Taganka in the *Hamlet* Gulag', in D. Kennedy, ed., *Foreign Shakespeare*.

88 Samuel West, 44.

89 Lois Potter, 'This Distracted Globe: Summer 2000', *Shakespeare Quarterly* 41 (Spring, 2001): 124–32: 128–9.

90 Tim Carroll, 'Practising Behaviour to His Own Shadow', in *Shakespeare's Globe: a Theatrical Experiment*, C. Carson and F. Karim-Cooper, eds (Cambridge: Cambridge University Press, 2008), 40; Samuel West, 51.

91 Robert Stephens, *Knight Errant; Memoirs of a Vagabond Actor* (London: Hodder & Stoughton Ltd, 1995), 180.

92 Croall, 79.

93 'Interview with Suzuki Tadashi' (6 April 1995), with Takahashi Yasunari, Anzai Tetsuo, Matsuoka Kazuko, Ted Motohashi and James Brandon', in M. Ryuta et al, eds, *Performing Shakespeare in Japan*, 200; Litvin, 144.

94 Adrian Kiernander, 'John Bell and a Post-colonial Australian Shakespeare, 1963–2000', in J. Golder and R. Madelaine, eds, *O Brave New World: Two Centuries of Shakespeare on the Australian Stage* (Sydney: Currency Press, 2001), 240.

95 Ruru Li, 'Six People in Search of "To be or not to be": Hamlet's Soliloquy in six Chinese Productions and the Metamorphosis of Shakespeare Performance on the Chinese Stage', in P. Trivedi and M. Ryuta, eds, *Re-playing Shakespeare in Asia*, 127–9.

96 Huang, 248.

97 Andy Lavender, *Hamlet in Pieces: Shakespeare Reworked by Peter Brook, Robert Lepage, Robert Wilson* (London: Nick Hern Books, 2001), 189, 218.

Chapter 4

1   Acting editions of *Hamlet* 1676, 1703, 1718, 1751 and 1773
    are reprinted in facsimile (London: Cornmarket, 1969). For
    his acting editions of 1763 and 1772, see Garrick 1981a and
    1981b.

2   This can be viewed online: https://www.youtube.com/
    watch?v=Mp_v_dP8s-8 [accessed 2 April 2015].

3   The comment sits oddly with the swashbuckling final scene,
    where Hamlet sweeps from a height of fifteen feet, as if on
    wings, to his revenge (cf. 1.5.29–31).

4   And, somewhat to my regret, in the 2104 Manchester
    production I began with.

5   The exception was David Garrick's altered version of the play
    in 1772 (see Lois Potter in this volume (56–7)).

6   The Folio text of 1623 completes the thought: 'Is't not perfect
    conscience / To quit him with this arm? And is't not to be
    damned / To let this canker of our nature come / In further
    evil?' (5.2.67–70)

7   For a detailed account, see Tony Howard, *Women As Hamlet*
    (2007): 140–57.

8   See Margreta de Grazia, *'Hamlet' Without Hamlet* (2007) for
    a more detailed case for this possibility.

9   Quantitative analysis shows how little space women occupy in
    Hamlet (see Franco Moretti, *Distant Reading* (2013): 215–17).

10 For Ophelia through time, see Elaine Showalter, 'Representing
    Ophelia' (1985) and Kaara L. Peterson and Deanne Williams,
    eds, *The Afterlife of Ophelia* (2012).

Chapter 5

1   Unless otherwise stated, quotations from *Hamlet* are taken
    from the second quarto text of the Arden edition of *Hamlet*,
    A. Thompson and N. Taylor, eds (London: Thomson Learning,
    2006).

2   Yoshio Sugimoto, *An Introduction to Japanese Society*, 2nd edn (Cambridge: Cambridge University Press, 2003), 28.

3   Bert Cardullo, ed., *Akira Kurosawa: Interviews* (Jackson: University of Mississippi Press, 2008), 17.

4   See Joan Copjec, 'Introduction', in J. Copjec, ed., *Shades of Noir: A Reader* (London: Verso, 1993), x.

5   Rachael Hutchinson, 'Orientalism or Occidentalism?: Dynamics of Appropriation in Akira Kurosawa', in S. Dennison and S. H. Lim, eds, *Remapping World Cinema: Identity, Culture and Politics in Film* (London: Wallflower, 2006), 180.

6   Elise K. Tipton, *Japan: A Social and Political History*, 2nd edn (London: Routledge, 2008), 173, 175.

7   Stephen Prince, *The Warrior's Camera: The Cinema of Akira Kurosawa* (Princeton: Princeton University Press, 1999), 184.

8   Michael Almereyda, *William Shakespeare's 'Hamlet': A Screenplay Adaptation* (London: Faber, 2000), 133.

9   Fredric Jameson, *Postmodernism, or, the Cultural Logic of Late Capitalism* (London: Verso, 1991), 44.

10   See *Hamlet*, A. Thompson and N. Taylor, eds, Appendix 1, 466.

11   At the time of writing, the DVD of *The Banquet* is fairly widely available (e.g. through Amazon), while *Prince of the Himalayas* can be obtained through the Namse Bangdzo Bookstore, http://www.namsebangdzo.com [accessed 3 November 2015].

12   Susan Zimmerman, 'Killing the Dead: The Ghost of Hamlet's Desire', *Shakespeare Jahrbuch* 140 (2004): 87.

13   Sheng-mei Ma, *East-West Montage: Reflections on Asian Bodies in Diaspora* (Honolulu: University of Hawaii Press, 2007), 66.

14   Gary G. Xu, *Sinascape: Contemporary Chinese Cinema* (Lanham, MD: Rowman and Littlefield, 2007), 40.

15   Linda Charnes, *Hamlet's Heirs: Shakespeare and the Politics of a New Millennium* (London and New York: Routledge, 2006), 9.

16 Molly Hand, review of *Ye Yan/The Banquet* (dir. Xiaogang Feng), *Shakespeare*, 4.4 (2008), 433.

17 Grigori Kozintsev, *Shakespeare: Time and Conscience*, trans. Joyce Vining (London: Dennis Dobson, 1967), 216.

18 See *Hamlet*, A. Thompson and N. Taylor, eds, 16.1 t.n.

19 John Collick, *Shakespeare, Cinema and Society* (Manchester and New York: Manchester University Press, 1989), 139.

20 Mark Thornton Burnett, Courtney Lehmann, Marguerite H. Rippy and Ramona Wray, eds, *Great Shakespeareans: Welles, Kurosawa, Kozintsev, Zeffirelli* (London and New York: Bloomsbury, 2013), 105.

21 Kozintsev, *Shakespeare*, 35; Collick, *Shakespeare*, 130.

22 Kozintsev, *Shakespeare*, 238.

23 Interview between Mark Thornton Burnett and Varuzh Karim Masihi, 15 October 2014.

24 Margaret Litvin, *Hamlet's Arab Journey: Shakespeare's Prince and Nasser's Ghost* (Princeton: Princeton University Press, 2011), 53–4, 79–83, 129–30.

25 Burnett et al., *Great Shakespeareans*, 134.

26 Fatemeh Sadeghi, 'The Green Movement: A Struggle against Islamist Patriarchy?', in N. Nabavi, ed., *Iran: From Theocracy to the Green Movement* (New York: Palgrave, 2012), 125.

27 David Waines, *An Introduction to Islam*, 2nd edn (Cambridge: Cambridge University Press, 2003), 254.

BIBLIOGRAPHY

Adelman, Janet (1992), *Suffocating Mothers: Fantasies of Maternal Origin in Shakespeare's Plays, 'Hamlet' to 'The Tempest'*. London: Routledge.

Almereyda, Michael (2000), *William Shakespeare's 'Hamlet': A Screenplay Adaptation*. London: Faber.

Althusser, Louis (1971 [1970]), 'Ideology and Ideological State Apparatuses', in B. Brewster, trans., *Lenin and Philosophy and Other Essays*, 121–73. London: NLB.

Atwood, Margaret (2001), 'Gertrude Talks Back', in *Good Bones and Simple Murders*, 16–19. New York: Doubleday.

Banham, Martin, Rashni Mooneeram and Jane Plastow (2002), 'Shakespeare in Africa', in S. Wells and S. Stanton, eds, *The Cambridge Companion to Shakespeare on Stage*. Cambridge: Cambridge University Press.

Barber, Frances (1988), 'Ophelia in *Hamlet*', in R. Jackson and R. Smallwood, eds, *Players of Shakespeare* 2: *Further Essays in Shakespearean Performance*, 137–50. Cambridge: Cambridge University Press.

Barker, Francis (1984), *The Tremulous Private Body: Essays on Subjection*. London: Methuen.

Bartolovitch, Crystal (2012), 'Marx's Shakespeare', in C. Bartolovitch, J. E. Howard and D. Hillman, eds, *Marx and Freud: Great Shakespeareans*, 7–61. London: Continuum.

Bate, Jonathan (1992), *The Romantics on Shakespeare*. Harmondsworth: Penguin.

Bate, Jonathan (2007), 'The Case for the Folio'. Available online: www.rscshakespeare.co.uk

Bate, Jonathan and Eric Rasmussen, eds (2007), *The RSC Shakespeare Complete Works*. London: Macmillan.

Bednarz, James P. (2001), *Shakespeare and the Poets' War*. New York: Columbia University Press.

Belsey, Catharine (1985), *The Subject of Tragedy: Identity and Difference in Renaissance Drama*. London: Methuen.

Berkoff, Steven (1989), *I am Hamlet*. London: Faber and Faber.

Berry, Ralph (2008), '*Hamlet* Then and Now: An Overview', in
F. Occhiogrosso, ed., *Shakespearean Performance: New Studies*,
40–9. Madison, NJ: Fairleigh Dickinson.

Bertram, Paul and Bernice W. Kliman, eds (1991), *The Three-Text
'Hamlet': Parallel Texts of the First and Second Quartos and
First Folio*. New York: AMS Press [2nd edn 2003].

Bevington, David (2011), *Murder Most Foul: 'Hamlet' Through the
Ages*. Oxford: Oxford University Press.

Bloom, Harold (1998), *Shakespeare: The Invention of the Human*.
New York: Riverhead.

Bloom, Harold (2003), *Hamlet: Poem Unlimited*. New York:
Riverhead.

Boas, Frederick S., ed. (1901), *The Works of Thomas Kyd*. Oxford:
Clarendon Press.

Booth, Stephen (1969), 'On the Value of *Hamlet*', in N. Rabkin,
ed., *Reinterpretations of Elizabethan Drama*, 137–76. New
York: Columbia University Press.

Bourus, Terri (2014), *Young Shakespeare's Young Hamlet: Print,
Piracy and Performance*. London: Palgrave Macmillan.

Bradley, A. C. (1904), *Shakespearean Tragedy: Lectures on
'Hamlet', 'Othello', 'King Lear' and 'Macbeth'*. London:
Macmillan.

Bradley, A. C. (1909), 'Hegel's Theory of Tragedy', in *Oxford
Lectures on Poetry*, 69–92. London: Macmillan.

Bradley, A. C. (1929), 'English Poetry and German Philosophy in
the Age of Wordsworth', in *A Miscellany*, 105–38. London:
Macmillan.

Bradshaw, Graham (1987), Shakespeare's Scepticism. Brighton:
Harvester.

Brandon, James R. (2001), 'Shakespeare in Kabuki', in M. Ryuta, I.
Carruthers and J. Gillies, eds, *Performing Shakespeare in Japan*,
33–53. Cambridge: Cambridge University Press.

Brennecke, Ernst (1964), *Shakespeare in Germany 1590–1700, with
Translations of Five Early Plays*. Chicago: University of Chicago
Press.

Brockbank, Philip, ed. (1985), *Players of Shakespeare* 1.
Cambridge: Cambridge University Press.

Bucknill, Sir John Charles (1859), *The Psychology of Shakespeare*.
London: Longman, Brown, Green, Longmans and Roberts.

Bucknill, Sir John Charles (1860), *The Medical Knowledge of Shakespeare*. London: Longman and Company.

Buffery, Helena (2007), *Shakespeare in Catalan: Translating Imperialism*. Cardiff: University of Wales Press.

Burke, Edmund (1757), *A Philosophical Enquiry into the Origin of our Ideas of the Sublime and Beautiful*. London: R. and J. Dodsley.

Burkhardt, Sigurd (1968), *Shakespearean Meanings*. Princeton, NJ: Princeton University Press.

Burnett, Mark Thornton, Courtney Lehmann, Marguerite H. Rippy and Ramona Wray (2013), *Great Shakespeareans: Welles, Kurosawa, Kozintsev, Zeffirelli*. London and New York: Bloomsbury.

Bynum, W. F. and Michael Never (1986), 'Hamlet on the Couch: Hamlet is a Kind of Touchstone by which to Measure Changing Opinion – Psychatric and Otherwise – About Madness', *American Scientist* 74 (4): 3906.

'Byron and Shelley on the Character of Hamlet' (1830), in *The New Monthly Magazine and Literary Journal*. London: Henry Colburn and Richard Bentley.

Calderwood, James L. (1983), *To Be and Not To Be: Negation and Metadrama in 'Hamlet'*. New York: Columbia University Press.

Campbell, Lily Bess (1930), *Shakespeare's Tragic Heroes: Slaves of Passion*. Cambridge: Cambridge University Press.

Cardullo, Bert, ed. (2008), *Akira Kurosawa: Interviews*. Jackson: University of Mississippi Press.

Carroll, Tim (2008), 'Practising Behaviour to His Own Shadow', in C. Carson and F. Karim-Cooper, eds, *Shakespeare's Globe: A Theatrical Experiment*. Cambridge: Cambridge University Press.

Carter, Angela (1992 [1991]), *Wise Children*. London: Vintage.

Cavell, Stanley (1987), *Disowning Knowledge in Six Plays of Shakespeare*. Cambridge: Cambridge University Press.

Charnes, Linda (2006), *Hamlet's Heirs: Shakespeare and the Politics of a New Millennium*. London and New York: Routledge.

Charney, Maurice (1969), *Style in 'Hamlet'*. Princeton, NJ: Princeton University Press.

Church, Tony (1985), 'Polonius in *Hamlet*', in P. Brockbank, ed., *Players of Shakespeare* 1, 103–14. Cambridge: Cambridge University Press.

Clare, Janet (2014), *Shakespeare's Stage Traffic: Imitation,
    Borrowing and Competition in Renaissance Theatre*. Cambridge:
    Cambridge University Press.

Clarke, Mary Cowden (1854 [1850–2]), *The Girlhood of
    Shakespeare's Heroines: In a Series of Tales*, 3 vols. New York:
    C. S. Francis.

Clayton, Thomas, ed. (1992), *The 'Hamlet' First Published (Q1,
    1603): Origins, Form, Intertextualities*. Newark: University of
    Delaware Press.

Clemen, Wolfgang (1951), *The Development of Shakespeare's
    Imagery*. London: Methuen.

Collick, John (1989), *Shakespeare, Cinema and Society*. Manchester
    and New York: Manchester University Press.

Collier, Jeremy (1698), *A Short View of the Immorality and
    Profaneness of the English Stage, Together with the Sense of
    Antiquity upon this Argument*, 2nd edn. London: Keble, Sace
    and Hindmarsh.

Conklin, Paul S. (1968), *A History of 'Hamlet' Criticism
    1601–1821*. New York: Humanities Press.

Copjec, Joan (1993), 'Introduction', in J. Copjec, ed., *Shades of
    Noir: A Reader*. London: Verso, ix–xii.

Critchley, Simon and Jamieson Webster (2013), *The Shakespeare
    Doctrine*. London and New York: Verso.

Croall, Jonathan (2001), *Hamlet Observed: The National Theatre
    at Work*. London: NT Publications.

Cummings, Brian (2014), *Mortal Thoughts: Religion, Secularity
    and Identity in Shakespeare and Early Modern Culture*. Oxford:
    Oxford University Press.

Cunningham, Vanessa (2008), *Shakespeare and Garrick*.
    Cambridge: Cambridge University Press.

Curran, John E. (2006), *'Hamlet', Protestantism, and the Mourning
    of Contingency*. Farnham: Ashgate.

Daniell, David (1990), *'Hamlet'*, in S. Wells, ed., *Shakespeare: A
    Bibliographical Guide*, 201–21. Oxford: Clarendon Press.

Dawson, Anthony (1985), *Hamlet*, Manchester: Manchester
    University Press.

Dennis, John (1712), *An Essay on the Genius and Writings of
    Shakespeare*. London: Lintott.

Derrida, Jacques (1976 [1967]), *Of Grammatology*, trans.
    G. Chakravorty Spivak. Baltimore: Johns Hopkins University
    Press.

Derrida, Jacques (1994 [1993]), *Specters of Marx: The State of the Debt, the Work of Mourning, and the New International*, trans. P. Kamuf. New York: Routledge.

Dietrich, Julia (1992), *'Hamlet' in the 1960s: An Annotated Bibliography*. New York: Garland.

Dobson, Michael (1992), *The Making of the National Poet: Shakespeare, Adaptation, and Authorship, 1660-1769*. Oxford: Clarendon Press.

Dobson, Michael, ed. (2006), *Performing Shakespeare's Tragedies Today: the Actor's Perspective*. Cambridge: Cambridge University Press.

Dowden, Edward (1875), *Shakspere: A Critical Study of His Mind and Art*, 3rd edn. New York: Harper and Brothers.

Duncan-Jones, Katherine (2001), *Ungentle Shakespeare*. London: Arden.

Duncan-Jones, Katherine (2010), *Shakespeare: An Ungentle Life*, London: Methuen Drama.

Duncan-Jones, Katherine (2011), *Shakespeare: Upstart Crow to Sweet Swan*, 1592–1623. London: Arden.

Dusinberre, Juliet (1996 [1975]), *Shakespeare and the Nature of Women*, 2nd edn. London: Macmillan.

Edwards, Philip, ed. (1985), *Hamlet*. Cambridge: Cambridge University Press.

Edwards, Philip (2005), *Pilgrimage and Literary Tradition*. Cambridge: Cambridge University Press.

Eliot, T. S. (1950 [1919]), 'Hamlet and his Problems', in *The Sacred Wood*, 95–103. London: Methuen.

Ellmann, Richard (1987), *Oscar Wilde*. London: Hamish Hamilton.

Empson, William (1953a), '*Hamlet* When New', *The Sewanee Review* 61 (1): 15–42.

Empson, William (1953b), '*Hamlet* When New (Part II)', *The Sewanee Review* 61 (2): 185–205.

Erne, Lukas (2003), *Shakespeare as Literary Dramatist*. Cambridge: Cambridge University Press.

Everett, Barbara (1990), *Young Hamlet: Essays on Shakespeare's Tragedies*. Oxford: Clarendon Press.

Farley-Hills, David, ed. (1997), *Critical Responses to 'Hamlet' 1600–1790*. New York: AMS Press.

Farmer, Richard (1821 [1767]), *Essay on the Learning of Shakespeare*, 3rd edn. London: T. and H. Rodd.

Farren, George (1829), *Observations on the Laws of Mortality and Disease, and on the Principles of Life Insurance. With An Appendix, Containing Illustrations of the Progress of Mania, Melancholia, Craziness, and Demonomania, as Displayed in Shakespeare's Characters of Lear, Hamlet, Ophelia, and Edgar.* London: Dean and Munday.

Fayard, Nicole (2006), *The Performance of Shakespeare in France Since the Second World War: Re-Imagining Shakespeare.* Lewiston, NY: Edwin Mellen Press.

Felman, Shoshana (1977), 'To Open the Question', *Yale French Studies* 55/56: 5–10.

Felperin, Howard (1990), '"Cultural Poetics" versus "Cultural Materialism": The Two New Historicisms in Renaissance Studies', in *The Uses of the Canon: Elizabethan Literature and Contemporary Theory*, 142–69. Oxford: Clarendon Press.

Ferguson, Margaret W. (1985), '*Hamlet*: Letters and Spirits', in P. Parker and G. Hartman, eds, *Shakespeare and the Question of Theory*, 292–309. New York: Routledge.

Ferry, Anne (1983), *The 'Inward' Language: Sonnets of Wyatt, Sidney, Shakespeare, Donne.* Chicago: University of Chicago Press.

Fineman, Joel (1986), *Shakespeare's Perjured Eye: The Invention of Poetic Subjectivity in the Sonnets.* Berkeley: University of California Press.

Flaherty, Kate (2011), *Ours as We Play It: Australia Plays Shakespeare.* Crawley, Western Australia: UWA Publishing.

Foakes, R. A., ed. (1971), *Coleridge on Shakespeare.* London: Routledge and Kegan Paul.

Foakes, R. A., ed. (1989), *Coleridge's Criticism of Shakespeare: A Selection.* London: Athlone Press.

Foakes, R. A. (1993), *Hamlet versus Lear: Cultural Politics and Shakespeare's Art.* Cambridge: Cambridge University Press.

Foakes, R. A., ed. (1997), *King Lear*, Arden Shakespeare, 3rd series. London: Arden.

Fontane, Theodor (1999), *Shakespeare in the London Theatre 1855–58* (trans. with an intro. and notes by Russell Jackson). London: Society for Theatre Research.

Ford, John (1980), *The Broken Heart*, ed. T. J. B. Spencer. Manchester: Manchester University Press.

Fotheringham, Richard, Christa Jansohn and R. S. White, eds (2008), *Shakespeare's World/World Shakespeares*. Newark: University of Delaware Press.

Freud, Sigmund (1979 [1909]), 'Notes Upon a Case of Obsessional Neurosis', in J. Strachey, trans., *Case Histories II*, vol. 9, The Penguin Freud Library, Harmondsworth: Penguin Books.

Freud, Sigmund (1979 [1915]), 'Mourning and Melancholia', in J. Strachey, trans., *On Metapsychology*, vol. 11. The Penguin Freud Library, 245–68. Penguin: Harmondsworth.

Freud, Sigmund (1985), *The Complete Letters of Sigmund Freud to Wilhelm Fliess, 1887–1904*, trans. and ed. J. M. Masson. Cambridge, MA: Harvard University Press.

Freud, Sigmund (1985 [1900]), *On the Interpretation of Dreams*, trans. J. Strachey, The Penguin Freud Library, vol. 4. Harmondsworth: Penguin.

Freud, Sigmund (1997 [1905–6]), 'Psychopathic Characters on the Stage', in J. Strachey, trans., *Writings on Art and Culture*, 87–93. Stanford: Stanford University Press.

Freud, Sigmund (1997 [1914]), 'The Moses of Michaelangelo', in J. Strachey, trans., *Writings on Art and Culture*, 122–50, Stanford: Stanford University Press.

Freud, Sigmund (1997 [1919]), 'The Uncanny', in J. Strachey, trans., *Writings on Art and Culture*, 193–233. Stanford: Stanford University Press.

Freud, Sigmund, 'Doestoevsky and Parricide' (1997 [1927]), in J. Strachey, trans., *Writings on Art and Culture*, 234–55. Stanford: Stanford University Press.

Frye, Northrop (1976), *Fools of Time: Studies in Shakespearean Tragedy*. London: Oxford University Press.

Furness, Horace Howard, ed. (1877) *A New Variorum Edition of Shakespeare: 'Hamlet'*, 2 vols. Philadelphia: Lippincott.

Garber, Marjorie (2010 [1987]), *Shakespeare's Ghost Writers: Literature as Uncanny Causality*. New York: Routledge.

Garrick, David (1963), *The Letters of David Garrick*, ed. D. M. Little and G. M. Kahrl, 3 vols. Cambridge, MA: Harvard University Press.

Garrick, David (1981a), *The Plays of David Garrick*, ed. G. M. Berkowitz, 4 vols, vol. 3. New York: Garland.

Garrick, David (1981b), 'Garrick's Adaptations of Shakespeare, 1759–73', in H. W. Pedicord and F. L. Bergmann, eds, *The Plays* of *David Garrick*, 7 vols, vol. 4. Carbondale: Southern Illinois University Press.

Gielgud, John (1991), 'The Hamlet Tradition', in J. Gielgud, with J. Miller, *Acting Shakespeare*. London: Pan Books. [First published in Rosamund Gilder, *John Gielgud as Hamlet*. London: Methuen, 1937.]

Goethe, J. W. von (1824 [1795]), *Wilhelm Meister's Apprenticeship*, trans. Thomas Carlyle, 3 vols. Edinburgh: Oliver and Boyd.

Golder, John and Richard Madelaine, eds (2001), *O Brave New World: Two Centuries of Shakespeare on the Australian Stage*. Sydney: Currency Press.

Golub, Spencer (1993), 'Between the Curtain and the Grave: The Taganka in the *Hamlet* Gulag', in D. Kennedy, ed., *Foreign Shakespeare: Contemporary Performance*, 158–77. Cambridge: Cambridge University Press.

González, José Manuel (2014), 'Women Playing Hamlet on the Spanish Stage', in G. McMullan, L. Cowen Orlin and V. Mason Vaughan, eds, *Women Making Shakespeare*. London: Bloomsbury.

Grady, Hugh (2009), *Shakespeare and Impure Aesthetics*. Cambridge: Cambridge University Press.

Grazia, Margreta de (2007), *'Hamlet' Without Hamlet*. Cambridge. Cambridge University Press.

Greenblatt, Stephen (2001), *Hamlet in Purgatory*. Princeton, NJ: Princeton University Press.

Greer, Germaine (2007), *Shakespeare's Wife*. New York: Bloomsbury.

Greg, W. W. (1917), 'Hamlet's Hallucination', *The Modern Language Review* 12 (4): 393–421.

Gregor, Keith (2010), *Shakespeare in the Spanish Theatre: 1772 to the Present*. London: Continuum.

Guntner, Lawrence (1993), 'Brecht and Beyond: Shakespeare on the East German Stage', in D. Kennedy, ed., *Foreign Shakespeare: Contemporary Performance*, 109–39. Cambridge: Cambridge University Press.

Halford, Sir Henry (1833 [1829]), 'Popular and Classical Illustrations of Insanity' in *Essays and Orations, Read and Delivered at The Royal College of Physicians; to which is added An Account of the Opening of the Tomb of King Charles I*, 2nd edn. London: John Murray.

Halliday, F. E., ed. (1949), *Shakespeare and His Critics*. London: Duckworth.

Halman, Talât S. (2014), 'Shakespeare Art in the Turkish Heart: The Bard in the Ottoman Empire and the Turkish Republic', in A. Deniz Bozer, ed., *Shakespeare 450*, 11–27. Ankara: Hacettepe University.

Halpern, Richard (1997), *Shakespeare Among The Moderns*. Ithaca, NY: Cornell University Press.

Hamer, Douglas (1970), 'Was William Shakespeare William Shakeshafte?', *Review of English Studies* n.s. 21 (81): 41–8.

Hamlet (1948) [Film] Dir. Laurence Olivier. UK: Two Cities Films.

Hamlet (1964) [Film] Dir. Grigori Kozintsev. USSR: Lenfilm.

Hamlet (1990) [Film] Dir. Franco Zeffirelli, USA: Carolco.

Hamlet (1996) [Film] Dir. Kenneth Branagh. USA: Castle Rock Entertainment.

Hamlet (2000) [Film] Dir. Michael Almereyda. USA: Double A Films.

Hamlet: The Drama of Revenge (1920) [Film] Dir. Svend Gade. Germany: Art-Film GmbH.

Hand, Molly (2008), review of *Ye Yan/The Banquet* (dir. Xiaogang Feng), *Shakespeare*, 4.4, 429–33.

Hapgood, Robert, ed. (1999), *Hamlet*. Cambridge: Cambridge University Press.

Hartwig, Joan (1983), *Parody as Structural Syntax: Shakespeare's Analogical Scene*. Lincoln: University of Nebraska Press.

Hawkes, Terence (1985), *'Telmah'*, in P. Parker and G. Hartman, eds, *Shakespeare and the Question of Theory*, 310–12. New York: Routledge.

Hazlitt, William (1817), *Characters of Shakespeare's Plays*. London: R. Hunter and C. and J. Ollier.

Heilbrun, Carolyn G. (1991 [1957]), 'The Character of Hamlet's Mother', in *Hamlet's Mother and Other Women: Feminist Essays on Literature*, 9–17. London: Women's Press.

Hibbard, G. R., ed. (1987), *Hamlet*. Oxford: Oxford University Press.

Hillman, David (2007), *Shakespeare's Entrails: Belief, Scepticism and the Interior of the Body*. London: Palgrave.

Hodgdon, Barbara (2013),'The Visual Record: The Case of *Hamlet*', in D. Wiles and C. Dymkowski, eds, *The Cambridge Companion to Theatre History*, 246–66. Cambridge: Cambridge University Press.

Holderness, Graham (2007), '"I Covet your Skull": Death and Desire in Hamlet', *Shakespeare Survey* 60: 223–36.

Holderness, Graham and Bryan Loughrey, eds (1992), *The Tragicall Historie of Hamlet Prince of Denmarke*. Hemel Hempstead: Harvester.

Holland, Norman N. (1976), *Psychoanalysis and Shakespeare*. New York: Octagon Books.

Hollingsworth, Mark (2012), 'Shakespeare criticism', in G. Marshall, ed., *Shakespeare in the Nineteenth Century*. Cambridge: Cambridge University Press.

Honigmann, Ernst (1985), *Shakespeare: The Lost Years*. Manchester: Manchester University Press.

Howard, Tony (2007), *Women as Hamlet: Performance and Interpretation in Theatre, Film and Fiction*. Cambridge: Cambridge University Press.

Huang, Alex C. Y. (2009), *Chinese Shakespeares: Two Centuries of Cultural Exchange*. New York: Columbia University Press.

Hudson, H. N. (1848), *Lectures on Shakespeare*, 2 vols. New York: Baker and Scribner.

Hunt, Marvin W. (2007), *Looking for Hamlet*. London: Palgrave Macmillan.

Hunter, G. K. (1959), '*Hamlet* Criticism', *Critical Quarterly* 1: 27–32.

Husain, Adrian A. (2004), *Politics and Genre in 'Hamlet'*. Oxford: Oxford University Press.

Hutchinson, Rachael (2006), 'Orientalism or Occidentalism?: Dynamics of Appropriation in Akira Kurosawa', in S. Dennison and S. H. Lim, eds, *Remapping World Cinema: Identity, Culture and Politics in Film*. London: Wallflower, 173–87.

Ioppolo, Grace (1991), *Revising Shakespeare*. Cambridge, MA: Harvard University Press.

Jackson, Russell and Robert Smallwood, eds (1988), *Players of Shakespeare 2: Further Essays in Shakespearean Performance*. Cambridge: Cambridge University Press.

Jameson, Anna (1903 [1832]), *Shakespeare's Heroines: Characteristics of Women Moral, Poetical, and Historical*. London: George Bell.

Jameson, Fredric (1991), *Postmodernism, or, the Cultural Logic of Late Capitalism*. London: Verso.

Jardine, Lisa (1989 [1983]), *Still Harping on Daughters: Women and Drama in the Age of Shakespeare*, 2nd edn. New York: Harvester Wheatsheaf.

Jenkins, Harold (1965), '*Hamlet* Then Till Now', *Shakespeare Survey* 18: 34–45.

Jenkins, Harold, ed. (1982), *Hamlet*, Arden Shakespeare, 2nd series. London: Methuen.

Johnson, Samuel (1765), *Mr Johnson's Preface to his Edition of Shakespear's Plays*. London: J. and R. Tonson et al.

Johnson, Samuel (1989), *Samuel Johnson on Shakespeare*, ed. H. R. Woudhuysen. London: Penguin.

Jolly, Margrethe (2014), *The First Two Quartos of 'Hamlet': a New View of the Origins and Relationships of the Texts*. Jefferson, NC: McFarland.

Jones, Ernest (1949 [1910/29]), *Hamlet and Oedipus*. London: Victor Gollancz.

Jones, John (1995), *Shakespeare at Work*. Oxford: Clarendon Press.

Joyce, James (1993 [1922]), *Ulysses*, ed. J. Johnson. Oxford: Oxford University Press.

Kahn, Coppélia (1981), *Man's Estate: Masculine Identity in Shakespeare*. Berkeley: University of California Press.

Kastan, David Scott (2014), *A Will To Believe: Shakespeare and Religion*. Oxford: Oxford University Press.

Kellogg, A. O. (1866), *Shakespeare's Delineations of Insanity, Imbecility, and Suicide*. New York: Hurd and Houghton.

Kelly, Charles Adams (2007), *The Evidence Matrix for the 1st Quarto of Shakespeare's Hamlet*. Michigan: Triple Anvil Press.

Kennedy, Dennis, ed. (1993), *Foreign Shakespeare: Contemporary Performance*. Cambridge: Cambridge University Press.

Kerrigan, William (1994), *Hamlet's Perfection*. Baltimore: Johns Hopkins University Press.

Kettle, Arnold (1964), 'From *Hamlet* to *Lear*', in A. Kettle, ed., *Shakespeare in a Changing World*, 146–71. London: Lawrence and Wishart.

Kiernander, Adrian (2001), 'John Bell and a Post-colonial Australian Shakespeare, 1963–2000', in J. Golder and R. Madelaine, eds, *O Brave New World: Two Centuries of Shakespeare on the Australian Stage*, 236–55. Sydney: Currency Press.

Klein, Lisa (2006), *Ophelia*. London: Bloomsbury.

Kliman, Bernice (1996), 'The enfolded *Hamlet*', *The Shakespeare Newsletter* extra issue: 1–44. Available online: http://www.global-language.com/enfolded.html

Knight, G. Wilson (2001 [1930]), 'The Embassy of Death: An Essay on *Hamlet*', in *The Wheel of Fire*, 17–19. London: Routledge.

Knight, G. Wilson (2001 [1947]), '*Hamlet* Reconsidered', in *The Wheel of Fire*, 338–66. London: Routledge.

Knights, L. C. (1960), *An Approach to 'Hamlet'*. London: Chatto and Windus.

Kökeritz, Helge and Charles Tyler Prouty, eds (1955), *Mr William Shakespeares Comedies, Histories, & Tragedies*. Oxford: Oxford University Press.

Kott, Jan (1964), *Shakespeare Our Contemporary*, trans. B. Taborski. London: Methuen and Co.

Kottman, Paul A. (2009), *Tragic Conditions in Shakespeare*. Baltimore: Johns Hopkins University Press.

Kozintsev, Grigori (1967), *Shakespeare: Time and Conscience*, trans. J. Vining. London: Dennis Dobson.

Kuhn, Thomas S. (1962), *The Structure of Scientific Revolutions*. Chicago: University of Chicago Press.

Lacan, Jacques (1977), 'Desire and the Interpretation of Desire in *Hamlet*', ed. Jacques-Alain Miller, trans. James Hulbert, *Yale French Studies* 55/56: 11–52. Also available in Shoshana Felman, ed., *Literature and Psychoanalysis*, 11–52. Baltimore: Johns Hopkins University Press.

Lacan, Jacques (2002 [1960]), 'The Subversion of the Subject and the Dialectic of Desire in the Freudian Unconscious', in B. Fink, trans., *Écrits*, 671–702. New York: W. W. Norton & Co. Ltd.

Lamb, Charles (1811), 'Theatralia. No. 1. – On Garrick, and Acting; and the Plays of Shakspeare, Considered with Reference to their Fitness for Stage Representation', in *The Reflector: A Quarterly Magazine*, 2 vols. London: John Hunt.

Lavender, Andy (2001), *Hamlet in Pieces: Shakespeare Reworked by Peter Brook, Robert Lepage, Robert Wilson*. London: Nick Hern Books.

Lawrence, D. H. (1916). 'The Theatre', in *Twilight in Italy*, 97–145. London: Duckworth and Co.

Lee, Hyon-u (2008), 'Dialectical Progress of Femininity in Korean Shakespeare since 1990', in R. Fotheringham, C. Jansohn and R.

S. White, eds, *Shakespeare's World/World Shakespeares*, 273–91. Newark: University of Delaware Press.

Lee, John (2000), *Shakespeare's 'Hamlet' and the Controversies of Self*. Oxford: Oxford University Press.

Lesser, Zachary (2015), *'Hamlet' After Q1: An Uncanny History of the Shakespearean Text*. Philadelphia: University of Pennsylvania Press.

Lesser, Zachary and Peter Stallybrass (2008), 'The First Literary Hamlet and the Commonplacing of Professional Plays', *Shakespeare Quarterly* 59 (4): 371–420.

Levin, Harry (1959), *The Question of Hamlet*. New York: Oxford University Press.

Lewes, George Henry (1875), *On Actors and the Art of Acting*. London: Smith Elder.

Lewis, C. S. (1945 [1942]), 'Hamlet: The Prince or the Poem?', 139–54, in *Proceedings of the British Academy*. London: The British Academy.

Li, Ruru (2010), 'Six People in Search of "To be or not to be": Hamlet's Soliloquy in Six Chinese Productions and the Metamorphosis of Shakespeare Performance on the Chinese Stage', in P. Trivedi and M. Ryuta, eds, *Re-playing Shakespeare in Asia*, 119–40. New York: Routledge.

Litvin, Margaret (2011), *Hamlet's Arab Journey: Shakespeare's Prince and Nasser's Ghost*. Princeton, NJ: Princeton University Press.

Ma, Sheng-mei (2007), *East-West Montage: Reflections on Asian Bodies in Diaspora*. Honolulu: University of Hawaii Press.

McDonald, Russ (2001), *Shakespeare and the Arts of Language*, Oxford: Oxford University Press.

Mack, Maynard (1959), 'The World of *Hamlet*', *Yale Review* 41 (1951–2): 502–23.

Mackenzie, Henry (1793 [1780]), 'Criticism on the Character and Tragedy of *Hamlet*' and 'Criticism on *Hamlet* Concluded', in *The Mirror. A Periodical Paper, Published At Edinburgh In The Years 1779 And 1780* (1793), 9th edn, 2 vols. London: A. Strahan, T. Cadell.

Mahood, Molly (1957), *Shakespeare's Wordplay*. London: Methuen.

Mallin, Eric S. (2007), *Godless Shakespeare*. London: Continuum.

Malone, Edmond (1790), *The Plays and Poems of William Shakspeare*, vol. 9. London: J. Rivington et al.

Marcus, Leah S. (1996), *Unediting the Renaissance: Shakespeare, Marlowe and Milton*. London: Routledge.

Marino, James J. (2011), *Owning William Shakespeare: The King's Men and Their Intellectual Property*. Philadelphia: University of Pennsylvania Press.

Marino, James J. (2014), 'Shakespeare's Father's Ghost', *English Literary Renaissance* 44 (1): 56–77.

Marston, Westland (2012 [1877]), *Our Recent Actors*, 2 vols, repr. Cambridge: Cambridge University Press.

Matsuoka, Kazuoko (1995), 'Metamorphosis of Hamlet in Tokyo', in Y. Uéno, ed., *Hamlet and Japan*, 227–33. New York: AMS Press.

Meek, Richard (2009), *Narrating the Visual in Shakespeare*. London: Ashgate.

Melchiori, Giorgio (1992), 'The Acting Version and the Wiser Sort', in T. Clayton, ed., *The 'Hamlet' First Published (Q1, 1603): Origins, Form, Intertextualisation*, Newark: University of Delaware Press.

Menzer, Paul (2008), *The 'Hamlets': Cues, Qs, and Remembered Texts*. Newark: University of Delaware Press.

Montagu, Elizabeth (1769), *An Essay on the Writings and Genius of Shakespear, Compared with Greek and French Dramatic Poets. With Some Remarks Upon the Misrepresentations of Mons. de Voltaire*. London: J. and H. Hughs.

Moran, Kim (2010), 'The Stages "Occupied by Shakespeare": Intercultural Performances and the Search for "Korean-ness" in Postcolonial Korea', in P. Trivedi and M. Ryuta, eds, *Re-playing Shakespeare in Asia*, 200–20. New York: Routledge.

Moretti, Franco (2013), *Distant Reading*. London and New York: Verso.

Morley, Henry (1974), *The Journal of a London Playgoer, with an Introduction by Michael Booth*, Leicester: Leicester University Press.

Munro, J., ed. (1932), *The Shakespeare Allusion-Book: A Collection of Allusions to Shakespeare from 1591 to 1700*, 2 vols. London: Oxford University Press.

Murray, Gilbert (1914), *Hamlet and Orestes: A Study in Traditional Types*. London: British Academy.

Neill, Michael (1997), *Issues of Death: Mortality and Identity in English Renaissance Tragedy*. Oxford: Clarendon Press.

O'Shea, José Roberto (2005), 'Early Shakespearean Stars Performing on Brazilian Skies: João Caetano and National Theater', in B. Kliman and R. J. Santos, eds, *Latin American Shakespeares*, 25–36. Cranbury, NJ: Associated University Presses.

Palfrey, Simon and Tiffany Stern (2011), *Shakespeare in Parts*. Oxford: Oxford University Press.

Pape, Walter and Frederick Burwick (1996), *The Boydell Shakespeare Gallery*. Bottrop, Germany: Peter Pomp.

Patai, Daphne and Will H. Corral, eds (2005), *Theory's Empire: An Anthology of Dissent*. New York: Columbia University Press.

Paulin, Roger, ed. (2010), *Great Shakespeareans: Voltaire, Goethe, Schlegel, Coleridge*. London: Bloomsbury.

Pearson, Hesketh (1950), *The Last Actor-Managers*. London: Methuen & Co. Ltd.

Pennington, Michael (1985), 'Hamlet', in P. Brockbank, ed., *Players of Shakespeare* 1, 115–28. Cambridge: Cambridge University Press.

Petersen, Lene (2013), *Shakespeare's Errant Texts: Textual Form and Linguistic Style in Shakespearean 'Bad' Quartos and Co-authored Plays*. Cambridge: Cambridge University Press.

Peterson, Kaara L. and Deanne Williams, eds (2012), *The Afterlife of Ophelia*. London: Palgrave Macmillan.

Pope, Alexander, ed. (1725) *The Works of Shakespeare*, 6 vols. London: Jacob Tonson.

Potter, Lois (2001), 'This Distracted Globe: Summer 2000', *Shakespeare Quarterly* 41: 124–32.

Potter, Lois (2012), *The Life of William Shakespeare: A Critical Biography*. Oxford: Oxford University Press.

Powell, Brian (2010), 'One Man's *Hamlet* in 1911 Japan: The Bungei-Kyokai Production in the Imperial Theatre', in T. Sasayama, J. R. Mulryne and M. Shewring, eds, *Shakespeare and the Japanese Stage*, 38–52. Cambridge: Cambridge University Press.

Prince, Kathryn (2012), 'Shakespeare and English Nationalism', in F. Ritchie and P. Sabor, eds, *Shakespeare in the Eighteenth Century*, 277–94. Cambridge: Cambridge University Press.

Prince, Stephen (1999), *The Warrior's Camera: The Cinema of Akira Kurosawa*. Princeton, NJ: Princeton University Press.

Prosser, Eleanor (1967), *Hamlet and Revenge*. Stanford, CA: Stanford University Press.

Pye, Christopher (2000), *The Vanishing: Shakespeare, the Subject, and Early Modern Culture*. Durham, NC: Duke University Press.

Rabkin, Norman (1967), *Shakespeare and the Common Understanding*. Chicago: University of Chicago Press.

Rabkin, Norman, ed. (1969), *Reinterpretations of Elizabethan Drama*. New York: Columbia University Press.

Raven, A. A. (1936), *A 'Hamlet' Bibliography and Reference Guide 1877–1935*. Chicago: University of Chicago Press.

Reiss, Benjamin (2005), 'Bardolatry in Bedlam: Shakespeare, Psychiatry, and Cultural Authority in Nineteenth-Century America', *English Literary History* 72 (4): 769–97.

Richardson, William (1797 [1774]), *Essays on some of Shakespeare's Dramatic Characters. To which is added, An Essay on the Faults of Shakespeare*, 5th edn. London: J. Murray and S. Highley.

Righter, Anne (1962), *Shakespeare and the Idea of the Play*. London: Chatto and Windus.

Robertson, J. M. (1919), *The Problem of 'Hamlet'*. London: George Allen and Unwin.

Robinson, Randal F. (1984), *'Hamlet' in the 1950s: An Annotated Bibliography*. New York: Garland.

Roger, Christine (2010), 'August Wilhelm Schlegel', in R. Paulin, ed., *Great Shakespeareans: Voltaire, Goethe, Schlegel, Coleridge*, 92–127. London: Bloomsbury.

Rose, Jonathan (2001), *The Intellectual Life of the British Working Classes*. New Haven: Yale University Press.

Rosenbaum, Ron (2006), *The Shakespeare Wars: Clashing Scholars, Public Fiascos, Palace Coups*. New York: Random House.

Rosenberg, Marvin (1992), *The Masks of Hamlet*. Newark: University of Delaware Press; and London: AUP.

Rowe, Eleanor (1976), *Hamlet: A Window on Russia*. New York: New York University Press.

Rowe, Nicholas, ed. (1709), *The Works of Mr. William Shakespear; in Six Volumes*, vol. 1, xxxi. London: Jacob Tonson.

Rymer, Thomas (1693), *A Short View of Tragedy; It's Original, Excellency, and Corruption*. London: Baldwin.

Ryuta, Minami (2010), '"What, has this thing appear'd again tonight?": Re-playing Shakespeare on the Japanese Stage', in P. Trivedi and M. Ryuta, eds, *Re-playing Shakespeare in Asia*, 76–94. New York: Routledge.

Ryuta, Minami, Ian Carruthers and John Gillies, eds (2001),
    Performing Shakespeare in Japan. Cambridge: Cambridge
    University Press.
Sadeghi, Fatemeh (2012), 'The Green Movement: A Struggle
    against Islamist Patriarchy?', in N. Nabavi, ed., *Iran: From
    Theocracy to the Green Movement*, 123–36. New York:
    Palgrave.
Sasayama, Takashi, J. R. Mulryne and Margaret Shewring, eds
    (2010), *Shakespeare and the Japanese Stage*. Cambridge:
    Cambridge University Press.
Scofield, Martin (1980). *The Ghosts of 'Hamlet': The Play and
    Modern Writers*. Cambridge: Cambridge University Press.   '
Scoloker, Anthony [An. Sc.] (1604), *Daiphantus, Or The Passions
    of Love*. London: Cotton.
Shakespeare, William (1847/54), *Hamlet*, trans. P. Meurice and
    A. Dumas. Paris: Pagnerre.
Shakespeare, William (1877), *Hamlet*, ed. H. H. Furness, 2 vols.
    Philadelphia: J. B. Lippincott Company.
Shakespeare, William (1996), *Hamlet: Screenplay and Introduction*,
    Kenneth Branagh. New York: W. W. Norton & Co. Ltd.
Shapiro, James (2005), *1599: A Year in the Life of William
    Shakespeare*. London: Faber and Faber.
Shaw, George Bernard (1932), 'Hamlet', from *Our Theatres in the
    Nineties*, 3 vols, vol. 3, 200. London: Constable and Co. Ltd.
    [Originally published in *The Saturday Review*, 2 October 1897.]
Showalter, Elaine (1985), 'Representing Ophelia: Women, Madness
    and the Responsibilities of Feminist Criticism', in P. Parker and
    G. Hartman, eds, *Shakespeare and the Question of Theory*,
    77–94. New York: Routledge.
Shurbanov, Alexander and Boika Sokolova (2001), *Painting
    Shakespeare Red: an East-European Appropriation*, Newark:
    University of Delaware Press.
Sillars, Stuart (2012), *Shakespeare, Time and the Victorians*.
    Cambridge: Cambridge University Press.
Small, Helen (1996), *Love's Madness: Medicine, the Novel, and
    Female Insanity 1800–1865*. Oxford: Clarendon Press.
Smith, D. Nichol, ed. (1963), *Eighteenth Century Essays on
    Shakespeare*, 2nd edn. Oxford: Clarendon Press.
Smith, Rebecca (1980), 'A Heart Cleft in Twain: The Dilemma
    of Shakespeare's Gertrude', in C. R. Swift Lenz, C. Thomas

Neely and G. Greene, eds, *The Woman's Part: Feminist Criticism of Shakespeare*, 194–210. Urbana: University of Illinois Press.

Snyder, Susan (1979), *The Comic Matrix of Shakespeare's Tragedies*. Princeton, NJ: Princeton University Press.

Some Remarks on the Tragedy of Hamlet Prince of Denmark, Written by Mr. William Shakespeare (1736). London: W. Wilkins.

Speght, Thomas, ed. (1598), *The Workes of our Antient and lerned English Poet, Geffrey Chaucer, newly printed*, British Library, Additional MS. 42518. Available online: http://www.bl.uk/treasures/shakespeare/playhamlet.html (accessed 30 April 2015).

Spencer, T. J. B. (1963), 'The Decline of Hamlet', *Stratford Upon Avon Studies*, 5: 185–99.

Sprague, Arthur Colby (1944), *Shakespeare and the Actors: The Stage Business in His Plays (1660–1905)*. Cambridge, MA: Harvard University Press.

Spurgeon, Caroline F. E. (1935), *Shakespeare's Imagery and What It Tells Us*. Cambridge: Cambridge University Press.

Stephens, Robert (1995), *Knight Errant; Memoirs of a Vagabond Actor*. London: Hodder & Stoughton Ltd.

Stern, Tiffany (2013a), '"If I could see the Puppets Dallying": *Der Bestrafte Brudermord* and Hamlet's Encounters with the Puppets', *Shakespeare Bulletin* 31 (3): 337–52.

Stern, Tiffany (2013b), 'Sermons, Plays and Note-takers: *Hamlet* Q1 as a "Noted" Text', *Shakespeare Survey* 66: 1–23.

Stockholder, Kay (1987), *Dream Works: Lovers and Families in Shakespeare's Plays*. Toronto: University of Toronto Press.

Stoll, Elmer Edgar (1919), *Hamlet: A Historical and Comparative Study*, Minneapolis: University of Minnesota.

Stříbrný, Zdeněk (2000), *Shakespeare in Eastern Europe*. Oxford: Oxford University Press.

Stříbrný, Zdeněk (2007), 'Recent Hamlets in Prague, and a Postscript', in Z. Stříbrný, *The Whirligig of Time: Essays on Shakespeare and Czechoslovakia*, ed. L. Potter, Newark: University of Delaware Press.

Stubbs, Imogen (2006), 'Gertrude', in M. Dobson, ed., *Performing Shakespeare's Tragedies Today: the Actor's Perspective*, 29–40. Cambridge: Cambridge University Press.

Sugimoto, Yoshio (2003), *An Introduction to Japanese Society*, 2nd edn. Cambridge: Cambridge University Press.

Swinburne, Algernon Charles (1880), *A Study of Shakespeare*. London: Chatto and Windus.

Swinburne, Algernon Charles (1909 [1905]), *Shakespeare*. Oxford: Oxford University Press.

Symington, Rodney (2005), *The Nazi Appropriation of Shakespeare: Cultural Politics in the Third Reich*. Lewiston, NY: Edwin Mellen Press.

Takahashi, Yasunari, Anzai Tetsuo, Matsuoka Kazuko, Ted Motohashi and James Brandon (2001), 'Interview with Suzuki Tadashi, April 6, 1995', in M. Ryuta, I. Carruthers and J. Gillies, eds, *Performing Shakespeare in Japan*, 196–207. Cambridge: Cambridge University Press.

Taranow, Gerda (1996), *The Bernhardt Hamlet: Culture and Context*. New York: Peter Lang.

Tassi, Marguerite A. (2011), *Women and Revenge in Shakespeare: Gender, Genre, and Ethics*, Selinsgrove, PA: Susquehanna University Press.

Taylor, Charles (1975), *Hegel*. Cambridge: Cambridge University Press.

Taylor, Neil (2012), 'An Actress Prepares: Seven Ophelias', in K. L. Peterson and D. Williams, eds, *The Afterlife of Ophelia*, 43–58. London: Palgrave Macmillan.

The Bad Sleep Well (1960) [Film] Dir. Akira Kurosawa, Japan: Kurosawa Productions/Toho Co.

Thompson, Ann and Neil Taylor, eds (2006), *Hamlet: The Texts of 1603 and 1623*, Arden Shakespeare, 3rd series. London: Thomson Learning/Bloomsbury.

Tipton, Elise K. (2008), *Japan: A Social and Political History*, 2nd edn. London: Routledge.

Tolman, Albert H. (1904 [1898]), 'The Views About Hamlet', in *The Views About Hamlet and Other Essays*. Boston: Houghton, Mifflin and Co.

Traversi, D. A. (1969 [1938]), *An Approach to Shakespeare 2: 'Troilus and Cressida' to 'The Tempest'*. London: Hollis & Carter.

Trivedi, Poonam, ed. (2005), *India's Shakespeare: Translation, Interpretation, and Performance*. Newark: University of Delaware Press.

Trivedi, Poonam and Minami Ryuta, eds (2010), *Re-playing Shakespeare in Asia*. New York: Routledge.

Tronch-Pérez, Jesús (2002), *A Synoptic 'Hamlet': a Critical-Synoptic Edition of the Second Quarto and First Folio Texts of 'Hamlet'*. València: Universitat de València.

Uéno, Yoshiko, ed. (1995), *Hamlet and Japan*. New York: AMS Press.

Updike, John (2000), *Gertrude and Claudius*. London: Hamish Hamilton.

Vaughan, Alden T. and Virginia Mason Vaughan (2012), *Shakespeare in America*. Oxford: Oxford University Press.

Vendler, Helen (1997), *The Art of 'Shakespeare's Sonnets'*. Cambridge, MA: Belknap Press.

Vickers, Brian, ed. (1974–81), *Shakespeare: The Critical Heritage: 1623–1801*, 6 vols. London: Routledge and Kegan Paul.

Vickers, Neil (2007), 'Coleridge and the Idea of "Psychological" Criticism', *British Journal for Eighteenth-Century Studies* 30: 261–78.

Vining, Edward P. (1881), *The Mystery of Hamlet*, Philadelphia: J. B. Lippincott.

Voltaire (Arouet, François-Marie) (1733), *Letters Concerning the English Nation*, trans. anon. London: Davis and Lyon.

Waines, David (2003), *An Introduction to Islam*, 2nd edn. Cambridge: Cambridge University Press.

Warley, Christopher (2008), 'Specters of Horatio', *ELH* 75, Winter: 1023–50.

Watson, Robert N. (1994), *The Rest is Silence: Death as Annihilation in the English Renaissance*. Berkeley: University of California.

Watts, Cedric (1988), *Hamlet*. New York: Harvester Wheatsheaf.

Weimann, Robert (1985), 'Mimesis in *Hamlet*', in P. Parker and G. Hartman, eds, *Shakespeare and the Question of Theory*, 275–91. New York: Routledge.

Weis, René, ed. (1993), *King Lear: Parallel Text Edition*. London: Routledge.

Weis, René (2007), *Shakespeare Revealed: A Biography*. Edinburgh: John Murray.

Weitz, Morris (1964), *'Hamlet' and the Philosophy of Literary Criticism*. Chicago: University of Chicago Press.

Wells, Stanley and Sarah Stanton, eds (2002), *The Cambridge Companion to Shakespeare on Stage*. Cambridge: Cambridge University Press.

Wells, Stanley and Gary Taylor, eds (1987), *William Shakespeare: A Textual Companion*. Oxford: Clarendon Press.

Wells, Stanley and Gary Taylor, with John Jowett and William Montgomery, eds (1986), *William Shakespeare: Complete Works*. Oxford: Oxford University Press.

Werder, Karl (1907 [1875]), *The Heart of Hamlet's Mystery*, trans. E. Wilder. New York: G. P. Putnam's Sons.

Werstine, Paul (1988), 'The Textual Mystery of *Hamlet*', *Shakespeare Quarterly* 39: 1–26.

Werstine, Paul (2002), '"The Cause of this Defect": *Hamlet*'s Editors', in A. F. Kinney, ed., *'Hamlet': New Critical Essays*, 115–33. New York: Routledge.

West, Samuel (2006), 'Hamlet', in M. Dobson, ed., *Performing Shakespeare's Tragedies Today: the Actor's Perspective*, 41–56. Cambridge: Cambridge University Press.

Wickham, Glynne, Herbert Berry and William Ingram, eds (2000), *English Professional Theatre, 1530–1660*. Cambridge: Cambridge University Press.

Wilde, Oscar (1905 [1891]), 'The Decay of Lying', in *Intentions*. New York: Brentano's.

Wiles, David and Christine Dymkowski, eds (2013), *The Cambridge Companion to Theatre History*. Cambridge: Cambridge University Press.

Willems, Michèle (2007), 'The Mouse and the Urn: Versions of Shakespeare from Voltaire to Ducis,' *Shakespeare Survey* 60: 231–41.

Willems, Michèle (2010), 'Voltaire', in R. Paulin, ed., *Great Shakespeareans: Voltaire, Goethe, Schlegel, Coleridge*, 5–43. London: Bloomsbury.

Williamson, C. C. H., ed. (1972 [1950]), *Readings on the Character of Hamlet; 1661–1947*, 2nd edn. New York: Gordian Press.

Wilson, J. Dover, ed. (1934), *Hamlet*. Cambridge: Cambridge University Press.

Wilson, J. Dover (1959 [1935]), *What Happens in Hamlet*. Cambridge: Cambridge University Press.

Wilson, Richard (2004), *Secret Shakespeare: Studies in Theatre, Religion and Resistance*. Manchester: Manchester University Press.

Wilson, Richard (2007), *Shakespeare in French Theory: King of Shadows*. London: Routledge.

Wright, George T. (1981), 'Hendiadys and *Hamlet*', *PMLA* 96 (2): 168–93.

Xu, Gary G. (2007), *Sinascape: Contemporary Chinese Cinema*. Lanham, MD: Rowman and Littlefield.

Young, Edward (1759), *Conjectures on Original Composition*. London: A. Millar and J. Dodsley.

Zimmerman, Susan (2004), 'Killing the Dead: The Ghost of Hamlet's Desire', *Shakespeare Jahrbuch* 140: 81–96.

INDEX